Date Due

THE POETRY OF CHAUCER

THE POETRY OF CHAUCER

A GUIDE TO ITS STUDY AND APPRECIATION

BY

ROBERT KILBURN ROOT, 1877–

Professor of English in Princeton University

REVISED EDITION

NEW YORK

PETER SMITH

1950

PREFACE

DURING the last twenty years, the poetry of Chaucer has been attaining an ever increasing popularity. Not only in our colleges and universities, but among the lovers of good literature at large, the discovery has been made that the difficulty of Chaucer's language is by no means so great as at first appears, and that whatever difficulty there may be is richly compensated by the delights which his poetry has to offer. Meanwhile the scholars of Europe and America have been busy at the task of explaining what needs explanation, of investigating the problems of Chaucer's sources, and of determining the order in which his works were composed. It is the purpose of the present volume to render accessible to readers of Chaucer the fruits of these investigations, in so far as they conduce to a fuller appreciation of the poet and his work. For the benefit of those who wish to go more deeply into the subject, rather copious bibliographical references are given in the footnotes. Of Chaucer's biography we know little that is really significant; and that little has been frequently retold. It has, therefore, seemed better to omit any connected account of Chaucer's life, and to give in the discussion of the individual poems such biographical details as serve to illuminate them.

From the very nature of his task, the author's obligations are manifold. From Tyrwhitt down, there is hardly a Chaucerian scholar by whose labors he has not profited, as a glance at the footnotes will show. To Professor Ten Brink, to Professor Lounsbury, to

Professor Skeat, and to Dr. Furnivall and his collabo-
rators in the work of the Chaucer Society, his debt is
particularly large. In making quotations and citations,
Skeat's Student's Chaucer has been used; and the
order in which the several works of the poet are taken
up is, with one slight exception, that in which they are
there printed. This has seemed, on the whole, the most
convenient order; but the reader may take the chapters in any order he pleases. To my friends, Professor
Albert S. Cook of Yale University and Professor
Charles G. Osgood of Princeton University, I am
indebted for much valuable criticism.

R. K. R.

PRINCETON UNIVERSITY
May 25, 1906.

PREFACE TO REVISED EDITION

IT is now fifteen years since this book was first published, and these years have been extraordinarily fruitful of Chaucerian study. Important contributions have been made to our knowledge of Chaucer and of his relations to the literature and prevalent ideas of the Middle Ages, contributions which, it is pleasant to note, have been in large measure the work of American scholars. To Professor Kittredge and Professor Lowes of Harvard and to Professor Tatlock of Leland Stanford the debt of Chaucer-lovers is, and will remain, a large one. In some cases this new knowledge has led to a considerable revision of our earlier understanding of the essential purport of Chaucer's poetry. This is particularly true of the work of Chaucer's middle period — the *House of Fame*, *Troilus*, the *Legend of Good Women*, the translation of Boethius.

It was the original purpose of this book to render accessible to readers of Chaucer the fruits of scholarly investigation in so far as they conduce to a fuller appreciation of the poet and his work. If it is to continue to render this service, a thorough revision is now necessary. Such a revision is presented in the present volume. Where the new information is so fundamental that it essentially alters an earlier interpretation of the facts, the passage concerned has been rewritten, and new pages substituted for the old; where it is rather in the nature of additional light, which clarifies but does not alter, the new information is given in an appendix of 'Notes and Revisions' at the end of the volume. Chapters VI and VII, which deal with *Troilus* and the *House of Fame*, have been rewritten in their entirety. In addition, the pages numbered ix, x, 18, 40, 84, 85, 140–144, 167, 168, 184, 238–240, 291, 292 have been rewritten and substituted for the original pages. These changes have made necessary a new index; but the pagination of the volume has been so little disturbed that most references to the original edition will apply also to this. More than one quarter of the present volume is, therefore, new. It is hoped that with these revisions the book may continue to fill the place which has been accorded to it in the past. With it and with Skeat's *Student's Chaucer*, or better with Professor F. N. Robinson's edition soon to be published in the Cambridge Poets Series, the student or the general reader will have in his possession all that is essential to an understanding and appreciation of Chaucer's poetry.

It is a pleasure to record my gratitude to my friend, Professor Gordon Hall Gerould, for his help and counsel in the preparation of this edition.

R. K. R.

PRINCETON UNIVERSITY,
October, 1921.

A CHRONOLOGICAL SURVEY OF CHAUCER'S LIFE AND WORKS

(The few significant facts of Chaucer's life given below rest on documentary evidence, and may, therefore, be regarded as certain. The chronology of his works is far from certain; but the dates here given may be regarded as approximately correct.)

LIFE	WORKS
1340 Chaucer born in London. His father, John Chaucer, was a vintner, and was in some way connected with the court of Edward III. (The date, 1340, is conjectural.)	
1357 Attached, as a page (?), to the household of Elizabeth, Duchess of Clarence.	To this general period may be assigned the *Romaunt of the Rose*, and the 'balades, roundels, virelayes,' referred to in the Prologue to the *Legend of Good Women*.
1359 Serves in the English army in France, and taken prisoner by the French.	
1367 Granted a life pension for his services as valet in the king's household.	
	1369 *The Book of the Duchess.*
1372–73 First diplomatic mission to Italy.	
1374 Appointed Comptroller of the customs and subsidy of wools, skins, and leather for the port of London. (We know that in this year the poet was already married.) Leased a dwelling over the gate of Aldgate in London.	To the period from 1374 to 1379 may probably be assigned the *House of Fame*, and the poems later utilized as the *Monk's Tale* and the *Second Nun's Tale* of St. Cecilia.
1377 Diplomatic missions in Flanders and France.	
1378 Second journey to Italy in the king's service.	In the six years from 1380 to 1385 we may place the translation of Boethius, *Troilus and Criseyde* (not earlier than 1381), the *Parliament of Fowls* (1382?) and the story of Palamon and Arcite, known as the *Knight's Tale*, (shortly before 1385?).
1382 Appointed Comptroller of the petty customs. (This office he held in addition to his earlier office in the customs.)	

1385 Granted permission to exercise his office as comptroller through a permanent deputy.
Appointed Justice of Peace for the county of Kent.

1386 Member of Parliament for Kent. Gives up his London house (and resides at Greenwich?). Deprived (by a hostile faction at court?) of his offices in the customs.

1387 Death of Chaucer's wife.

1389 Appointed Clerk of the King's Works at Westminster.

1390 Clerk of the King's Works at Windsor, and member of a commission to repair the banks of the Thames between Woolwich and Greenwich.

1394 Granted an additional pension of 20 *l.* a year. (The poet seems, however, to have been in financial difficulty.)

1399 On the accession of Henry IV, Chaucer's pension again increased. He leases a house in Westminster.

1400 Chaucer's death.

1385–86 *The Legend of Good Women.*

Soon after 1386 were begun the *Canterbury Tales*, on which the poet probably worked intermittently till his death. Groups D, E, and F, which contain the discussion of marriage, seem to have been written later than 1393.

1391 *Treatise on the Astrolabe.*
1393 *Envoy to Scogan.*

1394–95 Revised form ('A' text) of Prologue to *Legend of Good Women.*

1396–97 *Envoy to Bukton.*
1399   *To his Empty Purse.*

CONTENTS

THE POETRY OF CHAUCER

CHAPTER I

CHAUCER'S ENGLAND

IT is five hundred years and more since Geoffrey Chaucer was 'nayled in his cheste,' and laid in what is now known as the Poets' Corner of Westminster Abbey. Many things have happened since that day: a new half-world has been discovered; mighty nations have had their birth; there have been wars and revolutions; the great world of science has been opened up, changing deeply our thoughts and beliefs, altering radically the conditions of our industrial and social life; one poet greater than Chaucer has arisen to grace our English tongue. Chaucer would have been intensely interested in all these things, could he have known them; but for him they did not exist. If we are to enter into the spirit of his poetry, we must forget for the time being the present-day world, and all that has happened in five hundred years, and live again in a day long dead. We must, with William Morris, —

> Forget six counties overhung with smoke,
> Forget the snorting steam and piston stroke,
> Forget the spreading of the hideous town;
> Think rather of the pack-horse on the down,
> And dream of London, small, and white, and clean,
> The clear Thames bordered by its gardens green.

When this leap into the dark backward and abysm of time has been accomplished, many of the comforts

and luxuries of modern life will be found missing:
houses are less comfortable; traveling is a slow and
dangerous process; there are no newspapers, no tele-
phones, no tea, coffee, or tobacco. Yet I fancy that
these things are not so indispensable as our modern
world thinks. For those of artistic tastes there is rich
compensation in the external beauty of the life around.
Nearly all the buildings of modern London which are
really works of art were standing in Chaucer's day;
many buildings of equal beauty were standing then
which have since perished. In place of the dingy,
ugly, monotonous buildings which now line the streets
of London town, stood picturesque houses of half-tim-
ber, decorated in bright colors. The throngs of people
passing through the streets must have been a constant
source of interest and pleasure; men did not then try
to efface themselves by sober suits of black or gray.
My lord passes by resplendent in bright colored silks
and velvets, his retainers clothed in their distinguishing livery; every trade has its peculiar costume. There
are processions and pageants, with banners and waving
plumes. Inside the houses one finds quaintly carved
furniture and splendid pictured tapestries. There is
a darker side to this picture, which we must also see
before we are done; but on the surface it is a gay and
beautiful life that we have entered. This is indeed
'merry England.'

There are many intellectual interests as well. The
right of the people to govern themselves in Parliament
is being fought out. The English Church is trying to
limit the usurpations of the papal power; Wiclif and
his poor preachers are sowing the seeds of the English
Reformation. English commerce is extending itself.
There is exciting news of the war with France.

Interesting from many varied aspects, the fourteenth

century is of particular significance to the student of literature and culture, because in it the movement of the Renaissance first assumed definite form, and our modern world began. But if the modern world had begun to assert itself, the mediæval world had by no means passed away. Side by side they stood, the old and the new, essentially hostile to each other, yet blended and intermingled through the whole range of society, often in most incongruous fashion. Because of their coexistence it is easy to compare and contrast them.

Any attempt at an inclusive definition of mediæval-ism and of the Renaissance is a perilous, perhaps an impossible, undertaking; but it is not so difficult to differentiate the two in their main characteristics and tendencies, always remembering that we have to do not so much with two periods of history as with two oppos-ing attitudes of mind, two habits of thought, which have always existed side by side, with now one, now the other, in the ascendant. The fundamental distinction, I think, lies in the fact that the mediæval mind has its gaze fixed primarily on the spiritual and abstract, that of the Renaissance on the sensuous and concrete. 'Me-diævalism proclaims that the eternal things of the spirit are alone worth while; the Renaissance declares that a man's life consists, if not in the abundance of the things he possesses, at any rate in the abundance and variety of the sensations he enjoys.' Though it is a char-acteristic of the greatest minds that they belong to no party, Dante and Shakespeare may be taken to repre-sent, in their dominant tendencies, the two habits of thought. In their power of poetic insight and obser-vation the two poets are nearly equal; but Dante, following the natural bent of his spirit, portrayed the world in terms of the abstract, through the language of

symbols; his great poem is a vision, and the personages of his drama are disembodied souls dwelling in a
realm of spirit; while Shakespeare shows us men and
women as concrete individuals, living and moving in an
actual, material world.

As a direct result of this basic distinction, we pass
to another which is of almost equal significance. In its
dealings with society and with humanity in general,
the mediæval tends towards communism, the Renaissance towards individualism; for the individual is a
concrete fact, the community is an abstract ideal. To
the mediæval mind, man is a member of a great spiritual family, the body of Christ, the Church catholic
and universal. His true happiness, temporal and eternal, is inseparable from the welfare of humanity as a
whole. ' For none of us liveth to himself, and no man
dieth to himself.' Thus Dante, in contrasting spiritual
and material benefits, explains that with material things
the larger the number who share in a benefit, the
smaller is the share of each; while with spiritual blessings, in particular the joys of Paradise, the larger the
number of souls who share, the greater is the portion
of each. To the mind of the Renaissance, then, bent on
the sensuous and material, the individual man, his personal strivings and accomplishment, becomes the main
interest. We have the thirst for personal fame, as
exemplified in the vanity of a Petrarch, replacing the
anonymous zeal of the cathedral-builders. We have
the national tendency, the idea of patriotism, as opposed
to the mediæval conception of a united Christendom,
a Holy Roman Empire. We have a splitting up of the
social body into small groups of individuals, but slightly
interested in one another's welfare. And as the consciousness of the whole community begins to fade, art
and literature become limited in their appeal, no longer

speaking to the whole people, but becoming the exclusive possession of the educated favored classes, a tendency which is clearly evident in Petrarch's scorn for compositions in the vernacular.

In the realm of thought, a precisely similar development takes place : the age of faith gives way to the age of reason. ' Faith is the evidence of things not seen,' that is, of the invisible world, the spiritual. Reason, of necessity, confines itself mainly to things which can be seen and handled; in a word, to the sensuous and material. Or, again, to relate this development to that suggested in the preceding paragraph, faith, or authority, rests on a communistic basis. A belief in the benevolence of God, or in the immortality of the soul, is based, apart from any supernatural revelation, on the universality of man's instinct that these facts are so. This universal instinct gains definiteness in the body of dogma held and taught consistently by the Church, an essentially communistic organization. According to the mediæval idea, the individual man has literally no right to think for himself; the right of private judgment, which lies at the very foundation of Protestantism, is nothing but a corollary of the individualism of the Renaissance.

In the domain of religion and conduct this ' right of private judgment' has had a curious twofold development. Among the more austere races of the north it gave rise to the Protestant Reformation, and, carried out to its logical conclusion, to that ' Protestantism of the Protestant religion ' which we call Puritanism. Protestantism is essentially the religion of the individual. This may be proved first of all by its tendency to break up into sects ; it is in its very nature centrifugal. The Protestant, again, is largely concerned with what he calls the salvation of his own soul, and in the process of achieving this he feels no need of priestly mediation; he insists, rather, on his direct and personal relation to the Deity. It is individualism in religion. The Protestant proceeds to create for himself, and with delightful inconsistency attempts to force upon others, a moral code of his own, harsh and unlovely, of which the Puritan observance of the Sabbath is a good example. At the opposite extreme from Puritanism is the other development of the Renaissance spirit, most conspicuous among the more passionate peoples of the south, in which men used their right of private judgment to overthrow all religion and morality. Morality conveniently divides itself into duty towards God and duty towards one's neighbor. If one doubts the existence of God, he disposes easily of one half of his duty; if he exalts his individual well-being at the expense of the common good of society, his duty towards his neighbor troubles him but little. And so we find in the Italian Renaissance a strong tendency towards irreligion and immorality, which may express itself in the moral laxity and religious indifference of a Boccaccio, or in the diabolic malignity of a Cæsar Borgia or a Catherine de Medici.

If, now, we try to balance up the profit and loss to civilization and culture which have ensued on the triumph of that Renaissance spirit, which is still dominant at the present day, we shall find the account a complicated one. To the heightened interest in material and sensuous things, and to the activity of the individual mind, we owe, of course, the whole of our modern science; to the same causes we owe a great part of our noblest literature and art, our Michael Angelo and our Shakespeare. This is no mean debt. Yet we must remember that this very art which we prize is a possession of only the few; the 'plain man' has no portion in it. Of what sort are the books and pictures which we produce for him? Art has been divorced from daily life. If we have greater poems and finer pictures than the Middle Ages knew, what of our carpets, our hangings, our furniture, our buildings, the dishes from which we eat? Then, too, we have to charge up against the Renaissance our complexity of life, our unsettled doubts, our ambitions and discontents. And, lastly, there is the hideous fact that our boasted civilization is largely a civilization of materialism, of selfishness and legalized greed. After studying the past and studying the present, we must strive to see both the benefits and the limitations which these two great world-tendencies have to offer, and, holding narrowly to neither, must so adjust and balance the two that we may attain to that golden mean which shall usher in the golden world.

In the light of these distinctions between mediævalism and the Renaissance, it will be well to pass in hasty review the great movements of the fourteenth century, political, social, religious, and literary, in order to see more clearly in what sort of a world Chaucer lived and worked.

Politically, the most significant movement, in England at least, is the trend towards national consciousness. Henry II, on his accession to the throne of England in 1154, controlled more than half of what is now France. Normandy he inherited from the Conqueror, Anjou from his father, Geoffrey; Aquitaine was his through the right of Eleanor his queen. Normandy and Anjou had been lost in the reign of King John (1199–1216); but Aquitaine was still a possession of the English crown when Edward III came to the throne in 1327. The national tendency, asserting itself in France, led the French king to the endeavor to bring all Frenchmen under his own control; and this was the ultimate cause of the Hundred Years' War, which began in 1337. The long continued war served to strengthen immeasurably in each country the budding instinct of patriotism. Men began to feel that they were Englishmen or Frenchmen; and the idea of a Holy Roman Empire faded gradually from their thoughts.

The battle of Crécy (1346) and of Poitiers (1356) had not only fanned the flame of patriotism, but, won as they were by the archery of English yeomen, they increased immensely the importance of the middle classes, and hastened the fall of feudalism. With this increased importance of the commoners went a corresponding increase in the power of Parliament, which reached its flood tide in the 'Good Parliament' of 1376. It is in this period that we first find clearly asserted the right of Parliament to vote taxes, on which as a corner-stone has since been built the edifice of English liberty.

This democratic tendency in English politics is even more plainly marked in the social and industrial development of the fourteenth century. With the rapid growth of commerce and manufacture, and the consequently increased importance of the towns, there arose a large and prosperous *bourgeois* class, which, being as it was entirely without the pale of the feudal system, hastened its disintegration. For a discontented serf could become a freeman by establishing a legal residence in one of the towns; and the vassal of higher station found himself overtopped in wealth, and consequently in influence, by the prosperous burgher. The emancipation of the laboring class from the bonds of serfdom was furthered by the great plague which swept over England, as over the rest of Europe, in 1348 and 1349. With half the population wiped out, the landowners found themselves with only half the former supply of labor, and only half the demand for their products. The price of labor rose, and the price of bread fell. The old feudal obligation of the serf to labor a certain number of days on his master's land had already, in large measure, been commuted into a money rent, and the laborers were not slow to take advantage of the opportunity to demand higher wages for their labor. The attempts to control the price of labor by legislation had little effect save to irritate the laborers, an irritation which reached its climax in the peasants' revolt of 1381. This revolt, suppressed by the courage and good judgment of the boy king, Richard II, though barren of any direct and immediate results, exerted a lasting influence on the temper of the lower classes, fostering in them a spirit of independence which made them no longer a negligible quantity in the life of the nation. They ceased to be merely a part of the social organism, and became, with their betters, individuals conscious of their individuality.

The new-born spirit of nationality, which was pervading all of English life, found striking expression in the relations of England with the Papacy. England had been formerly, of all nations, most loyal in its allegiance to the Pope ; but when in 1309 the seat of the Papacy was removed to Avignon, and the holy father himself became a creature of the French king, loyalty to the Pope came into conflict with hatred of France, and the new sentiment of national patriotism proved the stronger. Though the popes of the 'Babylonian captivity' seem not to have been wicked men, they were, at any rate, weak men ; and the papal court became a centre of luxury and vice. To support this luxury it became necessary to sell the Church's preferment; and England, where the Church owned in landed property alone more than one third of the soil of the realm, and received in dues and offerings an income amounting to twice the king's revenue, was a particularly rich field for papal simony. When foreigners, French and Italian, were preferred to the richest livings in England, and proceeded to spend their incomes abroad, the national pride, if not the national conscience, was aroused; and when a French pope, as the last court of appeal in matters of the canon law, set aside the decisions of English courts, the injury to English pride was still deeper. In 1351 was passed the Statute of Provisors, which aimed to stop the first of these abuses, and two years later the Statute of *Præmunire* was directed against the second.

This anti-papal agitation, though purely political in character, could not fail to shake also the religious authority of the Church. A pope who was a Frenchman, and therefore an enemy of England, could not command the full religious loyalty of Englishmen, especially when his court was notorious for its extravagance and profligacy. Not unnaturally the corruption at the head spread through the whole body; and we are unfortunately compelled to believe that the picture of clerical avarice drawn by Chaucer and his contemporaries is but little exaggerated. Though the Church has always taught that the unworthiness of the minister does not vitiate the efficacy of his spiritual ministrations, it was inevitable that even the untutored mind should question the value of an absolution bought with a price from a grasping and unscrupulous priest, and that questioning this, it should question further. If this was not enough, what must have been the consternation of the devout when, in 1378, the great schism of the west began, and Europe beheld two rival popes, each hurling anathemas at the other and at the other's supporters! Whichever pope you recognized, you were excommunicated by the other; and how was one to tell? England, of course, gave official recognition to Urban VI, the Pope of Rome, while France recognized Clement VII at Avignon; but the prestige of the papal name, and the authority of the Church as a whole, received a crushing blow. The more worldly, like Chaucer, laughed at the whole thing; the more devout either bewailed impotently, like Gower and Langland, the corruption they could not cure, or were driven, like Wiclif, into an open revolt, which was to be the precursor of the Protestant Reformation.

The corruption in the Church and its attendant moral laxity led to corruption in the whole social body. 'If gold rust, what shall iron do?' Chaucer's *Prologue* shows us a world in which avarice and deceit are all but universal, and the Prologue to the *Vision of Piers Plowman* bears witness only less vigorously to the same facts. The world, as Langland sees it, is indeed a 'fair field;' but the laborers are unworthy. His men are wandering in a maze, and everything is going wrong. Here are men at the plow, working hard, playing but seldom. What is the result of their work? They are winning what wasters destroy with gluttony. Pilgrims and palmers go on their journeys; and with what result? They have leave to lie all the rest of their lives. Friars, whose business it is to preach the gospel, gloze it to their own profit. Parsons and parish priests are forsaking their charges to go up to London and sing in chantries at Paul's. Bishops neglect their spiritual duties to take office under the King and count his silver. Gower, too, in the Prologue to his *Confessio Amantis*, reviews the condition of Church and State, and, less vigorously but no less clearly, portrays the same state of things: —

Lo, thus tobroke is Cristes folde,
Wherof the flock withoute guide
Devoured is on every side,
In lacke of hem that ben unware
Schepherdes, whiche her wit beware
Upon the world in other halve.
The sharpe pricke instede of salve
Thei usen now, wherof the hele
Thei hurte of that they scholden hele ;
And what schep that is full of wulle,
Upon his back, thei toose and pulle.

But if the world of fourteenth-century England was sadly out of joint, it was far from being stagnant. In its intellectual ferment the age had much the same character as the age of great Elizabeth. There was the same glow of patriotism and national consciousness consequent upon a series of brilliant victories against a foreign foe ; there was the same spirit of revolt against a foreign church ; and, though the forms of mediæval-ism still survived, there was at work the same leaven of new ideas and of a new conception of life, reinforced by a new interest in the works of classical antiquity, coming over-seas from Italy ; literature and art was breaking away from the conventional, and, under the influence of new models, was drinking again at the fountain-head of nature. For such periods of restless-ness and change have often given birth to great crea-tive literature.

Among a throng of lesser writers who contributed to the literature of fourteenth-century England, five stand out preëminent. There is the nameless author of *Sir Gawayne* and the *Pearl*, who, thoroughly medi-æval in his sympathies, infused new life into the old forms of the romance and the vision. There is Lang-land, who, though a mediæval in his habits of thought, had an independence of judgment, a vigor of expression, and a strong tinge of democracy, even of socialism, withal, which are essentially modern. There is Gower, at whom it is the fashion nowadays to laugh as ponderous and dull, but who has, nevertheless, a command of language, a mastery of metre, above all a faculty of simple, straightforward story-telling, which are far from contemptible, and which make his *Confessio Amantis*, when taken in small doses, at times really charming. There is the vigorous prose of Wiclif in his sermons and in his translation of the Bible, which is informed with the spirit of modern Protestantism, though tempered, to be sure, with some of the sweetness of mediæval Catholicism. If none of these is an author of the first importance, it is none the less true that nearly two hundred years were to elapse before any other English authors should arise to equal any one of them. Finally, there is Chaucer, the most perfect exponent of his age, who blended in himself both the old and the new, the mediæval and the modern, who not only represents his age, but, transcending its limitations, has become one of the foremost English poets for all time.

CHAPTER II

CHAUCER

IF the critic is to pass beyond the study of individual poems, and seek after a comprehensive estimate of a poet's whole work, or if he would wring from a series of writings the secret of the writer's soul, and strive to learn what manner of man he was and by what stages he became what he became, it is a question of the first importance to discover in what order his works were composed, and to determine, whenever possible, at least an approximate date for the composition of each. In the case of more modern authors, in general of those who lived after the invention of printing, the problem is usually solved by a mere inspection of the dates on the title-pages or in the prefaces of their volumes; but with authors like Shakespeare, who avoided publication by printing, and still more with authors like Chaucer, who never heard of the printing-press, the problem is more serious. The investigator must, as in any similar historical inquiry, collect and sift all the obtainable evidence of whatever sort. At times the evidence will consist of references in other books to the work in question; sometimes of allusions in the work itself to historical events of known date; oftener, and evidence of this third sort is least conclusive, and must be used with greatest caution, the argument must be based on the æsthetic qualities of the work itself, on metre, style, and general handling of the theme, which may indicate youth or maturity or decline of the poet's power.

For a few of Chaucer's writings, as, for example, the *Book of the Duchess*, the *Parliament of Fowls*, the *Legend of Good Women*, it is possible to assign approximate dates with a good deal of certainty. From the list of his own works given by Chaucer in the Prologue to the *Legend of Good Women*, we learn that the writings there mentioned were composed at some time earlier than the *Legend*. For the rest we are forced to piece together every available shred of evidence, and construct hypotheses which shall be as plausible as may be. In the succeeding chapters of this book, where Chaucer's writings are considered separately, such evidence and plausible hypotheses as we possess regarding the dates of the several works are considered in detail. The reader will discover that the evidence is often of the flimsiest. It is only necessary here to sum up in the mass what may be determined of the orderly development of Chaucer's art on the basis of the information, more or less trustworthy, which we actually possess.[1]

When it is remembered that the date of Chaucer's birth cannot be later than 1340, and that the earliest of his works for which we can assign a date, the *Book of the Duchess*, was not written till 1369, we are at once impressed with the fact that Chaucer's art was very late in coming to maturity. For the *Book of the Duchess*, though by no means a contemptible work, bears evident marks of youth and immaturity. What was Chaucer doing between 1360 and 1369? To this period it has been customary to assign the *Romaunt of the Rose*, or so much of it as may be considered

---

[1] The best general study of Chaucerian chronology is the essay by J. Koch, *The Chronology of Chaucer's Writings*, published by the Chaucer Society, London, 1890. Earlier, and therefore less trustworthy, is Ten Brink's *Chaucer : Studien zur Geschichte seiner Entwicklung und zur Chronologie seiner Schriften*, Münster, 1870. Ten Brink's later views on the subject may be found in two articles *Zur Chronologie von Chaucer's*

Chaucer's work; and though this assignment has been questioned,[1] the present writer is inclined to accept it as probable. In this period, too, we may assume, were written those 'balades, roundels, virelayes,' in praise of love, to which Chaucer refers in the *Legend of Good Women*, most of which have doubtless perished. To this general period belongs the *A. B. C.*, and possibly also *The Book of the Lion* and *Origines upon the Maudeleyne*, lost works to which Chaucer refers at the end of the *Parson's Tale* and in the *Legend of Good Women* respectively. During this, the earliest period of his activity, the poet's models were for the most part French. The literary world in which he lived was a world of dream and lovely shadows, of abstractions and graceful conventions, through which his guide was Guillaume de Lorris. The *Book of the Duchess* is a pleasing and charming piece, but not a great poem; excellent as is its poetic execution, there is little to suggest the Chaucer that was to be. Critics have been accustomed to call this period the period of French influence. Like most generalizations, the term is convenient but dangerous. If we keep to the term, and for convenience' sake it is perhaps well that we should, we must be careful to remember that the French influence upon Chaucer does not cease with the close of the so-called French period. The Prologue to the *Legend of Good Women* is thoroughly in the school of Guillaume de Lorris; and in the *Canterbury Tales* the influence of the satirical method of Jean de Meun, the second of the two authors of the *Roman de la Rose*, is evident at every turn. It is the overwhelming pre-

Schriften, in *Englische Studien*, 17. 1–22, 189–200 (1892). The opinions advocated by these earlier students of the subject have been considerably modified by later investigations as to the date of particular poems.

[1] Cf. below, p. 56.

dominance of French influence in this early period which makes the term appropriate.

In 1373 and again in 1378 Chaucer was sent on diplomatic missions to Italy, and came for the first time into vital contact with the great intellectual movement of the early Renaissance. He felt the power of Dante's divine poem; he breathed the atmosphere of humanism which emanated from Petrarch and his circle; he found in Boccaccio a great kindred spirit, an author of keen artistic susceptibility, who in character and temperament had much in common with himself. He found in Italy not only a new set of models, superior in art and in depth of thought to those of France; he received as well a new and powerful intellectual stimulus, which set him to thinking more deeply on the problems of philosophy, and gave him a keener interest in the intricacies of human character. It follows naturally enough that the decade from 1375 to 1385 was one of unwearied literary production. Despite his somewhat arduous duties as an office-holder in the civil service, he found time to produce a series of works which would alone assure him a permanent place in English literature. In the domain of philosophy he made his translation of Boethius on the *Consolation of Philosophy*, one of the half-dozen most popular books during the whole of the Middle Ages, and one which entered very deeply into Chaucer's philosophy of life. Though he was already familiar with the doctrines of Boethius as they are represented in the *Roman de la Rose*, it is hardly to be questioned that the spur to work of this more serious character came to him from his Italian voyages. His newly found interest in human beings as individuals, in the more complex problems of character, bore fruit in his best sustained and most perfect work, *Troilus and Criseyde*.

To this decade, most probably to the earlier years of it, belongs the *House of Fame*, a poem written in the octosyllabic couplets of Chaucer's French models, and in its form a dream-vision of the same type as the *Book of the Duchess*, but thoroughly permeated with memories of Dante. Here and in the *Parliament of Fowls*, written in 1381 or 1382, Chaucer's artistic power has reached something very near to full maturity. In each of these poems an essentially slight theme is developed with the utmost wealth of wit and fancy; through each Chaucer's characteristic humor plays most deliciously. To the earlier years of this decade, also, will probably be assigned the legend of St. Cecilia, which was later to become the *Second Nun's Tale*, and possibly also the series of 'tragedies,' modelled on the *De Casibus Virorum et Feminarum Illustrium* of Boccaccio, later utilized as the tale of the Canterbury Monk. To the later years of the decade belong the *Parliament of Fowls* and *Troilus;* and at its very close, I believe, the story of Palamon and Arcite, which we know as the *Knight's Tale*. It is in these poems that the influence of Boccaccio is supreme. As the first period of the poet's activity has been called the period of French influence, so this second period has been called that of Italian influence. With the same proviso as before, that a great influence once felt never ceases to operate, this term also may be allowed to stand. Chaucer has not forgotten his French models; but the influence of Italy is predominant.

To the final period of Chaucer's art belong his greatest work, the *Canterbury Tales*, begun soon after 1386, and, on the borderland of the period, the unfinished work which may be thought of as a sort of propædeutic to this, the *Legend of Good Women*, a collection of tales introduced by the most charming of dream-vision allegories, which may safely be dated 1385 or 1386. If we speak

of this as the period of Chaucer's originality, we must
carefully define what we mean by the term original.
For nearly every tale in the *Legend* and in the *Book
of Canterbury* a definite original may be found; nor is
the idea of either collection essentially Chaucer's own.
Chaucer, like Shakespeare, seldom troubled himself to
invent a plot. For a majority, perhaps, of the ideas to
be found in these works Chaucer is indebted to 'olde
bokes.' The striking difference between this period
and the two which preceded is that no single influence
is predominant, no single influence save that of the
poet's own personality. From the *Roman de la Rose*,
from Boethius, from Italy, from ancient Rome, Chaucer
borrows at will; but he has ceased to be a pupil, and
has become a master. In a sense he is no longer influenced from without; he has absorbed and assimilated
and made his own. Thoughts which were once the
thoughts of Boethius or Jean de Meun or Boccaccio
are now his thoughts. He has included and tran-
scended.

Among the individual authors from whom Chaucer
drew the material which he thus took up into himself,
four stand out preëminent. They are Boethius, Jean de
Meun, Boccaccio, and Ovid. From Boethius he drew
the major part of his philosophy, his insistence on a
stoical superiority to Fortune and her whims, his interest in the problem of foreknowledge and free-will,
his platonic belief that true nobility springs only from
greatness of soul. Wherever Chaucer moralizes or phi-
losophizes, the chances are strong that a similar passage
may be found in the *Consolation of Philosophy*.[1] To

---

[1] It must be remembered that the doctrines of Boethius are largely
reproduced in the *Roman de la Rose*, and that consequently it is often
impossible to determine whether Chaucer is borrowing at first or at
second hand. Since Chaucer was intimately acquainted with both
works, the question is one of little moment; for he cannot have failed

Jean de Meun, Chaucer's debt is manifold. From him he learned the highly effective satirical method which he uses in the General Prologue to the *Canterbury Tales* and in the prologues of the *Pardoner* and the *Wife of Bath*, from him he borrowed many of his ideas, in particular those which are tinged with radicalism or skepticism; still more important, he seems to have acquired from Jean de Meun that attitude of mind, that habit of thought, which became an integral part of his nature — the habit of looking at life from the standpoint of comedy, that curious blending of easy tolerance and biting sarcasm, which is saved only by the evident kindliness of his soul from the charge of downright cynicism. From Boccaccio and the Italian Renaissance Chaucer received, as we have already seen, an interest in individual humanity, a new and higher standard of artistic form, and a great intellectual stimulus, not to mention the plots of two of his most important compositions. To Ovid, to whose work the philosophical eagle in the *House of Fame* refers as Chaucer's ' owne book,' Chaucer was indebted largely and continuously. ' Altogether,' says Professor Lounsbury, ' Ovid may be called the favorite author of Chaucer in respect to the extent to which the material taken from him was embodied in productions of his own, written at long intervals of time apart, and upon subjects essentially different.' [1] Though Chaucer knew Virgil, and was not unacquainted with other Latin literature, classical antiquity appealed to him most strongly in the pages of Ovid. While drawing from him stories and allusions,

to recognize Boethius as the original source. He was probably not aware of the fact that the work of Boethius is little more than a compendium of the doctrines of earlier philosophers.

[1] *Studies in Chaucer*, 2. 251, 252. The quotation is from the chapter on ' The Learning of Chaucer,' a chapter of which the serious student of Chaucer cannot afford to be ignorant.

Chaucer must have learned also some of Ovid's ease and grace, his power of vivid description, his rich sensuousness of color and form.

Recognizing how great is Chaucer's debt to the work of those who went before him, one is tempted to ask what is left to Chaucer as his own. In one sense, little, in another sense, all. If originality be taken to imply newness, what was never known nor thought before, original minds have been very rare in the world's history, and have seldom expressed themselves in literature and art. The artist is not properly an investigator, a discoverer of truth; his function is rather to select and assimilate, and by new combination of ideas or by new and higher expression, to present the truth with greater cogency and to commend it to the emotions of his audience. He is, however, no mere purveyor of the truth; he, too, must be an original thinker, but original in the sense that he carries back the truth which he has learned to its origin, its fountain-head, in nature itself. Novelty is possible to very few; originality is possible to many. It is not necessary that we should drink from a new river of truth, but that we should drink its waters at the fountain-head, the *origo*, unmixed and unsullied. When Chaucer retells Boccaccio's story of Troilus and his faithless love, he does not merely translate; neither does he paraphrase and adapt. Accepting the plot of the *Filostrato*, he creates the characters anew from his own independent knowledge of human nature, giving to them new sentiments, new motives, impelling them often to new actions, and consequently to new situations. Chaucer's Troilus and Criseyde and Pandarus are as original, perhaps more original, than their prototypes in Boccaccio. So is it when he borrows a thought from Boethius or Jean de Meun. In this sense Chaucer is a great original poet; in this sense, and in this sense alone, may we assert the originality of Shakespeare. If Chaucer's indebtedness seems greater than Shakespeare's, it is first because the range of his intellect is less universal, and secondly because he drew from a smaller number of sources. We of to-day draw our ideas from such a multitude of writers that our resultant philosophies are mosaics, wherein it is all but impossible to distinguish the origin of this bit and of that; Chaucer had relatively few sources from which to draw, and his indebtedness to each of these is consequently much larger.

Having seen the principal sources whence the poet's ideas were drawn, and the process by which these ideas were made his own, it will not be very difficult to frame some general notion of his ideals and beliefs, of his attitude toward the world about him, of what may be called his philosophy of life. Not that Chaucer ever fashioned for himself a complete and consistent 'system' of philosophy; he was as far as possible removed from any purpose of deliberate didacticism; he was conscious of no burning 'message' to be delivered through the medium of his art; but it is none the less possible to gather from his works a fairly definite idea of his intellectual and spiritual constitution.

If the distinction be indeed legitimate, Chaucer's mind is remarkable rather for its breadth than for its depth, for the extent of its interests rather than for the intensity of its convictions. If Chaucer is not a profound thinker, he is at any rate marked by an eager intellectual curiosity, an openness to ideas, which is evident at all periods of his life. In the domain of science one notices first of all his interest in astronomy and the related pseudo-science of astrology. His works abound in allusions astronomical and astrological. Like Dante and Milton, he prefers to tell his times and seasons by the great clock of the starry heavens and by the calendar of the zodiac. So minute and definite are these allusions in the majority of cases that we must depend on the professed student of astronomy for their elucidation. From such elucidations we learn that the allusions are not only definite but accurate. The crowning proof of the poet's astronomical attainments is furnished by his *Treatise on the Astrolabe*, written in his later years for the use of 'litel Lowis my sone.' Though his acquaintance with physical science was less extensive, the discourse of the eagle in the *House of Fame* includes an admirable exposition of the theory of the transmission of sound; and a similar perception of scientific principles, though with humorous application, is shown in the concluding episode of the *Summoner's Tale*. That Chaucer had delved somewhat deeply into the mysteries of alchemy is shown by the tale of the Canon's Yeoman. Still another topic, on the borderland of science, in which he betrays a lively interest is the cause and significance of dreams.[1]

In the realm of philosophy and metaphysic there was one problem which had for Chaucer a powerful fascination, the problem of God's foreknowledge and the freedom of man's will. On this topic the disappointed Troilus argues with himself at weary length; on this topic, and on the related topic of man's inability to choose for himself, Arcite discourses in the *Knight's Tale* (A. 1251–1274); to the same topic the *Knight's Tale* reverts near its close in a long speech by Theseus. Some years later Chaucer opened the question again, this time in playful mood, in the tale of the Nun's

---

[1] This interest, which Chaucer shares with many of his contemporaries, is to be traced to the popularity of Macrobius's commentary on the *Somnium Scipionis* of Cicero. For an account of this work, see below, p. 65.

Priest. Somewhat closely allied with this problem of foreknowledge and predestination is the equally insoluble problem of the existence of evil in a world governed by an all-powerful and benevolent God. It is this problem which troubles the faithful Dorigen in the *Franklin's Tale*, when she contemplates 'thise grisly feendly rokkes blake' which line the coast of Brittany, and threaten shipwreck to her husband returning from over-seas (F. 865–893). With more of bitterness and less of faith, the woeful prisoner, Palamon, vexes the same baffling question in the *Knight's Tale* (A. 1303–1333) : —

> Th' answere of this I lete to divynis,
> But wel I woot, that in this world gret pyne is.

Chaucer does not solve these questions — who indeed shall solve them ? — neither does he in his discussion of them pass much beyond his master Boethius. What is significant for our purpose is not his answers, for Chaucer is not primarily a philosopher, but the evidence which these discussions bear to his eager intellectual curiosity.

In the poet's attitude towards these various interests of science and metaphysic, in his attitude towards all the interests of life, one plainly discerns a tendency towards skepticism. It is easy to exaggerate this tendency; and some of Chaucer's critics, among them Professor Lounsbury, have laid upon this trait an emphasis which seems to me undue. Nevertheless, the point is not one to be neglected. Interested as he is in astronomy, Chaucer had learned, at least at the time when he wrote the *Franklin's Tale*, to distrust utterly the claims of astrologers and magicians. The magician of the story had a book, —

> Which book spak muchel of the operaciouns,
> Touchinge the eighte and twenty mansiouns

> That longen to the mone, and *swich folye,*
> *As in our dayes is nat worth a flye.*[1]

That Chaucer did not take very seriously the claims of
the alchemists, the *Canon's Yeoman's Tale* may bear
witness. It must be remembered that the majority even
of the more intelligent of Chaucer's contemporaries,
and of his successors for several generations to come,
believed firmly in both of these so-called sciences. Of
the supernatural in myth and story, Chaucer makes, of
course, large use in his works; and usually he is artist
enough to give to the supernatural the air of verisimili-
tude; but once, at least, when telling in the *Legend
of Dido* of the supernatural mist by which Æneas was
made invisible on his entrance into Carthage, he feels
called upon to screen himself from any charge of undue
credulity : —

> *I can nat seyn if that it be possible,*
> But Venus hadde him maked invisible, —
> *Thus seith the book,* withouten any lees.[2]

That Chaucer was capable of questioning some of the
tenets even of orthodox Christianity, we shall see a little
later on.

Coupled with this tendency to skepticism is a notice-
able tinge of radicalism. This, again, must not be exaggerated; Chaucer was no revolutionist; he had no desire
to subvert the existing order of things, either civil or
ecclesiastical. But the speech of the transformed hag
at the close of the *Wife of Bath's Tale,* and the balade
of *Gentilesse,* betray a strong leaven of democracy,
which is further evident in the lively and sympathetic
interest in the lower classes shown not infrequently
in the *Canterbury Tales.* Even more radical in its

---

[1] Chaucer expresses a similar opinion in his *Treatise on the Astrolabe,*
2. 4. 58–61 : ' Natheles, thise ben observauncez of judicial matiere and
rytes of payens, in which my spirit ne hath no feith.'

[2] *Legend,* 1020–1022.

tendency is the discussion of celibacy, that cherished
ideal of mediæval Catholicism, found in the *Wife of
Bath's Prologue*, and touched on again in the *Monk's
Prologue* and in the Epilogue to the *Nun's Priest's
Tale*.

Though it has been a comparatively easy matter to
discover Chaucer's attitude towards many of the interests of his day, it is difficult, perhaps impossible, to
determine with any exactness his attitude towards Christianity and the Catholic Church; for of his inmost convictions and hopes Chaucer, like other modest men,
speaks but seldom, and with reserve. We must not be
misled, as were the reformers of Henry VIII's time, by
the bitterness of Chaucer's attacks on the corruptions
of the Church, into classing him with Wiclif as one of
the forerunners of the Reformation. A contemporary
writer of unquestioned orthodoxy, John Gower, ful-
minates with equal bitterness, if with less effectiveness,
against precisely the same abuses; and Langland, who
in his treatment of the clergy is at one with Chaucer and
Gower, is always a faithful son of the Church. From
a great mass of independent testimony, we are compelled
to the belief that Chaucer's picture of wholesale corruption is but little overdrawn. It is entirely conceiv-
able that Chaucer, like Gower, should, while remaining
loyal to the Church, deplore its abuses. If Chaucer has
shown us unworthy churchmen, has he not also painted,
with all apparent sympathy, the portrait of an ideal
pastor, the ' povre persoun of a toun ' ? As regards the
vital doctrines of Christianity, Chaucer maintains a
discreet silence, from which nothing can be inferred
one way or the other. Professor Lounsbury has made
much [1] of the opening lines of the Prologue to the
Legend of Good Women : —

[1] *Studies in Chaucer*, 2. 512. The whole of the section entitled ' Chau-

> A thousand tymes have I herd men telle,
> That ther is joye in heven, and peyne in helle ;
> And I acorde wel that hit is so;
> But natheles, yit wot I wel also,
> That ther nis noon dwelling in this contree,
> That either hath in heven or helle ybe,
> Ne may of hit non other weyes witen,
> But as he hath herd seyd, or founde hit writen.

This Professor Lounsbury considers a skeptical utterance. But taken in the light of its context, the passage
is capable of an interpretation directly the opposite.
Chaucer is arguing that we must give 'feyth and ful
credence' to books, even when they relate things beyond the pale of our personal experience, just as we
believe in the joys of heaven and the pains of hell,
though no man living has ever tasted of either. Equally
inconsequent is any argument drawn from the lines
in the *Knight's Tale* which have to do with Arcite's
death (A. 2808–2814) : —

> His spirit chaunged hous, and wente ther,
> As I cam never, I can nat tellen wher.
> Therfor I stinte, I nam no divinistre ;
> Of soules finde I nat in this registre,
> Ne me ne list thilke opiniouns to telle
> Of hem, though that they wryten wher they dwelle.

Chaucer may surely decline to accompany his personages 'through the strait and dreadful pass of death'
without being accused of infidelity as to the life beyond.
A somewhat stronger case may be made out for Chaucer's doubt as to the efficacy of the absolution granted
by the corrupt clergy of his day. After his merciless
exposure of the methods of the Summoner in the General Prologue, he says : —

cer's Relations to Religion' deserves careful reading. To the present
writer Professor Lounsbury seems to have laid undue emphasis on
Chaucer's chance remarks.

Of cursing oghte ech gilty man him drede —
For curs wol slee, *right as assoilling saveth.*

This is unquestionably an ironical utterance; but one satirical remark must not be allowed to weigh too heavily, until it has been proved that Chaucer did not write the *Parson's Tale.* The doctrine of transubstantiation, openly combated during Chaucer's lifetime by the reformer Wiclif, the poet nowhere questions.

That Chaucer's mind betrays a tendency towards skepticism, or at least towards criticism, no one will doubt. His restless intellectual curiosity led him to question many things in heaven and earth; and under the influence of the new spirit of the Renaissance, he began no doubt to exercise the 'right of private judgment.' But that he was and remained, in his beliefs and hopes, in all essentials, a Christian and a loyal Catholic, there is no reason to deny and no adequate reason to doubt. Of the essentially religious nature of his character such works as the Boethius translation, the *Parson's Tale*, the Lawyer's tale of Constance, and the Prioress's story of the 'litel clergeon' furnish sufficient proof. The essential rightness of his moral judgment no one familiar with his work can seriously doubt. Some of his work, dealing as it does with flagrant immorality, is of questionable propriety; but with one or two exceptions, there is no attempt to show sin in other than its true light. Even these exceptions are to be explained as due to an excess of the spirit of comedy, rather than to a perverted moral judgment. In the little that we know of Chaucer's life, there is nothing that is inconsistent with the high virtues of 'trouthe and honour, fredom and curteisye,' or with the essentially Christian virtue, humility of heart.

Right as are his moral judgments, quick as he is to perceive evil, Chaucer is never touched by the spirit of the reformer. He was capable, doubtless, of sympathizing with a Langland or a Wiclif, but he never set himself consciously to further their work. He sees the corruption of the Church, and clearly recognizes the evil of it; but who is he to set the crooked straight? There has been always, since the close of the Golden Age, evil in the world; in one form or another evil will always exist. It is so, apparently, that God made the world. If there is always evil, there is always also good; the worst hypocrites in the *Canterbury Tales* have in them somewhat of good, something even lovable. The good is always admirable; and the evil, though deplorable, is so very amusing. If this is not the best possible world, it is at least the best actual world, the world at any rate in which we must spend our threescore years and ten. Let us cleave to what is good, and laugh good-naturedly at what is evil. Above all, let us keep our hearts kind and tender, lacerated by no *sæva indignatio* at what we cannot cure. In this spirit of kindly tolerance Chaucer looked at the world about him. To the ardent reformer such an attitude as this seems merely base and pusillanimous; but in Chaucer it springs neither from weakness nor indifference, but from quiet conviction. The reformer is necessarily a protestant, a dissenter; Chaucer is essentially a Catholic, his spirit is the Catholic spirit — perhaps it may be shown to be essentially the spirit of Christianity. To the man of truly humble spirit his own importance in the universe seems but small, his own exertions of slight avail. He will live his own life in the world as well as he can. Sedulously removing the beams from his own eyes, he will give to the world whatever of good he can, and see to it that his own small influence be an influence towards righteousness; for the rest, he will leave the salvation of the world in the competent hands of the God

who has created it. Chaucer has said all this himself
in what is one of his noblest utterances, the *Balade de
Bon Conseyl*, to which has been given the title *Truth*.

> Tempest thee noght al croked to redresse,
> In trust of hir that turneth as a bal:
> Gret reste stant in litel besinesse;
> And eek be war to sporne ageyn an al;
> Stryve noght, as doth the crokke with the **wal**.
> Daunte thyself, that dauntest otheres dede;
> And trouthe shal delivere, hit is no drede.
>
> That thee is sent, receyve in buxumnesse,
> The wrastling for this worlde axeth a fal.
> Her nis non hoom, her nis but wildernesse;
> Forth, pilgrim, forth ! Forth, beste, out of thy stal !
> Know thy contree, look up, thank God of al;
> Hold the hye wey, and lat thy gost thee lede;
> And trouthe shal delivere, hit is no drede.

That is the Catholic spirit; that is the spirit that actuated Chaucer's life. Reformers may rail at this spirit
as they please, but they cannot prove that it is weak
or base.

One other line from the balade entitled *Truth*, not
included in the two stanzas given above, must be quoted
for the light which it throws on Chaucer's temper. It
is the line with which the poem opens : —

> Flee fro the prees, and dwelle with sothfastnesse.

In the Prologue to *Sir Thopas*, it will be remembered, when the Host calls upon Chaucer to tell his tale,
he accuses him of riding ever with his eyes upon the
ground, and urges him to approach nearer and look up
merrily : —

> ' He semeth elvish by his contenaunce,
> For unto no wight dooth he daliaunce.'

Again, in the *House of Fame*, the eagle says to Chaucer : —

' And noght only fro fer contree,
   That ther no tyding comth to thee,
   But of thy verray neyghebores,
   That dwellen almost at thy dores,
   Thou herest neither that ne this.'

The trait to which these passages all point is one highly
characteristic of Chaucer's nature, a certain aloofness
from the world of men and things. Though keenly interested, he never seems to have felt himself a part of
it. To the great peasants' revolt of 1381, the dramatic
dénouement of which in the streets of London he may
well have witnessed with his own eyes, he refers but
once, and then only playfully in three lines.[1] Though
the battle of Poitiers was fought in Chaucer's lifetime,
and though he himself had seen service in the fields of
France, he never sings the glory of the English arms.
Closely attached as he was to the royal court, he never
speaks of the great diplomatic struggle which was being
fought out between England and the Pope. Chaucer was
living the while in another realm, the realm of fantasy.
Not that he felt it necessary, like Wordsworth, to retire
to the solitude of some Dove Cottage; fond as he was
of wandering in the fields of a May morning, Chaucer
would have been quite miserable in Dove Cottage. He
lived the major part of his life in London, and held
important offices under the Crown. We have every
reason to believe that he discharged the duties of these
offices faithfully and efficiently. Neither did he close
his eyes to things about him; few English poets have
observed the ways of men so minutely and so accurately
as he. He could be a practical man of affairs, when that
was necessary; he was doubtless the most charming of
companions over a glass of canary or old sack. But by
temperament and choice he held aloof, not an actor but

1 B. 4584–4586.

a spectator, sympathizing but not sharing in the interests of the world. He was in the world, but not of it; and for this very reason, perhaps, he continues to live when the more active and conspicuous men of his age have become but a shadow and a name.

The intellectual curiosity and openness of mind which mark Chaucer's attitude towards the world in general are equally evident in his more exclusively literary activity. Never a profound scholar,[1] even when measured by the standards of his own day, he was, none the less, an omnivorous reader, and dipped more or less deeply into a great variety of books on widely diverse subjects. Professor Lounsbury has noticed the significant fact that a large number of his citations and allusions are drawn from the earlier pages of a work. In his reading, as in his writing, his curiosity was ever leading him into new courses; after the first flush of interest was spent, he found it hard to hold himself down to the completion of a work begun with all enthusiasm. In his mastery of foreign languages, too, the same trait is discoverable. Though he read Latin, French, and Italian fluently, he is often guilty, when held down to the stricter work of translation, of rather serious blunders. It is but fair to remember, however, that in the absence of adequate lexicons and grammars, strict verbal accuracy was not easy of attainment. Similarly, when we catch him at error in an allusion, it must be remembered that books were not then, as now, readily accessible, and that even a painstaking scholar, which Chaucer certainly was not, was obliged to trust to memory much more than was always safe. Boccaccio, who made much greater pretensions to scholarship than Chaucer, was capable of such

[1] See Professor Lounsbury's chapter on 'The Learning of Chaucer,' *Studies in Chaucer*, 2. 169–426.

a hybrid coinage as *Filostrato*, the title of his Troilus romance, which he took to mean 'laid low by love;'
and the ponderously learned Gower was not aware that
Tullius and 'Cithero' were one and the same person.[1] In view of this last slip, it may surely be forgiven to Chaucer if he similarly fails to recognize the
identity of Iulus and Ascanius.[2] Chaucer's works
abound, indeed, with inaccuracies and with shocking
anachronisms; but so, for that matter, do the works of
Shakespeare. Unfortunately, however, Chaucer has a
thoroughly mediæval love of parading his learning.
It is one of the few serious blemishes in his art that
he cannot refrain from long scholastic digressions, in
which he heaps up authority on authority, and even
suffers his personages to interrupt a passionate speech
with an explanation of some obscure term needlessly
introduced.[3]

But if Chaucer, despite his parade of learning, did
not read with scholarly thoroughness, he read with the
fine discrimination of the literary critic. Nothing can
be more untrue to Chaucer than to speak of him, as was
long the fashion, as an untutored genius, 'warbling
his native wood-notes wild,' attaining his artistic effects
by mere happy blunder or lucky intuition. He was a
conscious critic of his own work and of the work of
others. There is good reason to believe that he began
the series of 'tragedies' known to us as the *Monk's
Tale*, in all good faith as a serious work of art; but
later, when he incorporated the unfinished series into
the *Canterbury Tales*, he had already recognized its
essential literary badness, and through the mouths of
the Host and the Knight conveys his own just criti-

---

[1] *Confessio Amantis*, 4. 2648 ; 7. 1588-1698.
[2] *House of Fame*, 177-178.
[3] *Troilus and Criseyde*, 5. 897-899.

cism of the work. Similarly, he was not long in discovering the inherent flaw in the scheme of the *Legend of Good Women*, and abandoning it as a mistaken experiment.[1] The exquisite burlesque of *Sir Thopas* and the Host's common-sense criticism thereon show that he had accurately discerned the literary extravagances of the widely popular romance of chivalry. Still higher proof of his fine literary taste is furnished by the process of selection and rejection, alteration and addition, with which he utilizes the works which serve him as sources for his compositions.

The eclectic character of Chaucer's artistic procedure is strikingly shown in the variety of his experiments in versification. Metrically, to be sure, his range is very limited; he employs normally only the iambic rhythm; and, save in *Sir Thopas*,[2] his measure is always either tetrameter or pentameter, though ample variety is attained by skillful handling of the pauses, by not infrequent substitutions of trochee or dactyl for the normal iambus, by large use of the feminine ending, and by various drawing out of the sense from one verse into another. It is in stanza form that Chaucer experimented widely. Nine tenths or more of his verse composition is in one of three stanzas, — the octosyllabic couplet, characteristic of his earliest or French period, though reappearing in the *House of Fame;* the rime royal, or seven-line stanza of *Troilus and Criseyde*, which belongs in general to the second or Italian period; and the heroic couplet, in which was written his maturest work. The last two of these stanzas, of which the first continued to be widely employed until Shakespeare's youth, and the second is rivaled only by blank

---

[1] Cf. below, p. 145.

[2] Further exception should, perhaps, be made of two stanzas in *Anelida and Arcite* (lines 272–280, 333–341), where the pentameter is broken up by internal rimes.

verse in use and popularity, Chaucer was the first to
introduce into English literature. In his mastery of all
three he has never been surpassed. The minor poems
display several other stanzas. If the rimes of the seven
line stanza are repeated through three or four successive stanzas, we get the balade form used by Chaucer
so effectively in *Truth*, in *Gentilesse*, and in *Lack of
Steadfastness*. In the *A. B. C.* and in the *Monk's
Tale* appears an eight-line stanza, with rime-scheme
ababbcbc, which Chaucer apparently abandoned as less
pliable than the seven-line stanza of the rime royal.
This stanza, with the addition of a final alexandrine
riming *c*, becomes the famous Spenserian stanza of
the *Faerie Queene*. The *Complaint to His Lady* is
little more than an exercise in versification. The poem
begins with two stanzas of the rime royal; then shifts
into the *terza rima* of Dante, employed here for the
first time in English verse, and ends in a ten-line
stanza with rime-scheme *aabaabcddc*. The complaint
inserted into *Anelida and Arcite* is a highly artificial
arrangement of varying stanzas, with strophe and
answering antistrophe. Still another artificial form
borrowed from France is the triple roundel entitled
Merciles Beaute, with which should be grouped the
charming roundel introduced into the *Parliament of
Fowls*. When it is remembered that in some of these
artificial verse-forms it is necessary to find twelve
words riming with the same sound, and that in a few
instances the number is yet greater, Chaucer's mastery
of the art of riming is apparent; for seldom are we
conscious of any constraint due to the exigencies of
rime.

No less remarkable is the breadth and variety of
Chaucer's range, when his work is looked at from the
standpoint of its content. Preëminently, of course, his

fame rests on his power as a narrator, the power to tell an interesting story supremely well. His narrative method is characterized by straightforward directness and simplicity. Ordinarily, his stories have a single plot, one main thread of interest, which is taken up at the beginning and followed without interruption to the end. This is the method of Boccaccio and of mediæval story-telling in general; it is the method which William Morris adopted in his *Earthly Paradise*. The method of the modern writer of short stories is quite different from this, since his purpose is usually not so much to narrate a series of happenings as to create a single strong impression. His story will not begin at the beginning, and will seldom be conducted to its logical end; it will consist of a series of striking situations, presented not necessarily in their chronological order, with just so much of narrative as may be necessary to bind these situations together and make them understandable. To this modern method Chaucer approximates in the *Pardoner's Tale*, and in lesser measure in the *Knight's Tale*,[1] from which the reader carries away not so much the recollection of a narrative as the vivid memory of a few important scenes. Even when Chaucer clings more closely to the mediæval method of direct narration, he achieves a somewhat similar effect by a subtle shifting of emphasis. If one compares his stories of Virginia and of Constance with their originals, it may be seen how, by the addition of a few skillful touches, the interest of narrative has been subordinated to the strong impression of a noble character. With what admirable skill Chaucer could handle a more complicated plot, in which two independent intrigues are made to furnish each the catastrophe for the other, may be seen in the conduct of the *Miller's Tale*.

[1] Cf. what is said of these tales below, pp. 172, 227–230.

No less brilliant is Chaucer's art in description. From the merry May morning, gay with singing of birds and sounding of the huntsman's horn, in the *Book of the Duchess* to the matchless series of portraits in the Prologue to the *Canterbury Tales*, the vividness and variety of Chaucer's pictures are unsurpassed. It were idle to enumerate them, for the reader's memory will call up a score of unforgettable scenes. What is the *Knight's Tale* but a splendidly pictured tapestry, full of color and motion? Particularly remarkable in these descriptions is their scope and breadth. There is much more of definiteness than of vagueness in Chaucer's descriptive method; yet the mind is seldom wearied with a confusing catalogue of details. A few significant details give exactness to the picture, while suggesting a whole realm of things beyond. It is as though a veil were suddenly withdrawn, letting the scene burst instantly into view. Lowell has called attention to this quality of suggestiveness in the description at the beginning of the *Clerk's Tale:* —

> Ther is, at the west syde of Itaille,
> Doun at the rote of Vesulus the colde,
> A lusty playne, habundant of vitaille,
> Wher many a tour and toun thou mayst biholde,
> That founded were in tyme of fadres olde,
> And many another delitable sighte,
> And Saluces this noble contree highte.

Though not primarily a reflective poet, Chaucer is no less a master in this division of his art. Illustrations may be drawn from among his minor poems, and even more from among the moralizing passages of *Troilus* and the *Canterbury Tales*. The *House of Fame*, too, is essentially a work of reflection, though clothed in the form of an allegorical narrative.

Unfortunately, Chaucer never wrote a drama; but

that he might have been, had the dramatic form been developed in his time, one of the foremost of English dramatists, there can be no manner of doubt. A master of the art of characterization, skillful in his handling of dialogue, delighting in action, and keenly alive to the value of effective situation and climax, above all a master of constructive art, he is a dramatist in all but the fact. Evident in many of the *Canterbury Tales*, and still more manifest in the story of the pilgrimage itself, this dramatic power reaches its fullest expression in *Troilus and Criseyde*, a work which is better dramatically than Shakespeare's play on the same theme. The five books into which the poem is disposed correspond accurately to the five acts of the drama; the action rises to a climax in the third book, and falls to a catastrophe in the fifth. The poem consists of a series of dramatic scenes; and the story is carried forward almost entirely by means of dialogue. The characterization of Criseyde is as subtle as anything in Shakespeare; and Pandarus is hardly less remarkable. In virtue of this work alone, Chaucer has an unquestionable right to be considered as the forerunner of the great dramatic literature of Elizabeth and James.

After considering the range of Chaucer's power in narrative and dramatic art, it is surprising to find how limited is his power as a lyrist. Though in the *Prioress's Tale*, in the Lawyer's tale of Constance, and in the *Book of the Duchess* there is a distinctly lyrical note, Chaucer seldom enters the domain of the lyric proper. The best of his short poems, such as *Truth*, *Gentilesse*, and *The Former Age*, are reflective rather than lyrical, while the love poems, though charming in their way, are too conventional and artificial to touch us deeply. Almost alone in its fresh spontane-

ity, its authentically lyric quality, stands the roundel
sung by the choir of birds at the end of the *Parliament of Fowls*. Why this absence of lyric power, it
is hard to say. In the age of Elizabeth dramatic and
lyric went hand in hand. The fact must merely be
recorded as one of the limitations in Chaucer's genius.

The variety and breadth of Chaucer's art shows
itself again in his wide register of tone. For illustra-
tion one need not go beyond the limits of the *Canterbury Tales*. There is the romantic idealism of the
Knight's Tale and the high religious idealism of
the *Prioress's Tale* side by side with the Zolaesque
realism of the Miller and the Reeve. The Wife of
Bath's prologue is brutally frank in its realism; her
tale is a graceful tale of faerie. The delightful extrava-
ganza of Chanticleer and Partlet is introduced by a
realistic *genre* painting of the poor widow's cottage,
worthy of Teniers or Gerard Dou. In both of these
manners Chaucer seems equally at home. The dominant tone in the *Canterbury Tales*, as in Chaucer's
work as a whole, is that of humor; but Chaucer's
humor is as protean in its variety as any other of his
qualities. It ranges from broad farce and boisterous
horse-play in the tales of the Miller and the Summoner
to the sly insinuations of the *Knight's Tale* and the
infinitely graceful burlesque of *Sir Thopas*. Every in-
termediate stage between these extremes is represented,
the most characteristic mean between the two being
found, perhaps, in the tale of the Nun's Priest. The
only constant element in Chaucer's humor is its kindliness, its healthiness, its spontaneous freshness.

With a keen sense of humor is usually joined, as in
Thackeray and Dickens, a deep susceptibility to the
pathetic, and Chaucer is no exception to the rule; but,
unlike Dickens and Thackeray, he knows the delicate

line which separates pathos from sentimentality, and over this line he never steps. Troilus as he eagerly watches for the returning form of Cressid, Arcite taking his last leave of his kinsman and his love, Dorigen as she goes to keep her terrible tryst, Constance comforting her little son, Virginius dooming his daughter to the death that shall vindicate her honor, Griselda preparing for the wedding feast of the rival who is to supplant her, above all the matchless story of the murdered schoolboy singing his *Alma Redemptoris* — these show the touch of pathos in its purest form, and the list might be indefinitely extended. In any one of these instances a lesser poet would have become sentimental.

To the sublimer heights of tragedy Chaucer rarely ascends. Though the *Pardoner's Tale* moves us to tragic pity and fear, it does this rather by its accessories — the dreadful plague, the mysterious veiled figure, the suddenness of its catastrophe — than by any working out of inevitable moral law. Its effect is not so much that of tragedy as of superb melodrama. Chaucer called his *Troilus and Criseyde* a 'tragedie,' and he has handled his theme in the spirit of tragedy as the Middle Ages understood the term. The story moves forward relentlessly to an ever impending doom. But the poem has not the intensity of great tragedy. Its effect is rather a blending of pathos and tragic irony. Troilus has sought and achieved a great happiness which turns in his grasp to the bitterness of ashes. So it must ever be, Chaucer declares, with the 'false felicity' of temporal joy. It is Chaucer's constant sense of the irony of life, of the mockery which our ultimate achievement casts on rosy expectation, that dominates his more serious thought. This irony is most often a comic irony; but at times, as in *Troilus* or the *Pardoner's Tale,* it becomes essentially tragic.

> What is this world ? what asketh men to have ?
> Now with his love, now in his colde grave
> Allone, withouten any companye.

The author of these lines was surely capable of being serious; there are few lines in our literature more pregnant with the tragedy of life. But this note is never long sustained; where possible, it is avoided altogether. Capable of seriousness, Chaucer has deliberately chosen to portray the world through the medium of comedy.

> I woot myself best how I stonde,

are Chaucer's words when he refuses to compete for the favors of Lady Fame. I, for one, am ready to believe that Chaucer knew his own powers best, and am unwilling to quarrel with him for his choice of the comic spirit; for comedy such as his constitutes a 'criticism of life' as true within its limits as that of 'high seriousness' and the 'grand style.'

Of Chaucer's style it will not do to talk at great length, for its quality can be felt much better than it can be analyzed. It is so delicate, indeed, that any elaborate analysis seems in the nature of an impertinence. It is characterized preëminently by its simplicity. Though for his metre's sake the poet affects a slight archaism in the preservation of the final *e*, which was already beginning to disappear, his words are the words of every-day life. His sentences are short and loose, simple in their structure, free from awkward inversions and from any studied balance or antithesis. As his diction is simple, so is his thought. In his later work, at least, there is an almost complete absence of the strained conceits, the far-fetched metaphors, and elaborate puns, which mar much of Shakespeare's work; and this is the more remarkable when one remembers Chaucer's reverence for the authority of

Petrarch. Once in the *Franklin's Tale*, he finds him.
self betrayed into an overwrought metaphor : —

> For th'orisonte hath reft the sonne his light.

Instead of canceling the line, he lets it stand, and
adds : —

> This is as muche to seye as it was night.

To read Chaucer is to listen to the charming, gracious
conversation of a cultured gentleman who is also a
poet. At times his language is as terse and pregnant as
any in Shakespeare. Such is the line in the *Knight's
Tale* which shows us

> The smyler with the knyf under the cloke.

But ordinarily he has leisure to give his thought full
expression. He has 'the power of diffusion without
being diffuse.' His stories tell themselves away without apparent effort, even without apparent art, without
hurry, but without delay.

> A povre widwe, somdel stope in age,
> Was whylom dwelling in a narwe cotage,
> Bisyde a grove, stonding in a dale.
> This widwe, of which I telle you my tale —

There is nothing remarkable in these lines ; but they
are the very essence of literature, and no one can resist
their charm.

If Chaucer's style is marked by naturalness and
simplicity, let no one suppose that it is a careless style.
Artless as his lines seem, they are full of that highest art which effaces itself. In his perfect finish, his
unassuming elegance, Chaucer is essentially Gallic,
one may almost say Hellenic. With all his simplicity,
there is a quiet energy, a sureness of touch, a delicacy
of perception, which betray the master mind. Above
all, there is in Chaucer's style, as in the man himself,

a sanity and poise, a calm equanimity, which render it peculiarly grateful to the ears of our modern world, wearied with much wild talking.

No one will pretend, I suppose, that Chaucer is a poet of the first rank. He is not a great prophet like Dante, with a burning message which he must deliver; only rarely does he move one's whole emotional and moral nature as does Shakespeare. Though sharing in the fresh spontaneity which makes the Homeric poems a perpetual solace, he has not Homer's majesty; nor does he attain to the dignity and elegance of Virgil. As a comedian he will hardly rank with Cervantes and Molière. In intellect and in art he is inferior to all these; but among poets of the second rank his position is high. In the list of English poets other than Shakespeare, Milton is the only one who may be held to surpass him; and between two men so dissimilar in their powers one will hesitate to determine the preëminence.

The qualities which make for Chaucer's greatness have already been reviewed in the preceding pages, and will be considered again in more detail as they manifest themselves in individual works, in the chapters which follow; but the quality which distinguishes him preëminently is his sanity and poise. With the possible exception of Shakespeare, there is no English poet of power even commensurate with Chaucer's, who is so eminently sane. We are living in an age which is restless, in many respects unhealthy, insane. On one side of us is the dull sway of materialism, commercialism, money-getting; on the other side we still hear the frantic protests of a Carlyle and a Ruskin, the revolutionary rhapsodies of a Byron or a Shelley, we listen to the persistent self-analyses of a Wordsworth or a Coleridge, or to the beautiful but morbid imaginings of a Keats;

or, coming nearer to the present day, we hearken to the
strange dreamings of a Maeterlinck or the unsparing
iconoclasms of an Ibsen. I would not for a moment
be thought insensible to the greatness of these men ;
I insist merely that with all their varied greatness
there is infused a strain which is morbid and unhealthy.
The eighteenth century had sanity without poetry ; the
nineteenth had poetry without sanity ; Chaucer, like
the great Greeks, combined both.

We turn to Chaucer not primarily for moral guidance and spiritual sustenance, nor yet that our emotions
may be deeply and powerfully moved ; we turn to him
rather for refreshment, that our eyes and ears may
be opened anew to the varied interest and beauty of
the world around us, that we may come again into
healthy living contact with the smiling green earth
and with the hearts of men, that we may shake off
for a while ' the burthen of the mystery of all this
unintelligible world,' and share in the kindly laughter
of the gods, that we may breathe the pure, serene
air of equanimity.

CHAPTER III

THE ROMAUNT OF THE ROSE

It is thoroughly in accord with what we know of Chaucer's innate modesty that his first serious undertaking in literature should have been a translation rather than an original work ; and surely no better exercise than that of translation could have been found to develop a technical mastery of poetic form. The poem which Chaucer chose to translate was the widely popular *Roman de la Rose*, a work which offered a broad and varied scope to the young poet's powers of expression, and was, moreover, thoroughly congenial to his tastes and sympathies.

Though the Chaucerian *Romaunt of the Rose* extends to the no mean length of 7698 lines, it reproduces less than a third of its French original, for the *Roman de la Rose* contains in Méon's edition 22,047 lines of octosyllabic couplets. Of these, lines 1–5169 and 10716–12564 alone are translated. But if the English translation is only a fragment of its original, Chaucer's familiarity with the whole poem, and the influence which it exerted upon him, are so great, that the poem in its entirety is of the first importance to the student of Chaucer's work.

The *Roman de la Rose* is the work not of a single author, but of two authors, of two successive generations, utterly unlike in their ideals and temperaments. Of the first of these, Guillaume de Lorris, whose work extends to line 4068, we know very little ; and for that little we are indebted to the second poet, Jean de Meun, who continued his work. From the statements of the younger author we are able to calculate that Guillaume must have been born about the year 1200, and that the composition of the poem must have fallen between the years 1225 and 1230. His work is supposed to have been terminated by his early death. Of the place of his birth and of his residence we do not know. The little town of Lorris is a few miles east of Orleans; and Guillaume's name may indicate that as his birth-place; but we cannot be sure. If, as seems probable, he was a clerk, his education may have been received either at Orleans or at Paris. His dialect shows that he lived in the north of France; but in the absence of any critical edition of the *Roman*, it is impossible to be more exact.

Of Jean de Meun, who forty years after Guillaume's death undertook the continuation of his unfinished work, we know somewhat more. Jean Clopinel was born at Meun-sur-Loire, and died before November 6, 1305, on which date his comfortable house in Paris was deeded to the Dominicans of the rue St. Jacques. Since it can be shown from internal evidence that his continuation of the *Roman* was written between 1268 and 1277, M. Langlois fixes on the year 1240 as the approximate date of his birth. From his own statement in another work we learn that his life was an honorable and prosperous one, and that it had been his fortune to serve 'les plus granz genz de France.' He was an excellent scholar, widely read in Latin and French, and the author of several works, among which may be mentioned a trans-lation of the *Consolation of Philosophy* of Boethius, a book to which he is deeply indebted in the *Roman de la Rose*.

Two men more dissimilar in character than the authors of the *Roman* it would be hard to find.

Guillaume is essentially an idealist, a purist, cherishing the fair ideal of Middle Age chivalry, living in a world of dream and shadows. To him love is the great influence which ennobles and purifies the human heart, woman is a superior, well-nigh perfect being, little short of the divine, in whose service man may well expend all in him that is best and highest. His poem is a love story and a courtly treatise on the art of love. Five years and more ago, he tells us, as he lay on his bed one May morning, he dreamed a wondrous dream. In this dream he wandered out through the flowering fields, with the birds singing all about him, and came at last to a great garden all walled about, the garden of love. In the midst of the garden, hard by the fountain of Narcissus, stands a goodly rose tree, on which grows a bud which the poet longs earnestly to pluck. This is the allegorical device by which the poet shadows forth his love for the lady of his desire. The porter at the gate of the garden is Idleness. The *dramatis personæ* are, save the poet himself, such abstractions as Largesse, Fair-Welcome, Evil-Tongue, Jealousy, and Danger, or haughtiness. When allegory is but a literary device, it is always dangerous; but Guillaume thought in terms of allegory, and his allegorical personages, if shadowy, are none the less true and effective. Guillaume de Lorris is not a great poet; but he is a good poet, and one can hardly fail to enjoy the quiet loveliness of his work.

Jean de Meun is of quite a different stamp, so different, indeed, that it seems a mere caprice that he should have undertaken the continuation of such a poem as the *Roman de la Rose*. If Guillaume de Lorris is a conservative and an idealist, Jean de Meun is a realist and a revolutionist. To him the chivalric ideal is mere nonsense. In his democratic creed noble birth is but an

accident; personal worth is the only patent of true nobility. Woman is a vain and fickle creature, a snare for
men's feet. Love is but a game played for the prize of
sensual gratification. In crossing the line which divides
the work of the two authors, the reader plunges into a
totally different atmosphere. Jean de Meun has kept to
the machinery of Guillaume's poem; the same allegorical personages pass before us; the quest of the rose still
remains the ostensible theme of the poem; but the poet
uses the framework merely as a device for the introduction of his own ideas. There are long digressions on
various topics, philosophical and theological, wearisome
because of their prolixity, but excellent in their rea-
soning, and terse and effective in their diction. There
are bitter tirades against the frailty of woman, and
merciless attacks against the corruption of the clergy.
Jean de Meun's method in his satirical passages is of peculiar interest to the student of Chaucer; for it is the
very method so effectively employed in the *Canterbury
Tales.* In the person of False-Seeming, one of the most
masterful of Jean de Meun's characterizations and the
prototype of Chaucer's Friar and Pardoner, a friar
himself is made to expose, proudly and boastfully, the
iniquities of his order; while in the person of the Du-
enna, who becomes in Chaucer's hands the genial Wife
of Bath, is exhibited all the sensuality and cunning
craft which constitutes Jean de Meun's idea of woman.

In Guillaume de Lorris one is conscious of a sweet
and noble personality, coupled with a fairly true sense
of artistic form and poetical expression. One cannot
read a thousand lines of Jean Clopinel without realizing that he has to do with a masterful intellect. His
personality is not lovable, but commanding. Unquestionably inferior to Guillaume in artistic form, — for
his work seems often a mere hodge-podge of ideas, — he

as unquestionably surpasses him in range and in intellectual scope. For the graceful delicacy of Guillaume's diction, Jean de Meun offers a nervous, incisive, yet polished style, which is as superior to that of Guillaume as is Shakespeare to Spenser.

This strange composite poem exerted in its own century, and in the two centuries following, an enormous influence on the literature of Northern Europe, and no inconsiderable influence south of the Alps. Its wide circulation is attested by the fact that nearly two hundred manuscript copies have survived to the present day, many of which are found in England and in Germany. It was early translated into Flemish and into Italian, while somewhat later appeared the English version which is the subject of this chapter. In France it was kept before the public eye by its bitter antagonists no less than by its enthusiastic admirers. It is hardly an exaggeration to say that for two hundred years no important French author escaped its influence. In England its vogue was little less extensive. Without its suggestion Chaucer would not have been Chaucer, and English literature would have followed a different channel.

The reasons for this widespread popularity and far-reaching influence are not hard to fathom. The *Roman* is not, as is sometimes asserted, a great original creation. Guillaume did not invent the dream-vision form nor the use of allegory, any more than Petrarch invented the sonnet; the revolutionary doctrines of Jean de Meun did not spring unbegotten from his own brain. Those who will take the trouble to read M. Ernest Langlois's monograph [1] on the subject will find that every significant feature of the poem is paralleled in earlier works. The great achievement of Guillaume

[1] *Origines et Sources du Roman de la Rose*, Paris, 1890.

de Lorris and Jean de Meun is that they assimilated
and then crystallized into masterful poetic expression
a literary form and a set of ideas which were already
current and popular. Without Petrarch the sonnet
might still have survived as a literary form; but it
could hardly have achieved the great vogue which it
attained through his authority. It is a general law in
literature that widespread and long-continued popularity is possible only when an idea already popular
receives permanent expression at the hands of a master.
The *Roman de la Rose* was immediately recognized
as such a masterpiece, and became the medium through
which was effectively transmitted an influence which
might otherwise have spent itself ineffectually in a
couple of generations. Another source of its wide appeal may be found in the fact of its dual and diverse
authorship. The poem took its rise just before the
dawn of the Renaissance. During the centuries which
immediately followed, two tendencies, the mediæval and
the modern, were existing side by side. To those who
clung to the old ideals, Guillaume de Lorris made a
strong appeal; while the free-thinkers of the Renaissance could not but recognize a kindred soul in Jean
de Meun. The poem was wide enough in its scope to
appeal to all. Chaucer, for example, who exhibits in
his own development the transition from the mediæval to the modern, was first attracted by Guillaume
de Lorris, and only later felt the full influence of Jean
de Meun.

The chief interest of the *Roman de la Rose* for the
modern student lies in this its historical significance as
an expression of the varying ideals of the later Middle
Ages; but it has its absolute interest as well. Any one
who will read the poem through, either in the French
original or in the excellent English translation by Mr

F. S. Ellis,[1] will find many passages of vivid and charming description, of keen analysis, of telling satire, of much vital human interest, and of true literary power, to repay him for the many hours which even a hurried reading will demand.[2]

The English translation of the *Roman de la Rose*, which is preserved in a single manuscript in the Hunterian collection at Glasgow, was first included among Chaucer's works in Thynne's edition of 1532,[3] and was until 1870 universally accepted as a genuine work of Chaucer. Since that date the question of its authenticity has been one of the most vexed problems of Chaucerian scholarship; and even to-day scholars are not in full accord as to the solution.

That Chaucer made a translation of some portion at least of the *Roman*, we know on Chaucer's own authority. In the Prologue to the *Legend of Good Women* (B version, 328–331), the god of love says to Chaucer: —

> For in pleyn text, withouten nede of glose,
> Thou hast translated the Romaunce of the Rose,
> That is an heresye ageyns my lawe,
> And makest wyse folk fro me withdrawe.[4]

[1] London, 1900. (The Temple Classics Series, J. M. Dent & Co. 3 vols.)

[2] The best editions of the French text are those of M. Méon, Paris, 1814, and F. Michel, Paris, 1864. A new edition, which will doubtless supersede these, is promised by M. Ernest Langlois. The best literary study of the *Roman* is that by M. Langlois in the second volume of *Histoire de la Langue et de la Littérature française*, published under the direction of M. Petit de Julleville, Paris, 1896. Shorter and less detailed, but highly suggestive, is the chapter devoted to the *Roman* in *La Littérature française au Moyen Age*, by Gaston Paris, Paris, 1890. Reference has been made in a previous note to M. Langlois's *Origines et Sources du Roman de la Rose*, Paris, 1890.

[3] Thynne printed from a manuscript now lost, which, though somewhat more accurate than the Hunterian MS., does not differ markedly from it.

[4] Lydgate, moreover, in the *Fall of Princes*, mentions the translation among other works of Chaucer: —

Two questions at once suggest themselves : Did Chaucer ever complete his translation ? Is the fragmentary translation which we possess the work of Chaucer ? The first of these questions may be pretty safely answered in the negative. In the first place, the translation of so long a poem is a laborious and tedious task; and Chaucer, as we well know, was only too likely to weary of an undertaking before it was half completed. In the second place, had so popular a poet as Chaucer completed a translation of so popular a poem as the *Roman de la Rose*, it is highly improbable that the work would have been allowed to perish.[1]

The first scholar to raise the second question, that as to Chaucer's authorship of the existing English version, was the late Professor F. J. Child of Harvard, in a communication to the *Athenæum* for December 3, 1870 : ' I may add, that it will take a great deal more than the fact that the *Romaunt of the Rose* is printed in old editions, to make me believe that it is Chaucer's. The rhymes are not his, and the style is not his, unless he changed both extraordinarily as he got on in life. The translation is often in a high degree slovenly. The part after the break, from v. 5814 on, seemed to me, on a recent comparison with the French, better done than the middle ; and as the Bialacoil of the earlier portion is here called Fair-welcomyng, *perhaps* this part belongs to a different version.'

Professor Child did not pursue the question any further ; and it was several years before any detailed argu-

And notably [he] did his businesse
By great auise his wittes to dispose,
To translate the *Romaynt of the Rose.*

Quoted by Skeat, 1. 23.

[1] It is, perhaps, worthy of remark that the *Romaunt of the Rose* is not mentioned in the list of works of evil tendency which Chaucer repents of having written in the ' retractation' at the end of the *Parson's Tale.*

ment against the Chaucerian authorship appeared in
print. It was nearly twenty years before the important hint contained in his last sentence received further elaboration. The first important document in the
controversy appeared from the pen of Skeat in 1880,[1]
in which the argument against Chaucer's authorship
of the translation is based mainly on three grounds:
(1) The presence in the translation of imperfect rimes,
particularly the riming of words ending in -y with
words ending in -ye, such as do not appear in the poet's
unquestioned works; (2) the occurrence of words which
belong distinctly to a dialect more northern than that
of Chaucer; (3) differences in the vocabulary of the
translation from the vocabulary of Chaucer.[2]

Though the argument against Chaucer's authorship
of the translation did not pass unchallenged,[3] nothing
more of importance appeared till 1888, when it was
clearly proved that Child had been right in suspecting
that the portion of the translation which follows the
break at line 5810 is not by the author of the earlier
portion.[4]

[1] *Chaucer's Prioress's Tale*, etc., third edition, Oxford, 1880. The
essay is reprinted in the Chaucer Society's volume of *Essays on Chaucer*, pp. 439–451. That the question had already been discussed is shown
by Thomas Arnold's communication to *The Academy*, July 20, 1878,
pp. 66, 67, and Skeat's answer, *The Academy*, August 10, 1878, p. 143.

[2] Of these arguments, the third is least sound. Cf. an article by Professor Cook in *Modern Language Notes*, 2. 143–146 (1887).

[3] The most important dissenting voice was that of Fick in *Englische
Studien*, 9. 161–167 (1886), who argued that the impure rimes and
northern forms were to be explained on the ground that the translation
was a work of Chaucer's youth.

[4] F. Lindner in *Englische Studien*, 11. 163–173. The argument is based
on rime, on the change from Bialacoil to Fair-welcomyng, noticed by
Child, and on a number of false translations in the second part. Lindner is not ready to attribute either section to Chaucer, but favors the
first rather than the second. His article is in many particulars invalidated by the more thorough investigations of Kaluza. (See below.) In
a review of Kaluza's work in *Englische Studien*, 18. 104–105, Lindner

In the years 1892 and 1893 the controversy reached its culmination. In his *Studies in Chaucer*,[1] published in 1892, Professor Lounsbury combated stoutly and at great length the arguments against Chaucer's authorship of the whole translation; and in the same year he was ably answered by Professor Kittredge.[2] In the year following, 1893, the whole question was put upon a new footing, and all preceding arguments were in a measure invalidated by Professor Kaluza.[3] It is unnecessary to reproduce here in detail Kaluza's arguments, which a serious student of the question will read for himself; his conclusions alone need detain us. He has shown conclusively that the existing *Romaunt of the Rose* consists, not, as Child guessed and Lindner proved, of two dissimilar fragments, but of three. The first (Fragment A), including lines 1–1705, contains nothing in rime, dialect, or vocabulary to prevent its attribution to Chaucer. The second (Fragment B), lines 1705–5810, is much less faithful in its following of the French text, and includes within its limits nearly all of the false rimes and northern forms which had led earlier scholars to reject the whole translation. Fragment C, lines 5811 to end, returns in method of translation and in style to the manner of Fragment A,

gracefully admits his errors, and assents fully to Kaluza's position. See Skeat's communication to *The Academy* for September 8, 1888, pp. 153, 154.

[1] Vol. ii, pp. 3–166. Professor Lounsbury has never retreated from the position here maintained. He is, as far as the present writer knows, the only scholar who still asserts the Chaucerian authorship of the whole translation.

[2] *Harvard Studies and Notes in Philology and Literature*, 1. 1–65. See also Skeat in *The Academy* for February 27, 1892, pp. 206, 207.

[3] *Chaucer und der Rosenroman*, Berlin, 1893. Kaluza had previously communicated his discoveries to Furnivall, who in turn communicated them to *The Academy* for July 5, 1890, p. 11. See also Skeat's communications to the same paper for July 19, 1890 (pp. 51, 52), and August 15, 1891 (p. 137).

and contains only a small number of questionable rimes
and forms. Dr. Kaluza reaches the conclusion that
Fragments A and C are the work of Chaucer, and that
Fragment B is the work of an unknown poet of northern dialect, who, imitating as well as he could the manner of Chaucer, set himself to complete Chaucer's
unfinished work.[1] The main contentions of Kaluza's
study have been pretty generally accepted; and most
scholars now agree that Fragment A is by Chaucer, and
that Fragment B certainly is not. About Fragment C
there is still much dispute, Professor Skeat declining to
accept it as Chaucer's.[2] The present writer is inclined
to agree with Kaluza in thinking it genuine.[3]

It may be held as fairly certain, then, that, intimate
as was Chaucer's acquaintance with the whole of the
Roman de la Rose, and great as was the influence it
exerted upon him, he executed but a small part of his
projected translation of the work, and that his unfinished version was later continued by some poet of
Chaucer's school.

It remains to ask at what period of his career Chaucer's fragmentary translation was made. While the
whole of the existing translation was held as Chaucer's
work, its imperfect rimes led students to attribute it

[1] In *Essays on Chaucer*, published by the Chaucer Society, pp. 675–683,
Skeat assigns the dialect of Fragment B to ' some county not far from
the Humber, as Lancashire, Yorkshire, or Lincolnshire.' The date of
the fragment he thinks to be later than 1400 and earlier than 1440. It
has recently been urged by J. H. Lange in *Englische Studien*, 29. 397–
405 (1901), that the author of Fragment B is Chaucer's disciple Lydgate. The argument is plausible, but not conclusive. Skeat has shown
(*Athenæum*, June 6, 1896, p. 747) that Lydgate was acquainted with
Fragment A.

[2] *Oxford Chaucer*, 1. 1–20.

[3] The latest attempt to prove Chaucer's authorship for the *whole*
translation is that of Miss Louise Pound in *Modern Language Notes*, 11.
92–102 (1896). The argument, which is based on the sentence-length
in Chaucer's genuine poems and in the *Romaunt*, is hardly convincing.

to the earliest period of the poet's activity. When, on the other hand, the whole work was considered spurious, this argument ceased to operate, and the fact that the *Romaunt* is mentioned in the Prologue to the *Legend of Good Women* in close association with the *Troilus* led Ten Brink to the conclusion that Chaucer's supposedly lost translation belonged to a period only slightly earlier than his *Troilus*.[1] To this conclusion Kaluza also assents.[2] Though the question probably is not capable of final proof, the present writer is inclined to hold to the earlier view, that Chaucer's translation belongs to the period of his youth. Though the portions of the work which may be attributed to Chaucer are of a high degree of excellence, easy and spirited,[3] they have not the power of his maturer work. The translation is a good one, but not a great one. There are, moreover, in Fragment C at least, a number of imperfect rimes that can be accepted as Chaucer's only on the assumption that the work is immature. Finally, it seems inherently more probable that an undertaking of this character should belong to the period of the poet's apprenticeship rather than to that of his developed art.[4] The association of the work with *Troilus* may be sufficiently explained as due to the similarity in the spirit of the two works.[5]

[1] *History of English Literature* (Eng. trans.), 2. 76, 77 ; and *Englische Studien*, 17. 9, 10.

[2] *Chaucer und der Rosenroman*, 1, 2.

[3] The first 1678 lines of the French poem are reprinted from Méon's edition in Skeat's *Oxford Chaucer*, 1. 93–164, parallel with Chaucer's version. The student is thus enabled to make his own comparisons between original and translation. The English version is but 27 lines longer than the French.

[4] Skeat, apparently, continues to regard the *Romaunt* as an early work. Cf. the *Oxford Chaucer*, 1. 11.

[5] For the date of the *Romaunt*, see also Koch's *The Chronology of Chaucer's Writings* (Chaucer Society), pp. 12–15.

CHAPTER IV

THE MINOR POEMS

THOUGH among the Minor Poems of Chaucer are numbered many of his latest as well as of his earliest productions, it is convenient to treat of them together in a single chapter. Nor is the departure from the chronological method which such treatment involves without its compensating advantages; for in their variety of theme and tone, and even more in their wide metrical range, they constitute an excellent introduction to Chaucer's longer and more sustained compositions. In the following pages the Minor Poems are considered severally in the approximately chronological order adopted in Professor Skeat's edition.

I. AN A. B. C.

Chaucer's *A. B. C.*, a 'song according to the order of the letters of the alphabet,' is merely a translation, as literal as the exigencies of rime and rhythm would permit, of a hymn to the Virgin included in *La Pèlerinage de la Vie Humaine* of Guillaume de Deguilleville, 'a Cistercian monk in the royal abbey of Chalis,' written about the year 1330. Of the date of Chaucer's translation we have no certain knowledge; but from the choice of subject and the manner of execution, it is safe to infer that it is among the poet's earliest works. It is merely a meritorious essay in verse composition. The introductory statement in Speght's Chaucer of 1602, where the *A. B. C.* was first printed, to the effect that it was made, 'as some say, at the

Request of Blanch, Duchesse of Lancaster, as a praier for her priuat vse, being a woman in her religion very deuout,' is not supported by any other evidence. The verse is iambic pentameter; the stanza contains eight lines, with the rime-scheme *ababbcbc*. The stanza of Chaucer's original contains twelve lines of octosyllabic verse, with only two rimes.

II. THE COMPLAINT TO PITY

The love-lorn squire, Aurelius, in the *Franklin's Tale*, tried to ease his heart by making 'manye layes, songes, *compleintes*, roundels, virelayes;' and, apparently, in his younger days, Chaucer had done the same. Whether the unhappy love expressed in the 'complaint' and described again at the beginning of the *Book of the Duchess* was a real and deep passion or not, we have no way of knowing. Don Quixote, when he would make himself a knight-errant complete, provided himself with a Dulcinea del Toboso whom he might serve as lady-love; and it is quite possible that when Chaucer would launch himself as a courtly poet, he found it expedient to do the same. Still we must not assume the truth of such a hypothesis merely because the expression of this love is clothed in artificial and conventional forms. Personally, I find the idea of a hopeless love, protracted through eight long years, out of harmony with the eminent sanity of Chaucer's nature. But who shall say?

We do not know the date of the *Complaint to Pity*, nor do we know whether or not it was original with Chaucer.[1] It is a conventional love poem on the French model, and is in all probability one of Chaucer's earliest extant works. It is interesting chiefly as

---

[1] Professor Skeat's attempt to find a parallel for the personification of Pity in the *Thebais* of Statius seems unnecessary.

being probably the earliest appearance in English verse of the seven-line stanza, with rime-scheme *ababbcc*, known as the rime-royal, which was later used in *Troilus and Criseyde*.

III. THE BOOK OF THE DUCHESS

The *Book of the Duchess*, or the 'Deeth of Blaunche the Duchesse,' as it is called in the Prologue to the *Legend of Good Women*, is the first of Chaucer's poems to which a definite date can be assigned. In September, 1369, died the Lady Blanche, daughter of Henry, Duke of Lancaster, and first wife of Chaucer's patron, John of Gaunt; and soon after her death, we may suppose, was written the poem which celebrates her virtue and bewails her loss. John of Gaunt and his lady were both twenty-nine years old; and if we accept the year 1340 as the approximate date of Chaucer's birth, this also was the age of the poet. Twenty-nine he was at least, perhaps older, so that if this be his first original work of any length, — and its immaturity lends credence to the belief, — Chaucer's genius was slow in its development. Keats, we remember, was but twenty-six when death took him away.

Chaucer's literary apprenticeship was worked out in the school of the *Roman de la Rose*, his translation of the poem being very likely his first serious venture into the field of letters; and the *Book of the Duchess*, like other work of his earliest period, is strongly under the influence of the allegorical love poetry of France. From that source, directly or indirectly, comes the whole machinery of the poem, its dream and vision, its singing birds, its flowery meads; from the same source are drawn some of the ideas also. Were not the walls of the chamber in which the poet dreamed that he awoke

> Peynted, bothe text and glose,
> Of al the Romaunce of the Rose ?

Of the same school of poetry is the Frenchman, Guillaume de Machault (1300?–1377), and from him, too,
Chaucer has borrowed here and there.[1] Machault's
Dit de la Fontaine Amoureuse, which Chaucer certainly knew, contains a long paraphrase of the story
of Ceyx and Alcyone; and it has been asserted that
this suggested the Proem of the *Book of the Duchess*.[2]
It is quite likely that Chaucer did consult Machault's
version of the story; but it is clearly demonstrable
that he also went directly to Ovid, and that he is more
indebted to the Latin than to the French. Though
the general spirit of the *Book of the Duchess* is of
the French school, its plot, if it may be said to have
a plot, is Chaucer's own. Of its 1334 lines, not more
than a hundred have been traced to a definite French
original.[3]

It is possible that the story of Ceyx and Alcyone
was originally an independent work. In the Prologue
of the *Man of Law's Tale*, at any rate, we read that

> In youthe he made of Ceys and Alcion;

but this may very well refer to the *Book of the
Duchess*, which, as we know, was made in Chaucer's
youth.

It is as a work of the poet's youth, a mark from which
one may measure his subsequent literary development,
Literary   that the *Book of the Duchess* deserves at-
Art.   tention. Intrinsically its value is but slight.
It is not lacking in beautiful and effective passages;

---

[1] See Sandras, *Étude sur G. Chaucer*, 291–294.

[2] The significant portions of the *Dit de la Fontaine Amoureuse* are
given by Ten Brink, *Studien*, 197–205. Ovid's version is found in *Metamorphoses*, 11. 410–748.

[3] Cf. Lounsbury's *Studies in Chaucer*, 2. 212.

but, taken as a whole, it furnishes but weary reading.
Distinctly graceful and pleasing is the story of Ceyx
and Alcyone, when judged purely on its own merits as
an imitation of Ovid; but so slight is its connection
with the main theme of the poem, that it constitutes
a serious breach of artistic unity. By far the most
charming passage of the whole work is the account
of the poet's supposed awakening, with the merry singing of the birds without the pictured windows of his
chamber broken by the sudden blast of the huntsman's
horn, all the varied life and motion of the hunt, the
flowers and trees and wild beasts of the greenwood.
It is not till the lonely knight begins to speak that
the poem sinks to its true level of mediocrity. Not
only are his speeches intolerably long, they are also
essentially artificial. If he may be forgiven his conventional diatribe against malicious fortune, and his
strange conceit of the game of chess, features borrowed from Machault, it is hard to overlook his unin-
termitted pedantry. He ransacks the treasure-house of
classical antiquity, and the Bible as well, to furnish
forth fit comparisons for his loss, and, not content with
this, stops now and then to explain a more recondite
allusion. He tells how he had made many songs to win
his lady's love : —

> Althogh I coude not make so wel
> Songes, ne knowe the art al,
> As coude Lamekes sone Tubal,
> That fond out first the art of songe;
> For, as his brothers hamers ronge
> Upon his anvelt up and doun,
> Therof he took the firste soun;
> But Grekes seyn, Pictagoras,
> That he the firste finder was
> Of the art; Aurora telleth so,
> But therof no fors, of hem two.

It is Chaucer, of course, and not the bereaved knight,
who is thus jealous of his reputation for philological
accuracy. 'But therof no fors, of hem two;' it is in
either case a serious lapse from literary taste. Lapses
of this sort Chaucer never wholly outgrew.

In passing judgment so harshly on the long speeches
of the knight, some exception must be made for the passage in which he describes the charms, spiritual as well
as physical, of the 'gode faire Whyte.' Of this Lowell
has spoken as 'one of the most beautiful portraits of
a woman that was ever drawn.' 'Full of life it is,' he
continues, 'and of graceful health, with no romantic
hectic or sentimental languish. It is such a figure as you
would never look for in a ballroom, but might expect
to meet in the dewy woods, just after sunrise, when you
were hunting for late violets.' [1] But even here one is
tempted to cry out on the score of prolixity.

Some attempt is made to create a sort of suspense by
withholding till the very end the fact that the knight's
loss of his lady is the irreparable loss of death; and
after the long-drawn-out speeches of the poem, a distinctly striking effect is produced by the abruptness of
the end, with its utter restraint : —

> 'She is deed !' 'Nay !' 'Yis, by my trouthe !'
> 'Is that your los ? by God, hit is routhe !'

I cannot agree with the majority of critics who see in
this ending proof that Chaucer tired of his work and
ended the poem hastily ; it seems to me rather a stroke
of deliberate art.

In its lack of good proportion and its frequent lapses
in taste, in the occasional roughness of metre which suggests the earlier alliterative line, in its lack of humor and
delicate irony, — for which, to be sure, there is little
opportunity, — we see that the *Book of the Duchess*

[1] *Conversations on some of the Old Poets*, p. 98.

stands at the beginning of Chaucer's development. In its graceful treatment of nature, its well-managed transitions, its skillful use of dialogue, in its portrait of noble womanhood and its occasional pathos, it gives promise of the splendid development to come.

IV. THE COMPLAINT OF MARS

The *Complaint of Mars* is a conventional poem, supposed to be sung by a bird on St. Valentine's Day, in which mythology and astronomy are curiously blent together to the greater glory of illicit love. There is nothing to indicate the date of its composition, nor have we any certain knowledge whether or not it was intended to celebrate an actual intrigue; though the old copyist, Shirley, appended to his manuscript copy of the piece the statement that some men say that it was made about my Lady of York, daughter to the King of Spain, and my Lord Huntingdon, sometime Duke of Exeter. The lady named was sister-in-law to Chaucer's patron, John of Gaunt, while my Lord Huntingdon afterwards married John of Gaunt's daughter, Elizabeth. Shirley further assures us in his heading to the poem that it was made at John of Gaunt's command. The *Complaint* has little claim to attention save for the fact that a somewhat difficult nine-line stanza is handled with a good deal of skill.

V. THE PARLIAMENT OF FOWLS

On the twentieth day after Christmas, in January, 1382, King Richard was married in the chapel of the palace at Westminster to the Lady Anne of Bohemia, a daughter of the Emperor Charles IV and a sister of Wenceslaus, King of Bohemia, 'who at this period had taken the title of Emperor of Rome.' Richard was but fifteen years old, and his bride was

Date.

but a few months his senior. For upwards of a year, Froissart tells us, Richard had been in treaty with King Wenceslaus, and the Lady Anne had been previously contracted to two German princes; so that the course of this diplomatic courtship had not been a very smooth one.

Though we cannot assert the fact with positive assurance, it seems very probable that it is the events of this royal courtship which Chaucer celebrates allegorically in his *Parliament of Fowls*. The 'formel egle,' which Nature holds on her hand, —

> Of shap the gentileste
> That ever she among hir werkes fonde,
> The most benigne and the goodlieste, —

would then represent the Lady Anne. The 'tercel egle,' 'the foul royal,' who declares his love for her, would stand for Richard, while the other two eagles, 'of lower kinde,' would be the two earlier suitors. The year of respite which Dame Nature grants, in which the 'formel egle' is to choose between her suitors, corresponds with the period over which the diplomatic negotiations were protracted. Chaucer is evidently celebrating a courtship in high life, and no other courtship of the period so well accords with the incidents of the poem. The maturity of Chaucer's literary art in the poem, furthermore, agrees very well with a date as late as 1382. That it cannot have been written later than 1385 is proved by the mention of it in the Prologue to the *Legend of Good Women*. It is not at all impossible that the delicate flattery of the *Parliament of Fowls* may have been directly responsible for the favor which Queen Anne showed to Chaucer three years later.[1]

Though its general form as a poem of the dream-

---

[1] Cf. p. 141.

vision type associates the *Parliament of Fowls* with
the essentially mediæval, French models of
Chaucer's earlier period, such as the *Ro-* Sources.
maunt of the Rose, and though the conception of
an assembly of fowls is probably of French origin,[1] the
poem shows overwhelming proof of the influence of
the new culture which came to Chaucer as a result of
his Italian journeys of 1373 and 1378.

After four introductory stanzas, Chaucer devotes fifty-
six lines to a synopsis of Cicero's *Somnium Scipionis*,
which he was reading before he fell asleep and dreamed
his dream. This work, a part of the *De Republica*,
was not known to Chaucer and to his contemporaries
in its original setting, for the *De Republica* was not
recovered till a later date, but was preserved as an extract in a copious commentary of Macrobius, a gram-
marian and philosopher of the fifth century. This book
was a very popular one with Chaucer and with the
Middle Ages in general, and exerted no small influence
on the *Divine Comedy* of Dante. The extract from
Cicero, if not the laborious commentary of Macrobius,
is fully worthy of the popularity it achieved.

In the section which follows on the synopsis of the
Somnium Scipionis, the predominant influence is that
of Dante, from whom the inscription over the gate
to the garden of love is freely adapted; though one
stanza, beginning with the line, —

> The wery hunter, slepinge in his bed, —

is translated from the late Latin poet Claudian. For
the description of the garden and its delights (lines 176–
294) Chaucer is closely indebted to the *Teseide* of
Boccaccio. It was at about this time, apparently, that

---

[1] As Skeat has noticed, one of the fables of Marie de France is entitled 'Li parlemens des Oiseax por faire Roi.' *Oxford Chaucer*, 1. 75.

Chaucer wrote his *Palamon and Arcite*, known to us as the *Knight's Tale ;* and finding that the stanzas of the *Teseide* here utilized were not necessary for his longer work, he thriftily turned them to account in the *Parliament of Fowls*.

The description of the Goddess Nature surrounded by all the birds of the air is adapted, as Chaucer himself tells us, from the *De Planctu Naturæ* of Alanus de Insulis, a Latin poet and divine of the twelfth century. In Alanus, however, the birds are merely depicted on the robe which Nature wears. As for the parliament itself, with its long debate, which constitutes the real substance of the poem, that is, so far as we know, Chaucer's own original production.

As the sources of the poem show a twofold influence, that of the departing Middle Age and that of the new Italian culture, so too in its literary workmanship one Literary may detect the transition from the more con-Art. ventional poetry of Chaucer's earlier period to the work of his maturer genius. Structurally considered, the work is far from perfect ; for the real action of the piece does not begin till nearly three hundred lines have rolled melodiously by. Beautiful as is the description of the garden of love, its length is both relatively and absolutely extravagant. Quite unnecessary to the action is the synopsis of the *Somnium Scipionis* with which the poem begins, an unfortunate bit of introductory machinery which Chaucer also employs, at greater length, in his earlier *Book of the Duchess*.

It is not till Chaucer has finished his introductions, and has left his authors well behind him, that the conventional gives place to the natural, and the poet's genius plays freely. The graceful and charming conceit of Dame Nature on her hill of flowers, with all the birds about her come to choose their mates, is well executed and well sustained. If we fail to enter with much enthusiasm into the emotions of the three rival eagles as they plead their amorous causes, we are at any rate highly entertained by the varying counsels of the four estates in this feathered parliament.

The birds of prey, who constitute the peers of the realm, take the matter quite seriously. If necessary, they are willing to see in the dispute fit cause for war. The fowls of lower degree, the *bourgeois* birds who feed on worms, the mercantile birds who occupy their business in the water, those of agricultural pursuit who feed on seeds, care more for their own well-being and for the expeditious transaction of business than for any punctilio of honor.

> But she wol love him, lat him love another !

cries the unsentimental goose, as spokesman for the water-fowl, while the cuckoo, of the worm-eating estate, goes even further : —

> 'So I,' quod he, 'may have my make in pees,
> I recche not how longe that ye stryve ;
> Lat ech of hem be soleyn al hir lyve.'

From these radical views the turtle dove, representing the more poetical class of those who feed on seeds, is inclined to dissent : —

> Yet let him serve hir ever, til he be deed,

an opinion which the duck considers merely laughable.

Though characterized quite humanly, Chaucer does not suffer us to forget that the parliament is only one of fowls, and the sudden 'Kek, kek ! kukkow, quek, quek' which breaks upon us serves as a delicious bit of humorous realism, after the passionate speeches of the three tercel eagles. As in its general structure the

Parliament of Fowls leads us to comparisons with the *Book of the Duchess* which preceded it, so in its treatment of birds who speak like men it leads us forward to the more finished art of the *Nun's Priest's Tale*.

VI. A COMPLAINT TO HIS LADY

Chaucer's *Complaint to his Lady* is apparently no more than a series of experiments in verse form. Beginning with two stanzas of seven lines, it shifts into the *terza rima* of Dante, and thence into a complex stanza of ten lines, with rime-scheme *aabaabcddc*. This is the first appearance of the *terza rima* in English verse, and probably its only appearance until English literature was again Italianized in the days of Wyatt and Surrey. As Mr. Heath suggests, the poem should not be taken too seriously.[1] It may have been written shortly after Chaucer's Italian journey of 1373.

VII. ANELIDA AND ARCITE

The fragment of *Anelida and Arcite* consists of a Proem of three stanzas, twenty-seven stanzas of seven lines each of the 'Story,' followed by a Complaint in fourteen stanzas of very elaborate metrical construction. After the Complaint, the 'Story' is resumed, but is broken off after a single stanza. Probably the work was never completed.

In line 21 Chaucer gives as his sources 'Stace, and after him Corinne.' Stanzas 4–7 are indeed from the *Thebais* of Statius; but who 'Corinne' may be, we do not know, — very likely the name is one of Chaucer's sheer inventions, — nor do we know any source for the story. But for six stanzas of the poem (1–3, 8–10) a source is easily discoverable. They are taken from the first and second books of Boccaccio's *Teseide*, the

[1] *Globe Chaucer*, p. xxxvii.

poem which served as the foundation of the *Knight's
Tale*. Since stanzas from the *Teseide* are also found
in the *Parliament of Fowls* and in *Troilus*, it is natural to infer that these three poems were written at
about the same time, when Chaucer was busy with
his *Palamon and Arcite*, later known as the *Knight's
Tale;* that is, soon after the year 1380.

Since the poem is a mere fragment, it is not possible
to say much of its literary qualities, save to call attention to the metrical skill and pleasing effect of the
Complaint which is incorporated into it. Neither can
we, while in ignorance of its source, venture to guess
how the story would have been concluded. Though also
a Theban at the court of Theseus, the Arcite of this
poem has nothing to do with the Arcite of the *Knight's
Tale*. It is not impossible that Chaucer may have
intended to celebrate some love story of the English
court, and that being busy with the *Teseide*, he chose
to shadow forth his real personages under names borrowed from the court of Theseus, inventing the name
Corinne to increase the obscurity of his allegory. Fragment as it is, the piece gives unquestioned proof of
Chaucer's power.

VIII. CHAUCER'S WORDS UNTO ADAM

I know no better way to illustrate Chaucer's half-seri-
ous, half-playful address to his copyist, than by quoting
the words of Petrarch to a friend to whom he wished
to send a copy of his own work on the *Life of Solitude:* 'I have tried ten times and more to have it copied
in such a way that, even if the style should not please
either the ears or the mind, the eyes might yet be grati-
fied by the form of the letters. But the faithfulness
and industry of the copyists, of whom I am constantly
complaining and with which you are familiar, have, in

spite of all my earnest efforts, frustrated my wishes. These fellows are verily the plague of noble minds. What I have just said must seem incredible. A work written in a few months cannot be copied in so many years! The trouble and discouragement involved in the case of more important books is obvious. . . . Such is the ignorance, laziness, or arrogance of these fellows, that, strange as it may seem, they do not reproduce what you give them, but write out something quite different.' [1]

One may assume that the poem was written soon after *Troilus* and *Boece*, which it mentions in the second line. It is written in the seven-line stanza of *Troilus*.

IX. THE FORMER AGE

Poets have always been ready to sing the praises of long ago, and to Chaucer, living in an age of continual warfare, of corruption and oppression, the ' blisful lyf, paisible and swete, led by the peples in the former age,' may well have appealed very strongly. Doubtless he was wise enough and practical enough to see the fallacies of a general ' return to nature,' and to recognize that civilization has brought its blessings as well as its curses; but he was also philosopher enough to see that ' covetyse ' was really at the bottom of all the most serious evils of his day, as it is of our own. The poem is founded on the fifth metre of the second book of Boethius's *Consolation of Philosophy*, and may profitably be compared with Chaucer's prose translation of the same passage. About twenty lines of *The Former Age* are directly taken from Boethius, while the remainder are Chaucer's own expansion of the theme. There is nothing to indicate the date of its composition.

---

[1] Robinson and Rolfe, *Petrarch, the First Modern Scholar and Man of Letters*, New York, 1899, pp. 27, 28.

The stanza consists of eight lines, with rime-scheme *ababbcbc*.

X. FORTUNE

Because the poem called *Fortune*, like *The Former Age*, is little more than a restatement of the teachings of Boethius,[1] it must not be inferred that it is a mere literary *tour de force.* Indirectly at first through the *Roman de la Rose*, and later from the *Consolation of Philosophy* itself, Chaucer assimilated the philosophy of Boethius into his own soul, and made it the guiding principle of his life. Trite though they be, the thoughts expressed in *Fortune* are noble thoughts; and they are nobly spoken forth, not only with art, but with conviction. Fortune may govern all things with her fickleness, but 'man is man and master of his fate.' Not only may a true man defy Fortune, he may learn from her frowns which of his friends are friends indeed, which things in life are really enduring. Before the poem closes, its stoicism becomes a Christian stoicism. The very uncertainty of things terrestrial, which we, 'ful of lewednesse,' call Fortune, is but part of the scheme of righteous Providence : —

> The hevene hath propretee of sikernesse,
> This world hath ever resteles travayle;
> Thy laste day is end of myn intresse:
> In general, this reule may nat fayle.

Whether the poem was called forth by some particular reverse of fortune or not cannot be known; but the definiteness of the refrain, —

> And eek thou hast thy beste frend alyve, —

and of the appeal to certain princes in the envoy, seems to suggest that this may have been the case. But who

---

[1] Cf. Boethius, Book II, Proses 1, 2, 3, 4, 5, 8, and Metre 1. Here and there the influence of Boethius seems to be at second hand through the *Roman de la Rose*. See Skeat's notes, *Oxford Chaucer*, 1. 542–547.

the friend may be, and what the occasion, it were idle to inquire.

Apart from the nobility of its thought and the elevation of its language, the poem is remarkable for the metrical skill which it betrays. The poem consists of three balades and an envoy. Each of the balades has three stanzas of eight lines each, with the rime-scheme *ababbcbc*, and the rimes are identical in each of the three stanzas; so that the rime ' b ' is repeated twelve times, while the rimes ' a ' and ' c ' appear six times each ; yet there is scarcely a line in which one is conscious of any conflict between versification and thought.

XI. MERCILESS BEAUTY

In the Prologue to the *Legend of Good Women*, it is said that Chaucer made many a hymn for love's holidays, —

That highten Balades, *Roundels*, Virelayes.

The roundel is a highly elaborate verse form, borrowed from France. The stanza contains thirteen lines, with rime-scheme *abbababbabbabb*, in which lines one and two are repeated as lines six and seven, and are again repeated with line three to form the last three lines of the stanza. The three roundels of this poem and the one near the end of the *Parliament of Fowls* are the only roundels of Chaucer preserved to us. *Merciless Beauty* is a charmingly graceful, but entirely conventional, love poem, after the French school, and perhaps imitated from a French original.[1]

XII. TO ROSEMOUNDE

The balade *To Rosemounde* was discovered by Professor Skeat in 1891, appended to a manuscript of *Troilus and Criseyde* in the Bodleian Library. This

[1] See Skeat, *Oxford Chaucer*, 1. 548.

may indicate that it was written at the same time as
the longer poem; but whenever written, it breathes
the same spirit of mingled seriousness and irony. It is
thoroughly characteristic of Chaucer's developed art.
There are three stanzas of eight lines each, with rime-
scheme *ababbcbc*, the rimes of the first stanza being
repeated in the second and third.

XIII. TRUTH

The balade of *Truth* is the best answer one may
give to the charge that Chaucer was incapable of ' high
seriousness.' Though suggested in part by Boethius,
the poem is essentially original, and expresses, I think,
the substance of Chaucer's criticism of life. Like Langland and Wiclif, Chaucer was fully conscious of the
evils of his time; nor was he, as one might hastily infer
from the humorous treatment of these evils in the
Canterbury Tales, indifferent to their gravity. When
Jacques invites Orlando to sit down and 'rail against
our mistress the world, and all our misery,' Orlando
answers: 'I will chide no breather in the world but
myself, against whom I know most faults.' Orlando's
attitude seems to have been Shakespeare's attitude, as
it was certainly Chaucer's. 'Werk wel thyself, that
other folk canst rede.' The world is bad, but who am
I, to set it right? the poet asks. Shall I not merely
fill my own soul with storm and tempest, and all the
while be striving 'as doth the crokke with the wal'?
The poet is gifted with a delicate and sensitive soul,
which, kept untainted, can give forth life and beauty
to his own age and to the ages in store. To spend it
all in mad protest against a wicked world — what shall
it profit? Fleeing from the press, renouncing the
'strenuous life' to dwell with truth, Chaucer showed
his age its true likeness, its good and evil. The world

might listen or not, as it pleased. After all there is a power stronger than we, making for righteousness : —

> Daunte thyself, that dauntest otheres dede ;
> *And trouthe shal delivere, hit is no drede.*

But beyond all this, what is this world that we should struggle so to set it straight?

> Her nis non hoom, her nis but wildernesse:
> Forth, pilgrim, forth! Forth, beste, out of thy stal !
> Know thy contree, look up, thank God of al;
> Hold the hye wey, and lat thy gost thee lede;
> And trouthe shal delivere, hit is no drede.

The poem consists of three stanzas and an envoy, all in the seven-line stanza, with the same rimes reappearing in each stanza and in the envoy.[1]

XIV. GENTILESSE

Though borrowed in its general conception, like *Truth,* from Boethius, and in part also from the *Roman de la Rose,* the balade of *Gentilesse* expresses Chaucer's own conviction as to true gentility, a conviction which is expressed again in the *Wife of Bath's Tale.* Trite enough in a democratic age like the present, these thoughts were more novel in the day of Chaucer, particularly when they came from one who dwelt near the court, that great centre of all the 'solemn plausibilities' of life. There are three seven-line stanzas, with rimes repeated throughout.

XV. LACK OF STEADFASTNESS

If the philosophy of 'Flee fro the prees' be accepted as representing Chaucer's true conviction, it is not surprising to find that he very seldom assumes the prophet's mantle, and attempts to scourge, save with the lash of comedy, the evils and abuses of his time. One of the

---

[1] For further remarks on this poem, cf. above, pp. 29, 30.

few exceptions to this rule is the vigorous balade, with its envoy to King Richard, entitled *Lack of Stead-fastness*. Covetise and the love of meed, the 'lust that folk have in dissensioun,' the decay of virtue and of mercy — these are the evils which are bringing the world to naught; and in this opinion Chaucer is at one with Langland, with Wiclif, and with Gower.

To assign even an approximate date for the composition of the poem is very difficult. In the Tanner manuscript of the minor poems it is headed with the words: 'Balade Royal made by oure laureal poete of Albyon in hees laste yeeres.' Following this hint, Chaucerian scholars have generally assigned it to the years between 1393 and 1399, during which Richard succeeded in alienating the loyalty and affection of most of his subjects. Mr. Pollard, however, suggests, with a good deal of reason, that from a dependent of the court such advice to his sovereign would have been prudent only at an earlier period, in 1389 perhaps, 'when the young Richard was taking the government into his own hands, and throwing over the tutelage of his guardian uncles with the support of all his people's hopes.' [1]

Professor Skeat asserts that the general idea of the poem was taken from Boethius, Book II, Metre 8; but the indebtedness, if any, was very slight. The poem is essentially original. The metre is the same as that of *Truth*.

XVI. ENVOY TO SCOGAN

The date of the playful *Envoy to Scogan* may, perhaps, be determined by the allusion in the second stanza to 'this deluge of pestilence,' which has been interpreted as a reference to the unusually heavy rains which, according to Stowe's *Annales*, fell in the autumn of 1393. 'Such abundance of water fell in

---

[1] Preface to the Globe Edition, p. xlix.

October, that at Bury in Suffolke the church was full
of water, and at Newmarket it bare downe walles of
houses, so that men and women hardly escaped drown-
ing.' [1] This deluge, Chaucer suggests, was due to the
tears of Venus shed over Scogan's impiety in love. The
date 1393 would agree, moreover, with the closing
stanza, in which Chaucer speaks of himself 'in solitarie
wilderness' at the mouth of the Thames, that is at
Greenwich, whither he had been dispatched in 1390 on
a commission to repair the banks of the river. That
the poem was written in Chaucer's later years is evident from his humorous mention of those 'that ben
hore and rounde of shape,' in the number of whom he
includes himself.

Of Scogan we know little. He is probably the
Henry Scogan, Squire, who was later tutor to the sons
of Henry IV. In a balade of his own, written, Professor
Skeat thinks, 'not many years before 1413,' Scogan
refers to Chaucer as 'my maistre Chaucier,' and proceeds to quote entire Chaucer's balade of *Gentilesse*.
There are six stanzas and an envoy, all in the seven-
line stanza. The rimes in each stanza are different.

XVII. ENVOY TO BUKTON

The date of the thoroughly characteristic *Envoy
to Bukton* is determined by the allusion in line 23
to the undesirability of being taken prisoner in Fries-
land, whither a company of English was dispatched in
August, 1396, to the aid of William of Hainault. [2] A
late date is further indicated by the reference to the
Wife of Bath. Of Bukton we know only that a Peter
de Buketon was the king's escheator for the County of

---

[1] *Oxford Chaucer*, 1. 557.

[2] See Froissart's *Chronicles*, Book IV, chap. 78. In the preceding
chapter we read that 'The Frieslanders are a people void of honor
and understanding, and show mercy to none who fall in their way.'

York in 1397. Apparently, Bukton was meditating a second marriage. Chaucer's sound advice on the subject, which seems to be at least half serious, need not be taken as proof that his own marriage had been particularly unhappy. It is clear, however, that Chaucer, now a widower, had no intention of falling again into 'swich dotage' if he could help it. There are three stanzas and an envoy of eight lines each, with rime-scheme *ababbcbc*.

XVIII. THE COMPLAINT OF VENUS

The *Complaint of Venus* consists of three balades, loosely joined together, and supplemented by an envoy. As Chaucer himself tells us in the envoy, the balades are translated from the French of Sir Otes de Graunsoun, a poet of Savoy, contemporary with Chaucer. As may be learned from a comparison with the French text, which is printed in Skeat's *Oxford Chaucer*,[1] the translation does not 'folowe word by word,' but is rather free. Since this complaint is associated in many copies with the *Complaint of Mars*, it has been assumed that the princess addressed in the envoy is the Princess Isabel of Spain and Duchess of York, whose love is celebrated in the earlier piece. If this be true, the date of composition will fall between 1390 and 1394; for in the latter year Princess Isabel died, and in the envoy Chaucer speaks of himself as already dulled by old age. The poem, which is of the conventional type, is chiefly interesting for its elaborate rime-scheme, admirably handled. Each of the three balades consists of three eight-line stanzas, riming *ababbccb*, with repeated rimes. The envoy has ten lines, riming *aabaabbaab*.

[1] l. 400–404. See also the articles on Graunsoun by Dr. A. Piaget, who first discovered the French originals, in *Romania*, 19. 237–259, 403–448.

XIX. THE COMPLAINT OF CHAUCER TO HIS EMPTY PURSE

This delightful poem, which with delicate humor applies the conventional language of amorous poetry to an empty purse, is probably among Chaucer's latest compositions. The envoy, at any rate, addressed to Henry IV as 'conquerour of Brutes Albioun,' cannot have been written earlier than September 30, 1399, when Parliament formally acknowledged, by ' free eleccioun,' Henry's right to the throne. It is, of course, possible that the preceding stanzas had been written at an earlier time. It is pleasant to know that this delicate appeal for help met with almost immediate reply. On October 3 Chaucer received an additional pension grant of forty marks from the royal treasury. There are three seven-line stanzas, with repeated rimes, and an envoy of five lines, riming *aabba*.

XX. PROVERBS

The two Proverbs attributed to Chaucer by the manuscripts are not of sufficient value to merit any discussion. Each proverb contains four octosyllabic lines, riming *abab*.

XXI. AGAINST WOMEN UNCONSTANT

Though there is no sufficient external evidence to prove this poem one of Chaucer's, it is so thoroughly Chaucerian in manner, and withal so charming and graceful, that one is strongly inclined to think that the manuscripts and the early editions are right in associating it with his genuine work. The idea of the poem and its refrain are from the French of Machault, an author with whom Chaucer was thoroughly familiar. The metre is Chaucer's favorite seven-line stanza, with repeated rimes.

XXII. AN AMOROUS COMPLAINT

As in the case of the preceding poem, there is no satisfactory evidence that *An Amorous Complaint* is by Chaucer, though it is certainly in his manner. The poem has not sufficient excellence to make the question an important one. The seven-line stanza is employed.

XXIII. A BALADE OF COMPLAINT

This poem, like the preceding, is of the conventional erotic type. It occurs in but one manuscript, and is not there attributed to Chaucer. Though superior to *An Amorous Complaint* in art, it is not a poem which we need consider very seriously. There are three seven-line stanzas, without repetition of rime. The accidental recurrence of the *c* rime of the first stanza as the *a* rime of the second is a metrical blemish which may be taken as an argument against its Chaucerian authorship.

XXIV. WOMANLY NOBLESSE

This poem, which is found in a single manuscript, was first printed by Professor Skeat in *The Athenæum* for June 9, 1894. If not deserving of the high praise bestowed upon it by Professor Skeat in the first flush of discovery, it is yet a charming and graceful bit of conventional love poetry. The rime-scheme is highly elaborate, but three rimes appearing in the entire piece. There are three stanzas of nine lines each, riming *aabaabbaa*, with repeated rimes, and an envoy of six lines riming *ababaa*, in which the same rimes again appear. The *a* rime is therefore repeated twenty-two times. It should be noticed, however, that Chaucer has prudently chosen very easy rimes.

CHAPTER V

BOETHIUS AND THE ASTROLABE

BOETHIUS DE CONSOLATIONE PHILOSOPHIE

DURING the whole extent of the Middle Ages there was no single work, save the Bible itself, which ex-
The erted so wide and continuous an influence on
Original. the thought of Europe as the dialogue of
Boethius on the *Consolation of Philosophy*. In England its influence may be traced from the very dawn of our literature; for the moralizing interpolations in *Beowulf* are in several instances to be traced to this source, and the *De Consolatione* was among the works which the great Alfred gave to his countrymen, translated into their own speech. Chaucer, as has already been seen, was permeated through and through with the teachings of Boethius, and his contemporaries felt this influence as strongly. What is true of England is true also of France and Italy and Germany. The direct influence of Boethius, moreover, was supplemented by an indirect influence, exerting itself through the channels of other books, notably of the *Roman de la Rose*. Through this channel, not improbably, Chaucer first met the doctrines of Boethius; and it is not impossible that the idea of Chaucer's translation was first suggested by a couplet of the *Roman* : —

> 'T would redound
> Greatly to that man's praise who should
> Translate that book with masterhood.[1]

[1] Ellis's translation, ll. 5344–5346.

Jean de Meun, at any rate, followed his own advice, and made a translation of the book into French.

The work fully deserved the popularity it attained, both in virtue of its inherent excellence and charm, and in virtue of the fascinatingly romantic life of its author. Additional authority was given to it by the tradition, now strongly questioned but never satisfactorily refuted, that its author was a Christian, and by the erroneous belief that he gave his life, a martyr for the true faith. Two or three centuries after his death, he was canonized as St. Severinus.

Anicius Manlius Severinus Boethius was born between the years 475 and 483 A. D., probably later than 480, and died in 524, his life falling in the exciting days of Odoacer and Theodoric. His family was one of high standing, which had for six centuries held office in the public service; his father, who died in the philosopher's boyhood, had been prefect of the city, prætorian prefect, and consul. Boethius married the daughter of his kinsman and guardian, Symmachus, a senator, and himself sat in the Senate. In the year 510 he was elected sole consul through the favor of Theodoric. In 522 the philosopher's two sons were made consuls together.

Though participating in affairs of state, Boethius's highest efforts were given to his books. His education was of the best, and his wide attainments included a knowledge of Greek. 'He translated the works of Pythagoras on music, of Ptolemy on astromomy, of Nichomachus on arithmetic, of Euclid on geometry, of Archimedes on mechanics. Finally, he sought to bring the whole of Greek speculative science within the range of Roman readers; and though he did not live to see the attainment of his ambition, he managed to give to the world in something less than twenty years, of which several were absorbed in the discharge of public duties,

more than thirty books of commentary on, and translation of, Aristotle.' [1]

From this life of distinguished service, Boethius was
snatched by a sudden tragic catastrophe. The Senate
was suspected by Theodoric of a treasonable intent
to restore the ancient liberties of Rome ; and Boethius
was chosen as the one to bear the full brunt of the royal
displeasure. Out of the mouths of notorious false witnesses, as Boethius insists, he was convicted of treason,
was imprisoned at Pavia, and, after a long imprisonment,
was put to death. It was during this period of imprisonment that he wrote the *Consolation of Philosophy.*

This, the latest and greatest of Boethius's writings,
is a dialogue between the author and the goodly lady
Philosophy, in alternating sections of prose and verse,
wherein are discussed those great problems of human
life which were brought vividly to the author's consciousness by his sudden and overwhelming misfortune,
coming as it did close on the heels of his highest prosperity. In briefest outline, the argument runs as
follows: As Boethius bewails in prison the wretchedness that has come upon him, suddenly appears to him
the majestic figure of Philosophy. 'When all the
universe is ordered by God,' the prisoner asks, 'why
should man alone wander at will?' Philosophy, in her
reply, asserts the absolute omnipotence of God (Book I).
It is not right to blame Fortune for our woes, for none
of the gifts of Fortune are really valuable. Fortune
really benefits man only when she frowns upon him,
thus teaching him what is the true good (Book II).
What, then, is this true good? It must include within
itself all the partial goods for which various men strive ;

---

[1] H. F. Stewart, *Boethius, an Essay*, Edinburgh and London, 1891,
p. 26. This volume of 279 pages may be most enthusiastically recom-
mended to any one who wishes to know more of Boethius and of his
philosophy.

and this absolute and perfect good, the sum of all partial goods, is God himself. Since all men instinctively seek happiness, and since happiness consists only in the true good, all men naturally seek God (Book III). But if God is the supreme good and is omnipotent, why do the wicked flourish? To this world-old question Philosophy answers in the spirit of Plato, that the wicked are not really powerful, that properly they do not even exist at all. They are no part of God, and God alone really exists. God, in his omnipotence, rules the world by his providence, Fate being merely his minister, the actual working out of his providence. Chance does not exist at all (Book IV). But if God's providence rules all things, what room is left for the free will of man? To God, who is the only eternal, superior to the accident of time, all things, past, present, and future, lie open in an 'everlasting now;' and all these things, being patent to his foreknowledge, have been ordered by him into a divine harmony. But to man, living under the condition of time, seeing only the past and present, blind to the future, there is at the moment a real freedom of choice. God foresees, but does not predestine; yet, since his foreknowledge is infallible, he overrules, not the choice, but the consequences of the choice. Thus the freedom of man's will is not inconsistent with God's overruling government (Book V).

The philosophy of the *Consolation*, though not untouched by Christian influence, is essentially pagan, an eclectic blending of Plato (and the Neo-Platonists) with Aristotle and the Stoics. Boethius is indeed the 'last of the Romans.' Noble and exalted as is the spirit which informs the dialogue, the consolation sought and received is not the consolation of the Christian; it is not a matter of faith, but of reason. It is curious that the subtle theological intellect of the Middle Ages should have accepted it with whole-hearted approval.[1]

To Chaucer the *Consolation of Philosophy* became the dominant influence in all his more speculative thought. Under its guidance he philosophized the story of Troilus and that of Palamon and Arcite; it is the thought of Boethius which he revitalizes in such *balades* as *Truth* and *Fortune* and *The Former Age*.[2]

There is no evidence which determines precisely the date of Chaucer's translation. It is included in the list The Trans- of the poet's works given in the Prologue to lation. the *Legend of Good Women*, and must therefore be earlier than 1386. Because of the very great Boethian influence on *Troilus*, and because of the fact that Chaucer mentions *Troilus* and his 'Boece' together in the lines addressed to Adam, his scrivener, it has been thought that the two works were executed at about the same time, i.e. shortly after 1380.

Chaucer used for his translation not only the Latin original, but also a French version, probably the work of Jean de Meun, which is preserved in two manuscripts of the Bibliothèque Nationale at Paris. As only a few excerpts from this translation have been printed, the precise extent of Chaucer's dependence on it has not been determined; but his debt seems to have been considerable.[3] Some of Chaucer's many glosses are taken

[1] The Latin text of the *Consolatio*, together with a seventeenth-century translation by 'I. T.' has been published in the Loeb Classical Library (1918), under the editorship of H. F. Stewart and E. K. Rand.

[2] For a most illuminating account of Chaucer's use of the *Consolation*, and for a discussion of his translation of the work, see B. L. Jefferson, *Chaucer and the Consolation of Philosophy of Boethius*, Princeton University Press, 1917.

[3] See M. H. Liddell's article in *Academy*, 1895, II. 227, and his notes in the Globe Chaucer. See also the discussion by B. L. Jefferson, *op. cit.* pp. 1–9. Dr. Jefferson's conclusions were independently corroborated by J. L. Lowes in *Romanic Review*, 8.383–400 (1917).

over from the French version; others are apparently from the commentary of Nicholas Trivet.[1]

Chaucer's translation is not free from blunders. For some of these the corruptions of his Latin text may be responsible; in the case of others he was certainly misled by the French version. But on the whole he has given a faithful and able rendering. The prose style of the translation, cumbersome and at times confused, and for our modern taste much too rhetorical, is in striking contrast with the directness and simplicity, the clearness and grace, of Chaucer's verse. Mr. Stewart says of it: [2] 'It is certainly not in prose that Chaucer's genius shows to best advantage. The restrictions of metre were indeed to him as silken fetters, while the freedom of prose only served to embarrass him.' Perhaps it would be better to say that for Chaucer and for his contemporaries prose offered not untrammeled freedom, but the intricacies of a literary medium not yet mastered. For the prose of Chaucer's translation, if not always felicitous, is anything but artless. It employs intricate alliteration, balance and antithesis, varied cadence of clause, and other 'colours of rethoryk.' At his best, Chaucer attains to a dignity and eloquence that suggest the perfection, three centuries later, of this same tradition of rhetorical prose in the hands of John Milton.

A TREATISE ON THE ASTROLABE

An astrolabe is 'an obsolete astronomical instrument of different forms, used for taking the altitude of the sun or stars, and for the solution of other problems in astronomy.' Chaucer's Treatise is an attempt to expound 'under ful lighte rewles and naked wordes in

[1] See the article by Miss K. O. Petersen, 'Chaucer and Trivet' *Publications of the Modern Language Association*, 18. 173–193 (1903).

[2] *Boethius, an Essay*, p. 227.

English,' the uses of the instrument and the elements of astronomy and astrology, for the benefit of ' litel Lowis my sone,' who had attained the 'tendre age of ten yeer.' As outlined in the Prologue, the work was to have consisted of five parts; but of these only the first and part of the second were completed. As the ' yeer of oure lord 1391, the 12 day of March ' is twice used [1] as an example in the ' conclusions ' of Part II, it is reasonable to assume that the year 1391 is the date of composition. Chaucer makes no claim to originality in his work : ' I ne usurpe nat to have founde this werk of my labour or of myn engyn. I nam but a lewd compilatour of the labour of olde Astrologiens, and have hit translated in myn English only for thy doctrine ; and with this swerd shal I sleen envye.' Professor Skeat has shown that the ' old astrologien ' from whom Chaucer has drawn the great bulk of his material is a Latin translation of a treatise by Messahala, an Arabian astronomer who flourished towards the end of the eighth century, entitled *Compositio et Operatio Astrolabie*. As the tables were to be calculated ' aftur the latitude of Oxenford,' it has been assumed that little Lewis was a student in the Oxford schools; beyond this we know nothing whatever about him, and it is not unlikely that he may have died before reaching manhood. Since the work has no literary value save that of clear exposition, and since the modern reader is little likely to attempt its perusal, it is not necessary to discuss it further, except to call attention to the charming character of the introductory sentences addressed by the author to his little son. [2]

[1] 2. 1. 6 and 2. 3. 18.

[2] The treatise has been edited by Mr. A. E. Brae, London, 1870, and again in 1872 by Professor Skeat for the Chaucer Society. Skeat's observations are repeated, in condensed form, in the *Oxford Chaucer*, 3. lvii-lxxx.

CHAPTER VI

TROILUS AND CRISEYDE

Of all the poems of Chaucer, not excepting the *Canterbury Tales*, none is more characteristic of his genius than is *Troilus and Criseyde*. In some ways it is his supreme masterpiece; for it is the only work of large dimensions, requiring a sustained effort of the poetical imagination, which he brought to completion. In mastery of constructive art, in perfect finish of execution, in portrayal of character and easy flow of action, above all in its dramatic objectiveness and vivid actuality, it will bear comparison with any narrative poem in the language.

Hitherto Chaucer had written, gracefully and wittily, in the school of French allegory and dream-vision. With *Troilus* he becomes the poet of living humanity. Though ostensibly a tale of Troy long ago, it makes but the scantest attempt to suggest the world of classical antiquity. Only the names are ancient; the characters, the manners, are modern and contemporary. Troy is but mediæval London, besieged as it might have been by the French. The parliament which King Priam convenes is an English parliament. Troilus might as well be son to Edward III. Its spirit and temper is that of the modern novel rather than of the mediæval romance. Were it written in prose, it would be called the first English novel.

To the taste of the modern reader, particularly at a first reading, it may seem in places tediously prolix; for considering its length there is comparatively little action. Its interest lies not in rapid action, but in a keen, minute, almost Richardsonian portrayal of character and situation. Its appeal grows with a second reading or a third. One ceases to be impatient at the slowness of progress, and looks eagerly in every stanza for subtle revelations of character and motive, for flashes of that ironical humor with which Chaucer has enlivened his essentially tragic theme, for lines of haunting poetic beauty. Perhaps the poem would be more effective still if it were somewhat condensed; but it is none the less true that from beginning to end there is not a stanza which is really irrelevant.

That *Troilus and Criseyde* was written and already known to English readers before 1386 we know from the references to it in the Prologue to the *Legend of Good Women*. There is, further, a presumption amounting to virtual certainty that Chaucer was not acquainted with Boccaccio's *Filostrato*, his primary source for *Troilus*, earlier than his first Italian journey of 1373. Within this period of a dozen years the poem cannot be dated with absolute certainty; but a variety of considerations points strongly to a date not earlier than 1382. For a date earlier than that the only important evidence is found in a passage of Gower's long French poem, the *Miroir de l'Omme*, where mention is made of 'la geste de Troylus et de la belle Creseide.' If Gower is alluding to Chaucer's poem, we must date *Troilus* before 1377; but it seems probable that Gower is thinking of some earlier version of the famous story, despite the fact that the sole surviving manuscript of the *Miroir* gives the name of the lady as 'Creseide' instead of 'Briseide,' the name under which she appears in Benoit and Guido. The most definite evidence for a later date is found in the plausible interpretation which sees a veiled compliment to the young

Date of Composition.

Queen Anne in a passage near the beginning of *Troilus* which describes Criseyde's beauty: —

> Right as our firste lettre is now an A,
> In beautee first so stood she, makelees.

Professor J. L. Lowes [1] was the first to suggest that this curious alphabetic simile, otherwise rather inept, refers to the use of Queen Anne's initial 'A' intertwined with the initial 'R' of her royal husband as a decorative device on courtly robes and tapestries. If this interpretation is correct — and it is supported by documentary evidence that the queen's initial was actually so used — the passage in question cannot have been written earlier than January 14, 1382, the date of Richard's marriage. A date between 1382 and 1384 is so thoroughly in accord with all the probabilities that it is accepted with a good deal of confidence. [2]

If written between 1382 and 1384, *Troilus* is a work of the poet's full maturity of mind and art; and its philosophic seriousness and superb mastery of execution corroborate the supposition. There is *Revision.* abundant testimony that Chaucer wrought out his masterpiece with painstaking care, and jealously sought to maintain its artistic integrity. Near its close he prays that the poem may escape the corruption of careless copyists: —

> And for ther is so greet diversitee
> In English and in wryting of our tonge,
> So preye I god that noon miswryte thee,
> Ne thee mismetre for defaute of tonge;

and in the lines addressed to Adam his own scrivener,

[1] 'The Date of Chaucer's Troilus and Criseyde,' *Publications of the Modern Language Association*, 23. 285–306 (1908).

[2] See Professor Kittredge's Chaucer Society volume, *The Date of Chaucer's Troilus*, 1908. For the argument in favor of an early date, see Professor Tatlock's *Development and Chronology*, pp. 15–34.

he represents himself as 'rubbing and scraping' the manuscripts of *Troilus* written by the careless scribe to correct their errors and bring them into textual conformity with his own 'making.' Nor was he content merely to correct scribal errors. The manuscripts of the poem which have survived to us show that even after its publication Chaucer continued to work over it, rewriting lines, substituting a more felicitous word, changing here and there the order of the stanzas. Most significant of these revisions is the addition of three new passages designed to heighten the philosophical tone of the poem. These are Troilus's hymn to love as the perpetual bond of all things in heaven and earth (3. 1744–1771), which is closely paraphrased from one of the metres of Boethius; the long soliloquy of Troilus on the conflict between divine foreknowledge and human freedom (4. 953–1085), which is also adapted from Boethius; and the three stanzas (5. 1807–1827) near the close of the poem, borrowed from Boccaccio's *Teseide*, which describe the flight to heaven of the soul of Troilus.

There is no evidence to determine the date of these revisions, which were certainly not all made at one time. The added passages seem to have been written at an early period; that on free will is referred to by Thomas Usk in his *Testament of Love* written about 1387. The manuscripts on which Skeat's text of the poem is based contain the greater part, but not all, of Chaucer's revisions.[1]

Of the many sources from which the Middle Age satisfied its thirst for stories, three stand out preeminent. There is first the 'matter of France' with its heroic tales of Charlemagne and Roland;

The Troy Story.

---

[1] For a full account of the problem of revision, see the present writer's Chaucer Society volume, *The Textual Tradition of Chaucer's Troilus*, 1916.

there is again the 'matter of Brittany' with its romances of the Table Round; and lastly, the source
with which we are immediately concerned, 'the matter of Rome the Great.' By this last phrase we are to
understand, of course, not merely Rome, but the
whole field of classical antiquity, — the wars of Alexander, the tale of Thebes, and above all, the 'tale of Troy
divine.'

A modern author who should wish to write of Troy
would turn first of all to Homer; but in the Middle Ages
Homer was little more than a name. There must always
have been a few scholars here and there who had some
knowledge of Greek, picked up perhaps on journeys to
the Levant; but for the vast majority of those who read
at all, Homer was accessible only in the *Epitome Iliados
Homericæ* of Pindarus Thebanus (first century), where
the events of the *Iliad* are condensed into 1100 lines of
Latin hexameter. But even if Homer had been more
easily accessible, it is doubtful whether he would have
satisfied the mediæval historian. To begin with, he
lived long after the events he undertakes to describe;
and then, too, his work bears the marks of evident falsehood, for who can believe that the gods came down to
earth and warred with men? Fortunately there was a
better authority than that of Homer, the authority of an
eyewitness, who himself took part in the expedition
against Troy. This important document is the *Ephemeris Belli Trojani* of Dictys the Cretan.

Dictys Cretensis was, so the preface of the *Ephemeris*
tells us, a dweller in Cnossus, who with Idomeneus and
Merion took arms against Troy. Realizing with rare
insight that the events which were passing by unheeded
of most would be of deep interest to the generations to
follow, Dictys kept a journal written in Phœnician characters. On the author's death, the six books of his chron-

icle were buried with him in a tin case, where they rested
undisturbed until the thirteenth year of the reign of
Nero, when they were fortunately exposed by an earth-
quake. A Greek, named Eupraxis, carried the manuscript to Rome, where, at the command of Nero, it was
transliterated into Greek characters, and from the Greek
version a Latin translation was made by one Septimius
Romanus. It is hardly necessary to suggest that this
story must not be taken too seriously. Whether the
work is really a translation from the Greek, or whether
the forgery was first launched in its present form, we
cannot say with certainty; but scholars are now inclined
to believe that the former is the case. The translation,
if translation it be, occupies 113 pages of Teubner text,
while the period covered begins with the birth of Paris,
and ends with the death of Ulysses. The prose style of
the author is fairly good, being to a great extent an
imitation of that of Sallust. The date of composition is
probably the fourth century A. D. The following passage
taken from chapter ix, describing the death of Troilus,
will give a fair idea of what the book is like: —

At post paucos dies Græci instructi armis processere in
campum lacessentes, si auderent, ad bellandum Trojanos.
Quis dux Alexander cum reliquis fratribus militem ordinat
atque adversum pergit. Sed priusquam ferire inter se acies,
aut jaci tela cœpere, barbari desolatis ordinibus fugam faciunt:
cæsique eorum plurimi, aut in flumen præceps dati, cum hinc
atque inde ingrueret hostis atque undique adempta fuga esset.
Capti etiam Lycaon et Troilus Priamidæ, quos in medium
perductos Achilles jugulari jubet indignatus nondum sibi a
Priamo super his, quæ secum tractaverat, mandatum.

Dictys was greatly preferred to Homer, because he
was more trustworthy, being, as we have seen, an eyewitness, and excluding all traces of the supernatural;

but there was one particular in which he was not perfectly satisfactory: he was a Greek, and, as such, prejudiced against the Trojans, who were our ancestors. It is not necessary, however, to trust to the narrative of a single prejudiced historian; by good fortune there was also an historian within the walls of Troy. The *De Excidio Trojæ Historia* of Dares the Phrygian gives us an authentic account of the war from the standpoint of the defeated Trojans.

Homer mentions (*Iliad*, 5. 9) one Dares, a rich man and blameless, a priest of Hephæstus. To him antiquity ascribed an *Iliad* older than Homer's. Of this lost work, probably the work of a sophist, the Latin version purports to be a translation made by Cornelius Nepos. A recently discovered papyrus proves that a Greek original really existed, of which the Latin version is a condensation; but the condensation was certainly not made by Nepos. Professor Constans, the editor of Benoit, characterizes the *Historia* as 'un assemblage disproportionné de maigres détails écrit en un latin barbare et horriblement monotone.' It cannot have been composed earlier than the sixth century A. D. That Constans has not been too hard on Dares may be shown by the following selection (chapter xxix): —

Postera die Trojani alacres in aciem prodeunt. Agamemnon exercitum contra educit. Prœlio commisso uterque exercitus inter se pugnat. Postquam major pars diei transiit, prodit in primo Troilus, cædit devastat, Argivos in castra fugat. Postera die exercitum Trojani educunt: contra Agamemnon. Fit maxima cædes, uterque exercitus inter se pugnat acriter. Multos duces Argivorum Troilus interficit. Pugnatur continuis diebus VII. Agamemnon indutias petit in duo menses.

Fifty-two pages of Teubner text are filled with such

wretched stuff as this! But despite its inferiority, Dares seems to have been more popular with the Middle Ages than Dictys. He was a Trojan, and therefore a countryman; he was at any rate mercifully brief; perhaps, as Ten Brink suggests, the very fact that the work is but an epitome made it all the more available for the expansion and adornment which the Troy story was to receive at the hands of Benoit de Sainte-More.[1]

In the latter half of the twelfth century, according to Constans between 1155 and 1160, appeared a work which lies at the foundation of the whole later development of the legend of Troy; this is the *Roman de Troie* of Benoit de Sainte-More. Of Benoit, as of so many authors of the Middle Ages, we know nothing with certainty; but his book is a very substantial, and to the student a rather appalling, fact of 30,316 lines of octosyllabic couplets. Using as his basis the brief epitome of Dares,[2] and supplementing the matter there found from Dictys and Ovid, and perhaps other authors still, Benoit has given us a detailed history, which begins with the Argonautic expedition, describes the rape of Helen, the gathering of the Greek hosts, and, after telling the events of the siege and fall of Troy, devotes 5000 lines to the return of the Greek warriors to their homes, ending with the death of Ulysses. One would not like to be compelled to read the *Roman* through from cover to cover; but taken in moderate doses, Benoit has a good deal of poetic charm. Compared with Dictys and Dares, Benoit is great literature.

A little more than a century after the appearance of the *Roman de Troie*, in 1287, an Italian named Guido

---

[1] There is some reason to believe that a much longer Latin version of Dares may have been extant in the Middle Ages, of which the existing *Historia* is a condensation.

[2] Or perhaps a longer version of Dares, now lost.

delle Colonne produced in turgid Latin prose a paraphrase of Benoit's French poem. Guido, who was careful to say nothing about his indebtedness to Benoit, not only succeeded in passing off his *Historia Trojana* as an original composition; but was until after the middle of the nineteenth century actually believed to be the original from whom Benoit drew the material of his *Roman*. Guido added little to the substance of the tradition; but because his work was in the universal language of Europe, it attained a wide circulation, was translated into many languages, and became the basis for several Middle English 'Troy Books,' of which Lydgate's is, perhaps, the most important.

Before considering the *Filostrato* of Boccaccio, the immediate source of Chaucer's *Troilus and Criseyde*, it will be necessary to look back once more over the ground already traversed, and notice the degree of prominence given by earlier authors to the figures of Chaucer's pair of lovers. Homer merely mentions in a single passage (*Iliad*, 24. 257) the chariot-fighter Troilus as one of the sons of Priam whom Ares has destroyed. Virgil devotes a few lines to an account of his death (*Æneid*, 1. 474–478). Criseyde, or Briseida as Benoit calls her, probably represents two Homeric personages: Briseis, the slave of Achilles, whose name appears in the accusative Briseida in *Iliad*, 1. 184, and Chryseis, daughter of the seer Chryses, who is taken from Agamemnon at the command of Apollo. The accusative of her name, Chryseida, occurs in *Iliad*, 1. 182. As the professor of legerdemain will take two thin rabbits, and, rubbing them together in his hands, present us with one particularly fat rabbit, so these two unimportant characters have combined to form the heroine of the mediæval tale of Troy. In Dictys and Dares, Troilus has become a more important figure among the sons of Priam, and Briseida is accorded some prominence; but there is no hint of any relationship between them.

It is to Benoit de Sainte-More, so far as we can determine, that must be given the credit of inventing the story of the faithful love of Troilus and the faithlessness of Criseyde. One must not suppose, however, that the story furnishes the central theme of his voluminous work. It is merely an episode, which, during about a third of his work, serves to relieve the annals of bloodshed. We first meet the episode at line 13065, when a parliament is held to decide upon the return of Briseida to the Grecian camp; the death of Troilus occurs a thousand lines before the end of the poem.[1] In the main the events recorded agree with those described in the latter half of the poems of Boccaccio and Chaucer. Though a King Pandarus is mentioned by Benoit as one of the councilors in the Trojan parliament, he bears no part in the determination of the fortunes of Troilus and his love.

It was the genius of Boccaccio which first recognized in the Troilus and Briseida episode of Benoit the material for a single and unified love story. 'Boccaccio seems to have known both Guido and Benoit; Italian translations of both were then in existence; and on their basis he built up one of his most charming works, the most perfect of his epic poems. . . . The story lay before him finished, as part of a richly organized whole, and his only creative work was that specially suited to the poet,

---

[1] Benoit's poem is available in the admirable edition of Léopold Constans, published in six volumes by the Société des Anciens Textes Français, Paris, 1904–1912. The last volume of this edition contains a very useful discussion not only of Benoit, but of the development of the Troy story as a whole. A summary of those parts of the poem which deal with Troilus and Briseide may be found in Professor Kittredge's Chaucer Society volume, *The Date of Chaucer's Troilus*, pp. 62–65.

viz., the exercise of selection, of spiritual penetration, of deepening the characterization, and of glorifying all by a poetic presentation. . . . This tender, sentimental tale (for the poet passes quickly over the conclusion, and all the warlike scenes) is presented by Boccaccio with great psychological discernment, and with the most personal participation, though here and there with a slight tinge of irony. A truly creative spirit is revealed by the way in which the details are worked out, and by the thousand little touches that make us interested in his characters. But all these touches converge to one point, all have the same tendency.' [1]

Benoit's episode, as we have seen, begins with the departure of the heroine for the Greek camp; and in consequence the main interest of the tale centers about her intrigue with Diomede, the Troilus story serving as little more than an introduction. All the earlier scenes of the *Filostrato* are Boccaccio's invention. To serve as motive force for this earlier part of the story, the poet has invented the character of Pandarus. The Pandarus of Boccaccio, to be sure, is a character in many ways different from the Pandarus whom we know from Chaucer; he is a young and sprightly Florentine gentleman, an intimate companion of Troilus, and a cousin to Criseida.

In the preceding section of this chapter we have traced the development of the Troy myth as a whole, and have seen how the genius of Boccaccio, Boccaccio, seizing on a single episode of Benoit's *Ro-* Chaucer, *man*, has made a new and independent ro- and Shake-mance, not of battles long ago, but of lovers and their speare. love. This new creation has become one of the great world-stories, both in virtue of its intrinsic interest and because of its use by three great world-poets: Boccaccio,

[1] Ten Brink, *History of English Literature* (Eng. trans.), 2. 88–90,

Chaucer, and Shakespeare. It is in the highest degree interesting to see how these three poets have altered or modified the theme, each in accordance with his own character and underlying literary purpose. Boccaccio is a thoroughgoing sentimentalist, and he has told the story, accordingly, with full sympathy. Troilo is a portrait of the poet himself, generous, high-spirited, enthusiastic, sentimental. He has been in love before; but on beholding Criseida in the temple, as Boccaccio first beheld Fiammetta, he loves her with all his soul. Pandaro is a gay, light-hearted, loose-principled gallant, such as Boccaccio may have known at the Neapolitan court. Criseida is a fickle beauty, and little more. Troilo is the central figure of the poem, and with his love longings in the earlier part of the tale, and still more with his later sorrow, the reader is asked to sympathize in fullest measure.[1]

When Chaucer approached the story, he was no longer young. Though he professes himself the servant of the servants of love, he dares not hope success in love himself, 'for myn unlyklinesse.' If he identifies himself with any of the persons of his story, it is with the ironist Pandar, rather than with the sentimental Troilus. He tells the story with more detachment than does Boccaccio. Into its fundamental tragedy he breathes a spirit of ironical humor, which is all but totally foreign to the Italian poem. Even as he recounts the idealism of Troilus and presents the inexhaustible charm of Criseyde, he is conscious of the bitter mockery of both which is to be provided by Criseyde's ultimate treachery. That such angelic beauty and womanly charm should reside in a nature so essentially shallow and unstable, that the

[1] An English translation of the pertinent parts of the *Filostrato* by W. M. Rossetti has been published by the Chaucer Society: *Chaucer's Troilus and Criseyde (from the Harl. MS. 3943) compared with Boccaccio's Filostrato*, translated by W. M. Rossetti, London, 1873.

youthful ardor and utter loyalty of Troilus should be expended on a woman capable of Criseyde's baseness, that is part of the mystery and mockery of human life. And so, if Chaucer's poem has much more humor than Boccaccio's, it has also a much higher seriousness, a seriousness which becomes at the end a philosophic interpretation of the action, and through it of the ultimate values of life. Criseyde's falsehood becomes a type of the fallacy of all earthly happiness. But if life is certain to deceive, it is none the less very interesting, very amusing; and Chaucer dwells with the subtle analysis of great comedy on the complications of his tragic plot, the interplay of motive, above all on the psychological problems of Criseyde's character. The result is a poem which is neither tragedy nor comedy, but a masterpiece of irony.

Though in a very different spirit, Chaucer has in general followed the outline of Boccaccio's poem. At times, for many stanzas together, he is content to follow its very words. But he has very appreciably expanded his original; *Filostrato* contains 5512 lines, *Troilus* has 8239. The greater part of Chaucer's additions are found in the second and third books. The whole episode of the meeting of the lovers at the house of Deiphebus has no counterpart in *Filostrato;* wholly original also is the elaborate stratagem by which Pandarus brings the lovers together at his own house.[1]

If Chaucer has transformed the spirit of the story from pathetic sentimentality to half-ironical humor,

[1] For the relation of *Troilus* to its sources see Professor Karl Young's Chaucer Society volume, *Origin and Development of the Story of Troilus and Criseyde*, 1908, and H. M. Cummings, *The Indebtedness of Chaucer's Works to the Italian Works of Boccaccio*, Princeton dissertation, 1916. Professor Young has argued that the episode of the first night of his lovers was suggested to Chaucer by an episode in the *Filocolo*, a prose romance of Boccaccio. Dr. Cummings has, I think with justice, thrown grave doubt on the probability of such indebtedness.

Shakespeare, in his *Troilus and Cressida*, has approached it in a spirit of bitter cynicism and blackest pessimism.[1] The love story, which is after all subordinate to the intrigues of the Grecian camp, has neither the romance of Boccaccio nor the humor of Chaucer; it is merely disgusting. Troilus remains much what he is in Chaucer; but Cressida has flung away every pretense of virtue, and is merely a confessed wanton. Pandarus has lost all his geniality and humor, and is merely repulsive. To crown all, the final worthlessness of Cressida, and the breaking heart of Troilus, are interpreted to us by the scrofulous mind of Thersites, whose whole function in the play is to defile with the foulness of his own imagination all that humanity holds high and sacred.[2]

Chaucer's main source for *Troilus* is the *Filostrato* of Boccaccio; it is, indeed, no exaggeration to say that the English poem is a free reworking of the Italian. Chaucer has, to be sure, with something of the scholar's instinct, gone back of his immediate original, and consulted for a point here and there the works of Benoit and of Guido. Though there is no proof that he used the prose Dares, he did use for the portraits of the *dramatis personæ* which he draws in the fifth book the twelfth-century paraphrase of Dares in Latin hexameters by the Englishman, Joseph of Exeter.[3] With the artist's instinct, he has reshaped his characters, and

'Lollius.'

[1] For the reasons which may have actuated Shakespeare's treatment of the story, see the essay by W. W. Lawrence in the Columbia University Press volume of *Shaksperian Studies* (New York, 1916), pp. 187–211.

[2] Those who wish to pursue the theme still further in English literature may read Dryden's version of *Troilus and Cressida*, in which the character of the heroine is vitally altered by a new interpretation put upon her relations with Diomed.

[3] See the article by R. K. Root, 'Chaucer's Dares,' *Modern Philology*, 15. 1–22 (1917). Chaucer seems to have known Dictys only by name.

added two important episodes to the plot; but his debt
to Boccaccio remains preponderant.

Nowhere, however, does he so much as mention Boccaccio's name. Instead, he professes to follow with strict
fidelity 'myn autour called Lollius.' Twice, once near the
beginning of the poem and again near its end, he mentions 'Lollius' by name; and he appeals to him by implication as 'myn autour' in half a dozen other passages.
The identification of this mysterious 'Lollius' is a problem which has hitherto baffled the critics; for, though
one can find actual authors who bear the name of Lollius, or something resembling it, none of them has written the tale of Troy. Our most probable guess is that
the notion that some one named Lollius had written of
the Trojan war is to be traced to a misreading of the
opening lines of one of the epistles of Horace, the second
epistle of Book I: —

> Troiani belli scriptorem, maxime Lolli,
> Dum tu declamas Romæ, Præneste relegi.

It seems clear that Chaucer did not invent 'Lollius' out
of whole cloth, that he really believed that some 'Tro-
iani belli scriptor maximus' named Lollius, a Latin poet
of long ago, had actually existed; for he mentions him
also in the *House of Fame*, along with Homer, Dares,
Dictys, and Guido delle Colonne, as one who bears up
the fame of Troy. Perhaps he thought that the Latin
work of 'Lollius,' which he had never seen, was the immediate source of the Italian *Filostrato*, that in following
Filostrato he was but following Lollius at second hand.
At any rate, Chaucer chose to cite as his chief authority
the work of 'Lollius,' a Latin poet of long ago, instead
of a contemporary work written in the vernacular of
Italy.[1] He could thus lend to his story an air of greater

---

[1] It is not at all impossible that Chaucer did not know who was the
author of *Filostrato*.

credibility, as though it were in all essentials authentic history. Nor was there anything in the literary ethics of the Middle Ages which demanded of Chaucer an acknowledgment of his actual debt. Every good story was regarded as common property. A mediæval author adduced authority whenever by so doing he could add credit to his own work, never in recognition of an obligation.[1]

In the proem to Book II, Chaucer warns his readers that there is more than one way to make love: —

> Eek for to winne love in sondry ages,
> In sondry londes, sondry been usages.

If it was necessary for the poet to forestall the possible criticism of fourteenth-century lovers to whom the speech and doings of his hero might seem 'wonder nyce and straunge,' it is much more necessary to forestall similar criticism from the modern reader. The art of love has, like every other art, its conventions; but these conventions change greatly in sundry ages and in sundry lands. The love of Troilus and Criseyde is told in accordance with the code of courtly love, the code which is assumed in the French romances of the twelfth and thirteenth centuries, in Chrétien de Troyes and Marie de France, the code which is allegorically presented in the *Roman de la Rose*.

Courtly Love.

One of the central features of this code is that ideal love is seldom if ever compatible with marriage. Modern readers of *Troilus* are sure to ask why Troilus did not marry Criseyde. If Troilus is a prince royal, Criseyde is at least a lady of excellent social standing, and apparently of wealth. There could have been no serious bar to

---

[1] For the latest discussion of the Lollius problem and for a review of earlier discussions, see G. L. Kittredge, 'Chaucer's Lollius,' *Harvard Studies in Classical Philology*, 28. 47–133 (1917). The interpretation given above is in essentials that of Professor Kittredge.

a marriage, had the lovers so wished. But the idea of marriage is never once suggested. In the code of courtly love marriage is an arrangement of convenience quite outside the region of romantic love. Marriage implies, theoretically at least, the subjection of wife to husband; and in the love of the romances the lady rules supreme, her lightest whim a law. A twelfth-century writer on the art of love, Andreas Capellanus, reports a decision of the Countess Marie of Champagne that love cannot exist between husband and wife, 'amorem non posse suas inter duos iugales extendere vires.' [1]

But courtly love is in no sense platonic. Far removed as it is from grossness and mere sensuality by its elaborate idealization, it seeks final consummation in the complete surrender of the lady. When Criseyde accepts Troilus as her lover, she grants by implication the bestowal of her ultimate favors. Nor does such a bestowal incur from the courtly poet the slightest hint of blame. The relation established is an ideal relation, with all the sanctity which modern feeling casts about an ideal marriage. Chaucer repeatedly tells us that the influence on Troilus of his love, both in the period of his despairing adoration and that of his final possession, was an ennobling one. In the field of battle against the Greeks he was a very lion; and among his friends in Troy his manner became so goodly and gracious 'that ech him lovede that loked on his face.' When Criseyde takes her farewell of Troilus just before she sets out for the Grecian camp, she tells him that it was not his rank and riches, nor yet his martial prowess, which first won her love, 'but moral vertue grounded upon trouthe.' [2]

---

[1] Andreæ Capellani *de Amore* libri tres, ed. Trojel (1892) p. 153. For a useful summary of the code of courtly love and a detailed study of its exemplification in the works of Chaucer, see W. G. Dodd, *Courtly Love in Chaucer and Gower*, Boston, 1913.

[2] See *Troilus*, 1, 1075–1082; 3. 1802–1806; 4. 1667–1673.

We are to accept the love of Troilus and Criseyde, then, as something pure and ideal like the love of Romeo and Juliet, even though it lack the sanction of wedlock. And yet this noble and ennobling union must be kept inviolably secret. Were it avowed and known, the lady's reputation would be irreparably soiled. Pandarus repeatedly warns Troilus that he must not blab; and when, after the Trojan parliament has decreed Criseyde's return to her father, Troilus urges that they flee together to some far land, Criseyde pleads her reputation against it: —

> And also thenketh on myn honestee,
> That floureth yet, how foule I sholde it shende,
> And with what filthe it spotted sholde be,
> If in this forme I sholde with yow wende.

So at all costs the union must be kept secret, and the meetings of the lovers must be clandestine. This irreconcilable conflict of standards, that a love which is regarded as not only right and proper but ideally noble should if known become the height of dishonor, marks the essential artificiality of the whole code of courtly love. But artificial or not, we must accept its postulates if we are to understand the fundamental problem of *Troilus*. We must not consider the clandestine and illicit love of Troilus as in any sense a derogation of his noble character; nor must we regard Criseyde's acceptance of his love, scrupulously concealed as it is from all eyes, as any reflection on her honor. Criseyde's sin is not that she becomes the mistress of Troilus, but that having pledged her love she becomes unfaithful. For in courtly love, as in the whole system of chivalric ethics, the greatest of the virtues is truth and loyalty, and the blackest crime is that of faithlessness. As Dante reserves the lowest pit of his *Inferno* for the treachery of Brutus and Cassius and Judas Iscariot, so the deepest condemnation of the courtly lover is visited on the faithless Criseyde, the renegade of true love.

It is in the light of these conventions of courtly love that one must analyze the character of Chaucer's heroine. In Book I we see Criseyde only at a distance; but even so we are captivated at first sight, as Troilus is, by her beauty and charm. We are touched, too, with pity for her in the trying situation in which she is placed, and with admiration for the fine dignity with which she meets it. Her father, Calchas, knowing by his magic art that Troy is doomed to destruction, has basely gone over to the enemy, and left his daughter to bear alone and unprotected the anger which the Trojan populace is ready to visit on all his kin. She is a widow, also, recently bereaved. And so, alone and in great peril, she throws herself on the protection of Hector, who chivalrously promises her full immunity. She is living, then, in strict retirement in her own stately house with three young nieces to bear her company, and so 'keeps her estate' that she wins the full respect and love of every one. But who could help loving a lady of such exquisite beauty?

> So aungellyk was hir natyf beautee,
> That lyk a thing inmortal semed she,
> As doth an hevenish parfit creature,
> That doun were sent in scorning of nature.

Not only is she beautiful, there is a queenly dignity and grandeur in her port.

April comes and with it the great feast of Palladion, the Trojan Easter day, when every one goes to church in his best clothes; and Criseyde in her simple widow's black goes too. Ever conscious of her father's shame, she takes an inconspicuous station near the door; but having yielded so much to her sense of disgrace, her proud spirit never falters. She has a 'ful assured loking and manere,' with just a touch of defiance in it. It is while she stands thus in the temple that Troilus sees her from afar, and is struck to the heart by her beauty and dignity.

This is all that we see of Criseyde in Book I; though her presence, to be sure, fills all the long scene of Troilus's feverish love-longing.

Book II may be called the book of Criseyde. An overwhelming proportion of its lines is directly dedicated to the unfolding of her character, and to the subtle analysis of her heart as the figure of Troilus gradually establishes itself there. On a May morning Pandarus goes on his embassy to Criseyde's house. He finds her in a 'paved parlour' with two other ladies, listening to the 'geste of the Sege of Thebes,' quite undisturbed by the fact that its author, Statius, was not to be born till near the middle of the first century A.D. He playfully asks if it is a book of love she is reading, and is laughingly answered by an allusion to his own unrequited love. No small part of Criseyde's charm is conveyed through these scenes with her uncle, scenes of playful badinage, in which her wit is quite the equal of his. Uncle and niece meet on the most gracious terms of long established affection and understanding, with free give and take of kindly banter.

In answer to Pandar's suggestion that she put away her book and rise up and dance, she reminds him that she is a widow: —

> It sete me wel bet ay in a cave
> To bidde, and rede on holy seyntes lyves;
> Lat maydens gon to daunce, and yonge wyves.

This protestation is hardly to be taken with full seriousness; and yet it suggests, I think, something of the truth. Criseyde has come to regard herself, in the life of quiet

seclusion which follows on her widowhood and her father's shameful treachery, as forever cut off from the
brighter things of life. It is a state of mind by no means
unfavorable to the discovery that she has won the love
of Troilus, when once she has had time to make the
necessary adjustments. Pandarus pays no attention to
her words, but immediately begins to play on her woman's curiosity by hinting at a great piece of news that
he could tell her if he would. He plays with his secret
through a dozen stanzas, insinuating into his speech the
praise of Troilus, the friendliest of princes, second only
to Hector in prowess. Then at last, after much teasing,
he tells her the news, giving her no chance to reply till he
has spoken ten stanzas of appeal and argument.

Was the news a complete surprise to Criseyde, or had
she during the month which had elapsed since the feast of
Palladion suspected the truth? We cannot say. Chaucer himself raises the question, but professes his uncertainty as to the answer. In any case she receives the
news calmly: —

> Criseyde which that herde him in this wyse,
> Thoughte, 'I shal fele what he meneth, ywis.'
> 'Now, eem,' quod she, 'what wolde ye devyse,
> What is your reed I sholde doon of this?'

But when Pandar has given his advice that she return
love for love, this cool deliberation melts into a passionate burst of tears and reproaches, that he, her uncle and
her best friend, should counsel her to love. These tears
are the natural reaction which follows on the first clear
recognition of the terrifying possibility that she, the
widow and the recluse, may begin again to live passionately. Her resentment is short-lived, and she listens
trembling to Pandar's threat that her hard heart will be
the death not only of Troilus but of himself as well. Is

there after all any evil in her uncle's advice that she smile on Troilus, when she has the solemn assurance that he means no 'harm or vilanye'?

> And if this man slee here himself, allas!
> In my presence, it wol be no solas.
> What men wolde of hit deme I can nat seye;
> It nedeth me ful sleyly for to pleye.

Criseyde has recovered her self-control. In the lines just quoted, and even more in the long soliloquy in which she weighs the pro's and con's of love, one realizes how complete this self-control is. There is in these speeches a tone of cool calculation which to many readers may seem unpleasant, a trait of character which appears again in the fourth book when she builds her hope for a speedy return to Troy on the avarice of her aged father. In appraising these speeches, it must be remembered that Criseyde is not a young girl, with the impulsive idealism of her maidenhood. Just how old she is we do not know, — Chaucer himself professes that he does not know either — ; but one feels that she is, in experience at least, older than Troilus. She has been married and is now a widow. 'I am,' she says, 'myn owene woman, wel at ese.' Though love of Troilus has already found lodgment in her heart, it does not sweep her off her feet. She does not so much fall in love as drift into love; but she drifts with her eyes open.

Pandarus takes his leave, too shrewd in his knowledge of Criseyde's character to press her to a decision. But he has made his effect, and the effect is powerfully heightened by the circumstances which follow. By great good fortune, Troilus himself is presented to her view, Troilus the mighty warrior returning from battle on his wounded charger. Here is a living argument. Criseyde considers his excellent prowess, his wit, his shape, his courtesy, and above all his love for her. Would it not be a pity to cause the death of such an one as he? And last of all her niece, Antigone, sings her song in praise of love, every word of which imprints itself on Criseyde's heart. 'And ay gan love hir lasse for to agaste than it dide erst.'

On the next day Pandarus returns to the attack with a letter from Troilus, which Criseyde at first refuses to receive, but at last consents to answer. Once more, this time by Pandar's appointment, the knightly Troilus rides by her window. Though she will write to her lover, she offers him only a sister's regard. She will not agree to speak to him: —

> it were eek to sone
> To graunten him so greet a libertee.
> For playnly hir entente, as seyde she,
> Was for to love him unwist, if she mighte,
> And guerdon him with nothing but with sighte.

It is a prime article in the code of courtly love, as in our modern conventions of love-making, that the lady must not let herself be too easily won. Troilus and Pandar have every reason to be satisfied with the result of these two days of wooing; for the lady has at least acquiesced in the courtship, and her words 'eek to sone' and 'if she mighte' suggest the promise of more to come.

Up to this point Chaucer's story follows essentially, though with greater elaboration of detail, that of his Italian model. But here Boccaccio's heroine consents, with merely formal protest, to receive her lover as soon as time and place shall serve, provided only that due secrecy be maintained; and the joy of the lovers is shortly consummated. For the character of Criseyde as Chaucer has conceived it, such a course of action would have been much too direct. It would have required a definite decision instead of a genial drifting with circumstance. It is a striking fact that Criseyde, with all her native self-assurance, never takes a single step of her own volition. And so, that she may seem to herself to have been ensnared rather than to have capitulated, Pandarus gives full play to his love of cunning stratagem.

It is a most ingenious stratagem, plausible in its devising, and skillfully controlled by the master strategist down to the smallest detail, which brings Criseyde to the feigned sick-bed of the truly love-sick Troilus at the house of Deiphebus, where Troilus first has the chance to plead his own cause. This meeting proves to be the decisive moment of the story; for Criseyde, though unable to make a decision, accepts completely a decision which has been made for her by the logic of events, or by the scheming of her uncle. She would very likely have refused to grant Troilus a private meeting; but here is the meeting devised without her consent. It is Troilus, not Criseyde, who is panic-stricken. She listens to his passionate declarations, quietly asks him to tell her 'the fyn of his entente,' and after listening to his reply, says slowly and deliberately: —

> ' I shal trewely, with al my might,
> Your bittre tornen al into swetnesse;
> If I be she that may yow do gladnesse,
> For every wo ye shal recovere a blisse';
> And him in armes took, and gan him kisse.

This is complete surrender, and Pandarus recognizes it as such. Criseyde has, to be sure, stipulated that her honor must not be compromised; but she acquiesces by her silence in Pandar's promise that he will shortly devise a secret meeting of the lovers at his own house, where they shall have full leisure 'to speke of love aright.'

It is in fulfillment of this promise that Pandarus invites Criseyde to supper at his house, and after refusing to let her return home in the downpour of rain, brings

Troilus to her bed. This scene is another masterpiece of Pandar's strategy; but it is a plot in which the apparent victim is at least an acquiescent accomplice. At an openly avowed meeting and consummation of her love, such as the Italian Criseida herself arranges, Chaucer's heroine would probably have balked. Her woman's modesty, or at least her shrinking from an irrevocable decision, is still to be overcome. The act must seem to her inevitable, not of her own choosing; and yet there can be no doubt that she accepted her uncle's invitation knowing well that Troilus was to meet her. Pandar's denial of her suspicion is a virtual acknowledgment of its truth. As to her acceptance of this denial, Chaucer himself professes ignorance: —

> Nought list myn auctor fully to declare
> What that she thoughte whan he seyde so,
> That Troilus was out of town yfare,
> As if he seyde therof sooth or no.

When we remember that Chaucer's 'auctor' does not relate this episode of the supper-party at all, it is not strange that he does not 'fully declare' the heroine's motives. Chaucer's assumed ignorance is only his characteristic way of hinting rather than asserting his own interpretation. Criseyde herself settles the question beyond any doubt. When Troilus clasps her in his arms and begs her to yield, she replies: —

> 'Ne hadde I er now, my swete herte dere,
> Ben yolde, ywis, I were now not here.'

Again Criseyde accepts with full frankness the accomplished fact. The events of this first night have been so devised by Pandarus that they seem inevitable as a decree of fate; but now irrevocably in her lover's arms, Criseyde avows that not fate nor fortune, but her own love has brought her there. It is a very subtle touch in Chaucer's portrayal of the woman's heart. To herself she must seem to have yielded only to inevitable fate; but to her lover she wished to be not a helpless victim but an offering of free love.

The last barriers of womanly reluctance have been overcome; and Criseyde loves Troilus as passionately and unreservedly as he loves her. Judged by the standards of courtly love, the relation now established between the lovers is an ideal and noble one. As Criseyde says, it is a love —

> ayeins the which that no man may,
> Ne oughte eek goodly maken resistence.

The relation must be kept secret, or her honor will be gone. That is one of the conditions of courtly love. But, save for a half-hearted reproach to Pandarus for his share in the matter, Criseyde has no regrets; nor does Troilus ever suggest that there is anything shameful in this clandestine love. Two or three years pass in unbroken happiness, until the August day when the Trojan parliament decrees that Criseyde be delivered over to her father, and all the lovers' weal is turned to woe. Up to this point, Criseyde's behavior has been above reproach. With scrupulous observance of all the conventions of courtly love, she has accepted as her lover a knight who in worth and chivalric prowess is second only to Hector; and she has loved him not sensually, but nobly and purely, won not by 'veyn delyt' but by his 'moral vertue grounded upon trouthe.'

But this lady whose loveliness and charm have captivated not only Troilus, but Chaucer and his readers as well, must in the sequel become a hissing and reproach, the shame of all her sex. She is false to Troilus and to her solemnly plighted word; she allows herself to be

wooed and won with most indecent haste by the masterful but cynical Diomede. By the slightest turn of fortune, this catastrophe might have been averted, and
the story given a pathetic but heroic end. In her grief
at the prospect of leaving Troilus, a grief the sincerity
of which we may not doubt, Criseyde falls into a death-
like swoon; and Troilus, believing her to be really dead,
draws his sword and is on the point of ending his own
life. Had he done so, Criseyde would, she tells us, have
slain herself with the same sword. Had events taken
this course, we should have had an ending like that of
Pyramus and Thisbe, or of Romeo and Juliet. Or a different woman in Criseyde's place might have accepted
Troilus's urgent proposal that they defy all, and in despite of Priam and his parliament flee to some foreign
land. Had Troilus taken things boldly into his own
hands and resolutely carried her off, she would probably have acquiesced; but he humbly leaves the judgment to her. It is one of those irrevocable decisions
which Criseyde is incapable of making. She thinks too
precisely on the event — the injury to her own reputation and to that of Troilus should he desert his be-
leaguered city in its need, the life of wandering exile
which would lie ahead for both of them. It is so much
easier to accept the circumstances which fate and fortune have shaped. And so she departs for the Grecian
camp with solemnly reiterated promises to return by
the tenth day, 'but if that deeth me assayle.'

But once in her father's tent, she finds that return
is not easy. Once more she thinks upon the event —
she may be taken as a spy, she may fall into the hands
of lawless men. She lacks the resolution necessary for
so bold a step. She still purposes to return — but not
to-day, nor yet to-morrow. And there is Diomede, the
sudden Diomede, who boldly begins his courtship be-

fore they reach the Grecian camp. He is no idealizing courtly lover, but a somewhat cynical man of the world, a mediæval Lovelace, whose motto is:—

He is a fool that wol foryete himselve.

Diomede does not lose his heart; he merely improves a good opportunity to win a lady's. All the greater will be his conquest if, as he suspects, she has a lover in Troy. He needs no intriguing Pandarus to help him; he spends no sleepless nights. With a man of such force and resolute will, the hesitating Criseyde is helpless. At first she neither accepts nor rejects his courtship. Once more she prefers to drift with circumstance. She does not cease to care for Troilus; but in her loneliness the company of Diomede is very pleasant. How, after all, shall she return to Troy; and is not the fate of the city, as Diomede tells her, certain destruction? On the very day of her promised return, when faithful Troilus is feverishly watching from the city walls for a first sight of her, she is listening not unwilling to the love-making of Diomede; and both Troilus and Troy town are slipping 'knotless' through her heart. In less than two months she has accepted completely the new inevitable.

Over the details of Diomede's courtship and Criseyde's infamy, her gift to him of the bay steed and of the brooch which had belonged to Troilus, Chaucer passes hurriedly, with continual appeal to the authority of 'the story' and of 'myn auctor.' With utmost reluctance, and of sheer compulsion, he narrates the shame of Criseyde as it stands recorded in his old books. Her indecision, her irresolute tendency to drift with circumstance, the trait of character which Chaucer sums up in the phrase, 'slydinge of corage,' have brought her to the depths of ignominy. Criseyde's damnation is complete.

Though Chaucer's chief interest in the story would seem to lie in the personality of Criseyde, it is none the less true that Troilus remains its central figure. He is at least titular hero. When Criseyde's unfaithfulness is accomplished, she fades from the story; the fortunes of Troilus are followed till his death, and with his death the poem ends. The subject of the poem, as set forth in its opening line, is the 'double sorrow of Troilus.' Its concluding moral is pointed as his soul, mounting the heavens, looks back and despises this wretched world that 'passeth sone as floures fayre.'

Troilus.

Boccaccio drew the character of Troilo as the type of his own passionate love for Fiammetta; and Chaucer has left it in all essentials unchanged, though appreciably ennobled. Troilus is the ideal lover of chivalric love, utterly faithful, utterly humble in his self-effacing subjection to his lady. So completely is he the lover that one is in danger of forgetting that he is also the intrepid warrior, 'hardy as lyoun,' 'save Ector, most ydrad of any wight.' To the shouting multitudes who acclaimed him as he passed through the streets on his way home from battle, he was not the sighing lover, but 'our Ioye, and next his brother holdere up of Troye.' And it is this Troilus, 'al armed save his heed,' mounted on his bay steed, whose image sank into the heart of Criseyde.

With Troilus the warrior the modern reader finds himself in immediate sympathy; but with Troilus the lover he is in danger of losing patience, unless he understand clearly what sort of a character Chaucer is portraying, unless he realize how the courtly lover of mediæval romance is expected to behave. His utter faithfulness to Criseyde, his unwillingness to doubt her good faith long after the shrewder Pandarus sees clearly that she will not return, needs no apology. It is a point in which the mediæval code of love is in full accord with the conventions of modern romance. It is the utter humility of Troilus, his complete subjection to his lady, his conviction of his own unworthiness, which may seem to the modern reader unnatural. And yet here also the mediæval and the modern code are not so far apart. Modern convention demands that the lover proclaim himself 'not nearly good enough' for his lady, and declare that he is 'the luckiest of men' to win her. If the friends of the modern lover are tempted to smile at him, so does Pandarus more than once smile at the extravagances of Troilus. Nor does Chaucer take Troilus quite seriously; he tells us that the first letter of Troilus was filled with 'thise othere termes alle that in swich cas these loveres alle seche'; and a few lines later he reports: —

> And after that he seyde, *and ley ful loude,*
> Himself was litel worth, and lesse he coude.

These protestations of unworthiness, however sincerely uttered, are actually nothing but lies. Troilus himself had once jested at the woes of hapless lovers.

Thoroughly in accord with the mediæval depiction of love are the pallor and sleeplessness and loss of appetite which afflict Troilus, his sighs and tears and the tremors which seize him when he is about to speak to Criseyde for the first time. They are the recognized symptoms of the lover's malady,[1] symptoms not wholly unknown in modern love-stories. Before we accuse this second Hector of unmanliness in the luxuriance of his grief, we must remember that he indulges in these sighs and tears only when alone or in the sympathetic company

[1] See J. L. Lowes, 'The Loveres Maladye of Hereos,' *Modern Philology,* 11. 491–546 (1914).

of his closest friend. From all others his woes are jealously guarded; nor did the Greeks discover any lack of manliness on the battle-field.

But even so, Troilus does luxuriate in his sorrow, which is only another way of saying that he is a good deal of a sentimentalist. With him emotion and desire become an end in themselves rather than a spur to action. Without the aid of Pandarus he would perhaps never have let Criseyde know. It is in his helplessness to further his own cause that Troilus ceases to be merely the typical lover and becomes individualized. This tendency to luxuriate in his own sorrow is the trait of character which, in league with fate, brings about his tragedy. In the first sorrow of his double portion he is supplied by Pandarus with the active force which he lacks. Through the tireless energy and devotion of his friend he breaks down Criseyde's reluctance to harbor love, and all is well. But in his second sorrow, when Criseyde must leave him, Pandarus can give no help beyond patient sympathy. It is no time for intrigue and skillful manipulation; if there was any way out for Troilus, it was through quick decision and resolute action. Of such action the sentimental Troilus is not capable. He defers the decision to Criseyde, who characteristically follows the path of least resistance. For himself, he can only withdraw to a temple and bitterly debate with himself the question of God's providence and man's free will. This long Boethian soliloquy has been regarded as a digression and an artistic blemish in the poem. Prolonged beyond its due proportion it may be; but it is no more a digression than are the soliloquies of Hamlet. It is thoroughly in accord with the character of Troilus as Chaucer conceived him.[1]

[1] See the article by Dr. H. R. Patch on 'Troilus on Predestination,' *Journal of English and Germanic Philology*, 17. 399–422 (1918).

For Troilus in his love for Criseyde there is no such thing as free choice. It was his destiny that he should love Criseyde; and from the moment that he confides in Pandarus, his destiny is in the hands of his friend.

It is with a mingling of pathos and irony that Chaucer depicts the closing scenes of Troilus's story. While Criseyde is receiving the advances of Diomede, Troilus is sadly revisiting the scenes of his former happiness, looking with the eyes of tender sentiment at the barred windows of her empty house. The tenth day comes, and we witness the feverish watching of Troilus. Pandarus encourages his hopes, but in his own heart he knows better. The evidences of Criseyde's faithlessness are at last too clear for even Troilus's credulity. His fair dream is shattered; the lady whom he has idealized in joy and sorrow has proved false. Nothing remains but his own integrity. His only hope is to seek release from the emptiness of a deceitful world by speedy death in battle. And so Troilus 'repeyreth hoom from worldly vanitee.' He has anticipated by a little the doom which hangs over his city and all his kin. He is the tragic victim of Fortune and of his own character.

The dominating personage of the poem is neither Criseyde nor Troilus, but Pandarus, prime mover of the plot during half the story and the hero's confidant throughout. It is his character, gay and genial, shrewd and ironic, which gives the poem its prevailing tone, the tone of humorous irony which all but overshadows the essential tragedy.

Pandarus.

This masterly figure, perhaps the finest example of Chaucer's art in portraiture, is almost wholly the English poet's original creation. The Pandaro of Boccaccio is a young man, the *cousin* of Criseida (and of Troilo also), a high-spirited gallant, not much differentiated, save in his fortunes, from the hero, Troilo. He acts as messenger and go-between for the lovers; but the much readier susceptibility of the Italian heroine makes unnecessary any elaborate scheming and artifice. And Pandaro is quite devoid of the humor which is so salient a quality of his English counterpart.

Though Chaucer has depicted the character of his Pandarus in minute detail, he has nowhere described his personal appearance; nor has he given any certain indication of his age. But the impression we receive is of a man distinctly older than either of the lovers. He is Criseyde's uncle, a relationship which suggests — though it does not necessarily imply — that he is some years her senior. The terms of charming intimacy and playful banter on which they meet, the trust and confidence which Criseyde reposes in him, again suggest the older man and the younger woman. But the difference in their ages need not be more than ten or a dozen years; for Pandarus is not old, hardly even middle-aged. He is at any rate not too old to play the courtly lover. He has loved 'gon sithen longe whyle' a lady whose heart pity for him has never softened. He, like Troilus, has times of sleeplessness and pallor, when he feels 'his part of loves shottes kene'; but for the most part he bears his sorrow easily. Criseyde rallies him about it; and Pandarus himself jokes about his 'jolly woe' and 'lusty sorrow' which will not let him sleep of a May morning, and humorously describes himself as hopping lamely behind in the dance of love. And yet we must not doubt that Pandarus is genuinely the unsuccessful lover; it is one of the ironies of his character that he can win a lady for his friend but not for himself.

He is young enough, also, to be the friend and inseparable companion of Troilus. He has, he tells us, loved Troilus 'in wrong and right' all his life. It is a

strong and loyal friendship, with no faintest suspicion
of self-seeking. To his friendship he sacrifices rest and
honor.

For from the mediæval point of view as well as from
the modern, the rôle which Pandar plays is one of infamy and dishonor; and he clearly recognizes that were
his actions to be known he would be regarded as guilty
of 'the worste trecherye' to his niece. She also regards
his advocacy of Troilus's love as a breach of faith.[1]
The conventions of courtly love hold Troilus free of
blame, and Criseyde so long as she remains true, but
not so her uncle, whom circumstance has placed in
the position of a father to her, or an elder brother, and
who betrays his trust. Had he been merely the friend
of Troilus, acting as confidant and messenger, it would
have been different; but as Criseyde's uncle, he should
have been her jealous guardian. His only defense is
that he acts from motives of pure friendship. Professor
Kittredge has put very clearly the tragic conflict of
duties which confronts Pandarus as the friend of Troilus
and the uncle of Criseyde. 'This double relation is the
sum and substance of his tragedy, for it involves him
in an action that sullies his honor to no purpose. Since
Cressida is faithless, he not only labors in vain, but
ruins his friend by the very success that his plans
achieve. This humorous worldly enthusiast has two
ideals, friendship and faith in love. To friendship he
sacrifices his honor, only, it seems, to make possible
the tragic infidelity of Cressida, which destroys his
friend.[2]

Though Pandar sacrifices all to the ideal of friendship, he is not like Troilus an idealist. He does not
sentimentalize his friendship, nor yet his own unre-

[1] See *Troilus*, 3. 271–279; 2. 410–413. Cf. *Filostrato*, 3. 8.
[2] *Chaucer and his Poetry*, pp. 139, 140.

quited love. It is one of his outstanding traits of character that he clearly faces the facts, that he sees things
as they are; if he deceives others, he never deceives
himself. His love for Troilus does not blind him to his
friend's foolish extravagance in love; he can laugh at
Troilus as he can laugh at his own hapless love-story.
Even while he is comforting Troilus through his ten
days' waiting for Criseyde's return, he sees clearly that
the hope of Troilus is vain: —

> But in his herte he thoughte, and softe lough,
> And to himself ful sobrely he seyde:
> 'From hasel-wode, ther Ioly Robin pleyde,
> Shal come al that that thou abydest here;
> Ye, farewel al the snow of ferne yere.'

Pandar 'softe lough.' He is always laughing, at himself,
at others, at the irony of life which he so clearly sees —
Mais où sont les neiges d'antan? —; and yet his laughter
does not preclude sympathy. More than once we see
him weep at the woes of others. In his blending of
ironical humor, clear vision, unfailing sympathy, he
has much in common with the poet who created him.

If there is much about him which is worldly, he is
also in the better sense of the word a man of the world.
Nothing could exceed the grace and charm of his manners and his conversation, playful, witty, full of shrewd
observation. He handles Troilus and Criseyde with
equal tact; he is easy master of every situation. Best
of all, he is never dull.

Troilus and Criseyde is a masterpiece not only in its
keen analysis of character, but in the skill with which
its plot is conceived and developed; its art   Narrative
is in the highest sense of the word dramatic.   Art.
Troilus first sees Criseyde on a morning in April;
Criseyde departs for the Grecian camp on an August

morning two years later.[1] But if the story extends over some three years, the actions narrated are confined to a few days, several of which are recorded in full detail, almost hour by hour. Three quarters of the lines of Book I are devoted to the events of two days — the day when Troilus first sees Criseyde in the temple and the day when he confides his secret to Pandarus. Beginning with Book II, nearly 5000 lines of the 8239 which constitute the poem are devoted to the events of eight days, presented in sets of two, a day and its morrow. These four groups of two center respectively on Pandar's first visit to Criseyde in his friend's behalf,[2] on the dinner party at the house of Deiphebus, on the stormy night when the lovers meet at the house of Pandarus, on Criseyde's departure from Troy. Over 900 lines are given to the nine days which follow Criseyde's departure from Troy. The great bulk of the poem is thus devoted to a few significant episodes, and the intervening intervals are dismissed with concise summary.

Each of these major episodes is transacted largely by means of dialogue in a series of essentially dramatic scenes. It will sufficiently illustrate Chaucer's method if we analyze one of them, the episode of Criseyde's departure, which fills the fourth book and the beginning of the fifth. It is divided into six scenes. The first is a brief scene at the Grecian camp, in which Calchas obtains the promise that Antenor shall be exchanged for Criseyde (4. 64–140). The scene then shifts to Troy, where a parliament is held to consider the ex-

---

[1] We are told, 5. 8–14, that there have been three spring seasons since Troilus began to love Criseyde. If one counts as one of the three the spring in which the story begins, the total lapse of time is two and a half years; if one counts exclusively of the first spring, another year must be added.

[2] Chaucer dates this visit as on 'Mayes day the thridde,' 2. 56.

change, and Criseyde's departure is decreed while Troilus listens in helpless silence (4. 141–217). There follows a long scene in which Troilus in his own chamber,
first alone and later with Pandarus, bewails his evil
fortune (218–658). This is balanced by a scene at
Criseyde's house in which the heroine laments the fatal
decree. During this scene she receives the farewell
visit of her lady friends, and with breaking heart listens
to their idle chatter, at what Professor Price has called
'a Trojan afternoon tea'[1] — an interlude which is a
most subtle blending of comedy and pathos. Later in
the scene she is joined by Pandarus. This scene extends
from line 659 to 945. It is followed by the scene in the
temple, where Troilus has withdrawn to meditate on
the problem of God's providence and man's freedom;
he is interrupted by Pandarus who brings the plan for
a farewell meeting at his house (946–1123). The book
closes with the long scene (1124–1701) of the lovers'
last night together, a scene which extends till dawn of
the following day. The final scene of the episode, Criseyde's actual departure from the city, is transacted in
the opening lines of Book V. More than 1800 lines are
devoted to the events of these two days.[2]

Boccaccio dedicated his *Filostrato* to Fiammetta, the
lady of his passionate heart; Chaucer dedicates his own
retelling of the story to 'moral Gower' and 'the philo-

---

[1] See his illuminating article, 'Troilus and Criseyde, a study in
Chaucer's Method of Narrative Construction,' *Publications of the
Modern Language Association*, 11. 307–322 (1896). Professor Price
finds that the action of the poem is arranged into fifty scenes, skillfully contrasted in emotional tone, of which thirty-two are conducted
by means of dialogue, nine are soliloquy or monologue, two are trio
scenes, while seven introduce a larger group of speakers.

[2] The student will find it interesting to make a similar analysis of
the other episodes, particularly that of the dinner party at the house
of Deiphebus.

sophical Strode.' Chaucer's friend, John Gower, had
not yet written *Confessio Amantis*, his great
collection of moralized tales; but his early
works, the French *Miroir de l'Omme* and the Latin *Vox
Clamantis*, are even more pronouncedly didactic. They
constitute an ethical analysis of the individual and
of society as a whole which amply justifies Chaucer in
characterizing their author as preëminently a moralist.
Chaucer's other friend, Ralph Strode, was a fellow of
Merton College, Oxford, a scholastic of some distinction, and the author of voluminous treatises on logic
and dialectic.

The Moral.

Chaucer directs his book, then, to a great moralist
and a learned professor of philosophy, begging them
'ther nede is to corecte'; and he leaves us in no doubt
as to the moral he would have us draw from it, or the
philosophy of life which permeates it. Boccaccio is
content to warn young lovers not to put trust too
lightly in every fair lady, many of whom are, alas, like
Criseida, 'unstable as leaf in the wind.' One must be
cautious, and choose a mistress who will be firm and
constant. Very different is Chaucer's moral: —

> O yonge fresshe folkes, he or she,
> In which that love upgroweth with your age,
> Repeyreth hoom from worldly vanitee,
> And of your herte upcasteth the visage
> To thilke god that after his image
> Yow made, and thinketh al nis but a fayre
> This world, that passeth sone as floures fayre.

Let us flee the vanities of the world, and set our love
on Him who in the fullness of His love died for us on
the cross, 'for he nil falsen no wight, dar I seye.' This
moral is reiterated in the passage where the slain
Troilus, as his soul mounts the heavens, looks back at
'this litel spot of erthe' and —

> fully gan despyse
> This wrecched world, and held al **vanitee**
> To respect of the pleyn felicitee
> That is in hevene above.

The noble stanzas which follow heavenward the soul of
Troilus have no counterpart in *Filostrato;* Chaucer has
appropriated them from another poem of Boccaccio, the
Teseide, his principal source for the *Knight's Tale.* Nor
were the stanzas present in the first edition of *Troilus;*
they constitute a deliberate addition made at the time
when Chaucer revised his finished work.

It is plain that Chaucer has done his utmost to make
the poem end, unlike the consistently worldly *Filostrato,*
with full emphasis on its moral and philosophical significance. The contrast with Boccaccio, which is so marked
in the conclusion of the poem, is also present, though
less strikingly, throughout *Troilus and Criseyde.* The
whole story is interpreted at every stage in accordance
with the philosophy of Boethius, a philosophy which
Chaucer seems to have adopted as his own — a profound sense of the transitoriness of all earthly happiness,
of the capriciousness of Fortune, that incalculable
power to whom is entrusted the working out of divinely
ordained destiny.

Chaucer calls his poem a tragedy; and tragedy according to the mediæval conception is, as the Monk of
the *Canterbury Tales* makes clear, the story of a man
cast down by Fortune from great prosperity and high
estate into misery and wretchedness. But in the Boethian philosophy Fortune is but executrix of destiny.
Professor Kittredge has pointed out how strongly Chaucer has emphasized the idea that his characters are involved in the mesh of inexorable fate. It is 'through
his destiny' that Troilus first falls in love with Criseyde.
It is destiny again which sends him riding 'an esy pas'

below Criseyde's window at the very moment when Pandarus has disposed the lady's thoughts to answer love by love: —

> For which, men say, may nought disturbed be
> That shal bityden of necessitee.

And Troilus and Criseyde are Trojans, citizens of a doomed city, marked by the gods for destruction. Calchas has already fled from the doom to come; and it is to save his daughter from a share in it that he secures her extradition from the city, and so precipitates the tragedy. Troilus, when the Trojan parliament issues its decree, sees the hand of destiny at work: —

> For al that comth, comth by necessitee;
> Thus to be lorn, it is my destinee.

And so he debates, through a long passage which Chaucer added in his recension of the poem, the question of man's freedom and God's foreknowledge, inclining in his argument towards the side of predestination.

If stern necessity rules supreme, if men are but the playthings of Fortune, then earthly happiness is but delusion.

> 'O god!' quod she, 'so worldly selinesse,
> Which clerkes callen fals felicitee,
> Ymedled is with many a bitternesse!
> Ful anguisshous than is, god woot,' quod she,
> 'Condicioun of veyn prosperitee.
> For either joyes comen nought yfere,
> Or elles no wight hath hem alwey here.
> . . . .
> Wherfore I wol deffyne in this matere,
> That trewely, for ought I can espye,
> Ther is no verray wele in this world here.' [1]

It is Criseyde who in these lines, closely modeled on

[1] 3. 813–836.

Boethius,[1] sets forth the doctrine of false felicity; Criseyde, who by her subsequent falseness points this same moral at the end of the poem, the moral that the world is but Vanity Fair and its pleasures merely transitory, that true felicity is to be found only 'in hevene above.'

Not only in its concluding stanzas, but throughout its course, Chaucer has moralized his song of courtly love in terms of the stoic philosophy of Boethius, and justified his dedication of the poem to 'moral Gower' and 'the philosophical Strode.' He has given to his story of what is, after all, an illicit love a high level of moral elevation, a level which is essentially maintained throughout the poem. This element of its art contributes in no small measure to our feeling that *Troilus and Criseyde* is a very great poem.[2]

[1] Book II, Prose iv. For a full discussion of the Boethian element in *Troilus*, see B. L. Jefferson, *Chaucer and the Consolation of Philosophy of Boethius*, pp. 120–130.

[2] See Professor Tatlock's article, ' The Epilog of Chaucer's Troilus,' *Modern Philology*, 18. 625–659 (1921).

CHAPTER VII

THE HOUSE OF FAME

THERE is no evidence which enables us to assign a precise date to the *House of Fame*. Since it is named among the poet's works in the Prologue to the *Leg-* Date and *end of Good Women*, it must have been writ- Sources. ten before 1386. The use made in it of the *Divine Comedy* indicates a date later than Chaucer's Italian journey of 1373. Within this range of a dozen years, the date may, though less certainly, be further limited to the period from June, 1374, to February, 1385, the period of Chaucer's active administration of his comptrollership of customs. It would seem to be to these exacting duties at the customs house that the eagle refers in the lines: —

> For whan thy labour doon al is,
> And hast ymaad thy rekeninges,
> In stede of reste and newe thinges,
> Thou gost hoom to thy hous anoon;
> And, also domb as any stoon,
> Thou sittest at another boke,
> Til fully daswed is thy loke.

In default of a more exact date, one would be glad to know whether the poem was written earlier or later than Chaucer's masterpiece of the so-called Italian period, the *Book of Troilus*. Even here, no certain conclusion is possible; and the evidence, such as it is, is too complicated to summarize in such a book as this. But the weight of scholarly opinion now inclines towards the belief that the *House of Fame* was written before

Troilus.[1] If so, it cannot have been written later than 1380.

Such leisure as was left to the poet from his reckonings at the customs house must have been diligently spent in poring over old books; for the *House of Fame* displays a very considerable and varied reading. It is a much more 'learned' poem than is the *Book of the Duchess*, written in 1369. It shows, first of all, a thorough acquaintance with Dante, from whom apparently came the suggestion of Chaucer's flight heavenwards in the talons of an eagle, as well as echoes from all three sections of the *Divine Comedy*. Even greater is the influence of Virgil. The main events of the *Æneid* are digested in the description of the carvings on the temple of Venus in Book I; and the description of Lady Fame in Book III is indebted to *Æneid*, 4. 173–183. To Ovid, *Metamorphoses*, 12. 39–63, is due the general conception of a House of Fame. The *Somnium Scipionis* of Cicero, with the commentary of Macrobius, supplied the introductory discussion of the nature of dreams. Other works the influence of which may be traced are the *Anticlaudianus* of Alanus de Insulis, and the *De Nuptiis Philologiæ et Mercurii* of Martianus Capella. There is no evidence that Chaucer knew the *Trionfo della Fama* of Petrarch.

No single source for the poem as a whole has been discovered, nor is it likely that any will be found. But in general form and structure it belongs clearly in the category of the dream-vision literature of mediæval France, and has much in common with the *Roman de la Rose*, the *Paradys d'Amours* of Froissart, and Chaucer's own *Book of the Duchess;* though its marked differences from any known poems of the type are very striking. There is no reason to doubt that Chaucer alone is re-

[1] See G. L. Kittredge, *Date of Chaucer's Troilus*, pp. 53–60.

sponsible for the central conception of his plot and for its development, even though he has cast it in the mould of the vision-poems of love-allegory, and has enriched it from his varied reading.[1]

Despite its debt in form and substance to 'olde bokes,' the poem impresses one first of all by its spontaneity, its ease of movement, its boundless energy of invention. It excels in that quality which eighteenth-century critics designated as 'wit,' which we to-day are more likely to call ingenious fancy. It modestly disclaims any pretense to poetic art: —

The Story.

> Nat that I wilne, for maistrye,
> Here art poetical be shewed;
> But, for the rym is light and lewed,
> Yit make hit sumwhat agreable,
> Though som vers faile in a sillable.

It will merely recount to us a most marvelous dream which the poet dreamed on the tenth day of last December. And so, half playfully, half seriously, Chaucer discusses in his first fifty lines the nature of dreams. Are they warnings of things to come, or the mere result of bodily disorders? It is a question which Chaucer was fond of raising. With what amused interest he would have investigated present-day methods of 'psychoanalysis' through interpretation of dreams! But though Chaucer raises the question, he leaves its determination to 'grete clerkes.' If dreams are really warnings, they warn 'to derkly' to be of much use. So he merely recounts his dream without attempting an interpretation of it.

Unmindful of Chaucer's caution, scholars have tried to read into his dream an elaborate allegorical meaning,

---

[1] See W. O. Sypherd, *Studies in Chaucer's House of Fame*, Chaucer Society, 1907.

a revelation of his own intellectual experiences and aspirations; but the trend of critical opinion to-day is to discredit these interpretations as over-ingenious, and to accept the poem at its face value as merely a wonderful dream. At most, one may take as revealing Chaucer's own more serious conviction his account of Lady Fame and her abode.

The word 'fame' is used in the poem with double meaning. One meaning is rumor, general report, the mysterious dissemination of tidings. Upon the basis of this general report, some strange power distributes to men their meed of glory or reputation; and this is the second meaning of the word 'fame.' It is with the first of these meanings in view that the magisterial eagle gives his scientific explanation of how all reports tend by their own nature to fly upwards to a single center set in the midst of heaven and earth and sea. But in the third book we see first the dwelling-place of the goddess of reputation or glory. The poetic imagery is easy of interpretation. The mount of ice is slippery of ascent, and in its nature so little permanent that the names upon it melt easily away. Only on the northern side, the direction of hardship and adversity, were there any names of endurance. The lady Fame herself is a wondrous 'feminyne creature,' *semper mutabile*, who, like Virgil's *Fama*, is of such varying stature that one moment she seems less than a cubit in height, and the next she touches the heavens. Mutable in her outward form, the lady is equally capricious in the bestowal of her favor. Perhaps the most brilliant touch of poetical fancy in the poem is the scene where the various companies of men, the deserving and the desertless, come to ask their boons of glory or oblivion, and are answered with no rule or reason, but merely as the whim of the moment may dictate.

The significance of all this is plain enough. Uncertain and evanescent in itself, fame or reputation is bestowed in so unreasonable a way that a man of reason and self-respect cannot but despise it. As Chaucer stood marveling at all this gear, some one addressed him:—

> And seyde: ' Frend, what is thy name?
> Artow come hider to han fame?'
> 'Nay, forsothe, frend!' quod I;
> 'I cam noght hider, graunt mercy!
> For no swich cause, by my heed!
> Suffyceth me, as I were deed,
> That no wight have my name in honde.
> I woot myself best how I stonde;
> For what I drye or what I thinke,
> I wol myselven al hit drinke.'

Chaucer deliberately repudiates all desire for glory; but for fame in the sense of tidings he has the keenest relish; and this desire is satisfied in the house of Rumor, the *domus Dedali*, to which he is now conducted. Here are tidings in abundance, false and true, of all sorts of happenings under heaven. Here are shipmen and pilgrims, pardoners and messengers, —

> With scrippes bret-ful of lesinges,
> Entremedled with tydinges.

The poem breaks off abruptly — either because Chaucer never finished it, or because a final leaf got lost from the original manuscript — leaving the poet in the house of Rumor; and there we find him again some ten years later, as he rides with a company of shipmen and pilgrims and pardoners, an unassuming but keenly interested spectator and auditor, on the road to Canterbury.

The first phase of this wondrous dream transacts itself in a marvelous temple of glass, on the walls of

which are pictured in true mediæval fashion all the
story of Æneas. The poet recognizes that it is the
temple of Venus —

> for, in portreyture,
> I saw anoon right hir figure
> Naked fletinge in a see.

It is because of the poet's devotion to love that Jupiter
sends down his great eagle to bear him aloft to the land
of Fame, where he can hear tidings of lovers and their
ways.

The second book is concerned with Chaucer's skyward
journey. The eagle who bears him none too securely in
his talons is no mere piece of narrative machinery, but
quite the most delightful personage of the poem. He
is a very learned eagle, and not in the least niggardly
about imparting his learning. With his helpless audience of one gripped in his two claws, he lectures most
academically on the theory of sound, and then inquires
with fine condescension: —

> Have I not preved thus simply,
> Withouten any subtiltee
> Of speche, or gret prolixitee
> Of termes of philosophye?

To this question Chaucer, taking the part of wisdom,
discreetly answers 'Yis.'

> 'A ha!' quod he, 'lo, so I can
> Lewedly to a lewed man
> Speke, and shewe him swiche skiles,
> That he may shake hem by the biles,
> So palpable they shulden be.'

Though the eagle speak with the tongue of men and
schoolmasters, the poet does not forget that he is a bird,
and reminds his readers of the fact by the delicious conceit — 'shake hem by the biles.'

Having lectured to his own great satisfaction on the wave-theory of sound, he is ready, nay eager, to discourse on the stars; but his audience rebels: —

> ' Wilt thou lere of sterres aught?'
> ' Nay, certeinly,' quod I, ' right naught;
> And why? for I am now to ol l.'
> ' Elles I wolde thee have told,'
> Quod he, ',the sterres names, lo,
> And al the hevenes signes to,
> And which they been.'

Every reader of poetry, he insists, should have at least an elementary course in astronomy, and what time so favorable as this when we are in the very midst of the constellations? It is only when his hearer urges that his eyes will not bear to look upon the stars in their blazing proximity, that the eagle reluctantly bridles his pedagogic zeal.

It would be idle to point out all the humorous touches of this aerial colloquy. If the reader cannot see them for himself, as Matthew Arnold would have said, *morietur in peccatis suis*. Not even in the *Nun's Priest's Tale* is Chaucer's humor more irresistible.

CHAPTER VIII

THE LEGEND OF GOOD WOMEN

THE *Legend of Good Women* marks the beginning of what is ordinarily called Chaucer's third period, the period which reaches full flower in the *Canterbury Tales*. Itself a collection of tales bound together by community of theme and by a common prologue, it may in deed be thought of as a direct precursor of the greater collection which follows. Chaucer has ceased to feel the overmastering influence of Italian models; and though the intellectual stimulus received from Italy was not to spend itself until his death, he is feeling about for a form of literary expression which shall be essentially his own. That the *Legend* was in some sort an experimental venture is suggested by the fact that it was left unfinished, crowded from its place in his attention by the vastly superior conception of the *Canterbury Tales*. But experiment though it be, it is far from being a failure. The nine legends which Chaucer wrote are good pieces of narrative, told with the poet's peculiar grace and charm ; while the Prologue is, in its beauty of imagery, its buoyant freshness of an English Maytide, in its general conception and execution, one of Chaucer's most successful and most beautiful productions.

The *Legend* consists of a series of tales, drawn from the storehouse of classical antiquity, recounting the fortunes of noble women, true in love, intro- duced by a prologue poem of the dream- vision type so popular in the allegorical literature of

Sources.

the Middle Ages. In the case of such a work, one need not look for any single source; one will ask rather what models Chaucer may have had before him, or what earlier works may have suggested the scheme of his poem. Two such works immediately suggest themselves: the *Heroides* of Ovid, a series of imaginary letters sent by heroines of mythology to their faithless lovers, and, nearer to Chaucer's own time, the *De Claris Mulieribus* [1] of Boccaccio, a collection of stories in Latin prose, wherein are epitomized the fortunes of famous women. The first of these works Chaucer certainly knew; and there is every probability that he was acquainted with the other.

In compiling materials for the individual legends, Chaucer seems to have done what any modern author would do under similar circumstances: he read all the accounts of his heroines which were readily accessible to him, and selected, adapted, and combined, as his literary taste impelled him. In the case of the first legend, that of Cleopatra, it is not very clear just what versions of the story Chaucer used. Perhaps a Latin translation of Plutarch's life of Antony was accessible to him; perhaps, too, he consulted the *Historia adversum Paganos* of Orosius (fifth century A. D.) and the *De Claris Mulieribus* of Boccaccio. Pretty certainly he was acquainted with the *Epitome Rerum Romanarum* of Florus, a Roman historian of the reign of Hadrian. The legend of Thisbe was drawn entirely from Ovid's account of the lady in *Metamorphoses*, 4. 55–166, though the source was used by Chaucer with characteristic freedom. The story of Dido is taken, of course, from Virgil, though a few lines (1355–1365)

---

[1] Similar in character, though wider in its scope, is the *De Casibus Virorum et Feminarum Illustrium* of the same author, used by Chaucer as the model for his *Monk's Tale*.

are from Ovid's *Heroides*, 7. 1–8. For the stories of
Hypsipyle and Medea Chaucer went, naturally enough,
to Ovid;[1] but he seems to have made even greater use
of the account given in the *Historia Trojana* of Guido
delle Colonne.[2] For the story of Lucretia Chaucer
himself refers us to Livy and to Ovid,[3] the latter of
whom is his principal source. The remaining legends
are based chiefly on Ovid, whose influence is the dominant one in the whole collection. Other works which
Chaucer may well have consulted are the fables of
Hyginus, the two works of Boccaccio mentioned above,
and the compendium of classical mythology by the
same author entitled *De Genealogia Deorum*.[4] Most
of the stories of the *Legend of Good Women* are also
told by Gower in the *Confessio Amantis;* so that one
may, if he pleases, see how a less gifted contemporary
uses the same material.[5]

For the Prologue the problem of sources is much less
clear. It seems to have been composed under the general influence of a school, rather than of any particular
models. This school is that of the French love-allegory, with its familiar devices of a dream-vision and
a court of love, and its unfailing accompaniments of
May-morning, singing birds, and springing flowers, of
which the *Roman de la Rose* is the great exemplar.[6]
From among the vast throng of French love-allegories
of this type, it is possible to segregate a small group

[1] *Metamorphoses*, 7. 1–296; *Heroides*, 6 and 12.

[2] Cf. above, p. 98.

[3] *Fasti*, 3. 461–516.

[4] Chaucer's indebtedness to the *De Genealogia* has been convincingly
proved by C. G. Child in *Modern Language Notes*, 11. 238–245.

[5] For a discussion of the sources of the *Legend* and of the relation
of Chaucer's work to Gower's, see the excellent article by M. Bech in
Anglia, 5. 313–382.

[6] For a very thorough account of this poetry, see Professor W. A.
Neilson's *The Origins and Sources of the Court of Love*, Boston, 1899.

which exerted a more particular influence on the Prologue.

Some twenty years before the probable date of
Chaucer's *Legend*, the French poet Guillaume de
Machault wrote a *Dit de la Marguerite*, wherein a lady
named Marguerite, very likely a mistress of Machault's
patron Pierre de Lusignan, king of Cyprus, is praised
under the figure of the flower whose name she bears.
The cult of the daisy was immediately taken up by
Machault's literary disciples, Froissart and Deschamps.
Froissart in his *Dittié de la Flour de la Marguerite* and
his *Paradys d'Amours* uses the same symbolism, with
extravagant praise of the daisy, in honor of another
Marguerite; and Deschamps carries the same device
even farther in his *Lay de Franchise*, and in several of
his balades. As the fashion gained vogue, this symbolism of the daisy was applied even to ladies whose name
did not happen to be Marguerite. So that one need not
be surprised to find in the Prologue to Chaucer's
Legend that the daisy is used to symbolize Alcestis,
and, through her, Chaucer's patroness, Queen Anne.[1]

With the work of all three of these poets Chaucer,
we know, was familiar; with Deschamps he had per-
sonal relations of peculiar interest; for a balade of
Deschamps is addressed to the ' grant translateur, noble
Geffroy Chaucier.' [2] From the balade itself we learn that
it was to be sent to Chaucer, together with other of
Deschamps's poems, by the hands of Sir Lewis Clifford.[3]
It is entirely possible that the *Lay de Franchise*, with

---

[1] For a discussion of the marguerite poems and their influence on
Chaucer, see the article by J. L. Lowes on the *Legend of Good Women*, in *Publications of the Modern Language Association*, 19. 593–683
(1904).

[2] The balade is reprinted entire in the *Oxford Chaucer*, 1. lvi, lvii.

[3] For an account of Clifford, see the article by Professor Kittredge
on ' Chaucer and some of his Friends,' in *Modern Philology*, 1. 1–18.

its praise of the marguerite, was one of the poems thus transmitted from the poet over-seas. However it reached him, we can be all but sure that the *Lay de Franchise*, and Froissart's *Paradys d'Amours*, and perhaps other of the marguerite poems, were in Chaucer's mind when he composed his Prologue.[1] It is to this group of marguerite poets, then, and to the still larger group of their countrymen who had written courtly allegories of love, that Chaucer is speaking in the familiar lines near the beginning of his poem : —

> Ye lovers, that can make of sentement;
> In this cas oghte ye be diligent
> To forthren me somwhat in my labour,
> Whether ye ben with the leef or with the flour.
> For wel I wot, that ye han herbiforn
> Of making ropen, and lad awey the corn ;
> And I come after, glening here and there,
> And am ful glad if I may finde an ere
> Of any goodly word that ye han left.

One need only say that Chaucer's gleaning was indeed rich.

In the Patent Rolls for the eighth year of the reign of Richard II, under date of February 17 [1385], there is a writ by which the king grants ' by special grace to our beloved Geoffrey Chaucer, comptroller of our customs and subsidies in the port of our city of London,' the privilege of appointing a permanent deputy to conduct the business which he had before been commanded to transact with his own hand. With what delicious sense of untrammeled freedom must Chaucer have closed his books of reckonings, and taken farewell of his not too congenial associates at the custom-house on Thames-bank. No

Date and Circumstances of Composition.

---

[1] Despite the contention of Dr. Lowes in the article cited above, these poems seem to me to have served as suggestions, rather than as definite sources.

longer need he crowd his study and his writing into the evening hours, after a day's work was already done.

Chaucer was at this time a man of forty-five or thereabouts, and already the most famous poet in England. He was the 'grant translateur' of the *Roman de la Rose;* he had celebrated the marriage of Richard and Queen Anne in the *Parliament of Fowls;* he had shown the free play of his wit and fancy in the *House of Fame;* above all he had published but a few years ago his great narrative poem, *Troilus.* We can imagine that *Troilus* had created no small sensation in courtly circles. Never before had Chaucer's readers seen in English, nor in French, a story of courtly love told with such vivid and convincing realism; and in this vivid story the heroine, Criseyde, becomes in the end a type of all that a lady should not be. It is likely enough that many a noble lady of the court reproached the poet, betwixt play and earnest, for drawing so unflattering a portrait of womankind.

In the Prologue to the *Legend*, King Cupid bitterly upbraids the poet for having translated the *Romance of the Rose*, 'that is an heresye ageyns my lawe,' and for having written disparagingly of Criseyde — 'that maketh men to wommen lasse triste.' Queen Alcestis, supreme type of womanly fidelity in love, pleads Chaucer's cause. Perhaps, since Chaucer is but a foolish poet at best, he has sinned by sheer inadvertence, 'gessing no malyce.' At any rate, he has written many other poems in praising of Love's name. She promises that he will never err again; and proposes that as penance he shall now write 'of wommen trewe in lovinge al hir lyve.'

These proceedings at the court of King Cupid are, of course, a literary device for introducing the series of legends which is to follow; and Chaucer has warned us that the whole scene is but a dream. One must be on one's guard against reading into scenes of poetic fiction a record of supposedly actual happenings; yet in this instance there is reason to believe that the events of the dream-vision reflect something of reality, that the task of writing a legend of good women was imposed on Chaucer by Queen Anne, as in the poem it is enjoined on him by Queen Alcestis.

That the poem was, at any rate, to be dedicated to Queen Anne is made clear in Alceste's command:—

> And whan this book is maad, yive hit the quene
> On my behalfe, at Eltham, or at Shene.

Chaucer's disciple, Lydgate, writing a generation later, asserts in the Prologue to his *Falls of Princes* that the *Legend* was made 'at the request of the quene.' Perhaps Lydgate is reporting authentic tradition; perhaps his statement rests only on his own interpretation of Chaucer's Prologue. Even on this latter hypothesis the evidence is significant. The modern critic would be less diffident of seeing in the poem a meaning found also by a nearly contemporary poet thoroughly conversant with the conventions of mediæval poetry.

It seems probable, also, that Chaucer's reverence for Queen Alcestis, and his passionate devotion to the daisy which is associated with her, were intended as a compliment to Queen Anne. In the lines which sing the praises of the daisy, Chaucer has echoed the language of the French poets who, under the type of the marguerite, have complimented living ladies. But Chaucer surpasses his French originals in the fervor of his devotion. He says of the daisy:—

> She is the clernesse and the verrey light
> That in this derke worlde me wynt and ledeth;
> The herte inwith my sorowful brest yow dredeth,
> And loveth so sore, that ye ben verrayly
> The maistresse of my wit, and nothing I . . .

> Be ye my gyde and lady sovereyne;
> As to myn erthly god, to yow I calle,
> Bothe in this werke and in my sorwes alle.

These lines, as Professor Lowes has pointed out, are closely modeled on a passage of fervent devotion in the Proem to *Filostrato*, where Boccaccio is addressing not a flower, but his lady Fiammetta.

It would be absurd to suppose that this extravagant devotion of Chaucer is bestowed on a mere flower of the field. It seems hardly less unreasonable to suppose that it is lavished upon the mythical person of Queen Alcestis. What's Hecuba to him, or he to Hecuba, that he should weep for her?

To the present writer the conclusion seems inevitable that under the twofold type of the daisy and of Alcestis the poet is praising some living lady. If so, it is highly probable that the lady is none other than Queen Anne, to whom, as we know from Chaucer's own words, the book was to be formally presented 'at Eltham or at Shene.' From this conclusion it need not follow that Alcestis is at all points to be equated with Anne, nor that had Chaucer carried out his intention to devote one of the legends to the story of Alcestis:—

> She that for hir husbonde chees to dye,
> And eek to goon to helle, rather than he —

he would have made her life in any way an allegory of the life of the queen. Alcestis is not an invariable symbol for Queen Anne, but rather a type of noble womanhood and wifely devotion which, Chaucer suggests, is again embodied in his youthful queen.[1] The daisy, then,

[1] The view that Alcestis typifies Queen Anne is supported by Tatlock, *Development and Chronology of Chaucer's Works*, pp. 102–120, and by B. L. Jefferson in *Journal of English and Germanic Philology*, 13. 434–443. It is opposed by Lowes in the article already cited, and by Kittredge in *Modern Philology*, 6. 435–439. A middle position is taken by Samuel Moore in *Modern Language Review*, 7. 488–493.

plays a double rôle. It is immediately the type of Queen Alcestis who is to appear in person later in the poem; but more subtly it also shadows forth the poet's royal patroness.

The Prologue to the *Legend of Good Women* has come down to us in two versions which present very considerable variations from one another. Hitherto this discussion has confined itself to the longer version, which modern editors have designated by the letter 'B' to distinguish it from the shorter 'A' version, found in a single manuscript (Cambridge University Library, Gg 4. 27).[1] That both of these versions are from Chaucer's own hand, no one has doubted; but the question as to the relative priority of the two versions was long in dispute. The 'A' version contains 90 lines not found in 'B,' lacks 124 lines which 'B' contains, presents transpositions of several important passages, and numerous slight alterations in individual lines. Particularly notable is the fact that 'A' omits entirely the couplet quoted above in which the poem is expressly dedicated to Queen Anne, and that the passage in which the poet expresses his devotion to the daisy is greatly modified, with complete suppression of many of its most ardent lines. Had this version alone survived, we should have had no grounds for seeing in the poem any special compliment to the queen. The daisy would have seemed to typify Alcestis and only Alcestis.

It is impossible to enter here into all the intricacies of the argument. It must suffice to say that virtually all scholars are now agreed that the so-called 'B' version is the earlier, and that it was written in 1385 or 1386,

The Two Versions of the Prologue.

---

[1] Recent critics sometimes designate the 'A' version by the symbol 'G' or 'Gg,' and the so-called 'B' version, the text of which is best preserved in MS. Faifax 16 of the Bodleian Library, by the symbol 'F.'

probably in the latter year. Deschamps's *Lay de Franchise*, which seems to have contributed to Chaucer's praises of the marguerite, was composed for May-day, 1385. This sets an early limit for the date of the 'B' Prologue. It was certainly written before the death of Queen Anne in 1394. By 1387, or shortly after, Chaucer was apparently engaged on the *Canterbury Tales*, and would have been most unwilling to undertake, even at royal request, another collection of tales based on a plan artistically so inferior.

When Queen Anne died in 1394, her royal husband tore down the palace at Shene, where she had died, and avoided everything which should remind him of his loss. It would seem that the so-called 'A' version of the Prologue, which suppresses the dedication to the queen and obliterates the compliment paid to her in the earlier version, was called forth by this event and by the king's attitude towards it. As the *Legend* was not completed, it had probably never been presented to the queen, never formally 'published.' The queen's death made the dedication no longer appropriate; and the king's attitude made unacceptable to him a poem designed to do her honor. To adapt his still unfinished work to these new conditions would seem to have been Chaucer's motive for revision. If so, the date of the 'A' version must be shortly after 1394, a date which is corroborated by other considerations.[1]

By the command of Queen Alcestis, Chaucer is to write 'a glorious Legende of Gode Wommen, maidenes Plan of and wyves' who were saints and martyrs in the Poem. the cause of true love. Cupid adds a further command that the legends shall conclude with the life of Alcestis.

[1] For a fuller discussion of the problem see Tatlock's chapter on the *Legend* in *Development and Chronology of Chaucer's Works*.

The finished poem, then, was to have consisted of the Prologue, followed by the legends of the nineteen ladies who form Alcestis's train, and concluded by the story of Alcestis herself. But Chaucer had a sad habit not unknown to us moderns, of undertaking a large task with boundless enthusiasm, and of tiring of it before the task was half performed. He wrote nine legends (the last unfinished), praising the virtue of ten of the noble ladies, and then the new and the better idea of the Canterbury pilgrimage took possession of his mind. With the intellectual impatience so characteristic of him, he started on the fresher task; and though intending to finish the *Legend*, as shown by his reference to it in the Prologue to the *Man of Law's Tale*, he laid it one side to wait for the more convenient day which never came. It is easy to see why the work was put aside. Charming as the Prologue is in its kind, it is after all only a dream, and forever inferior to the human reality and broad sweep of the Prologue to the *Canterbury Tales*. Moreover, since the tales were all to be told by the poet himself, there was no opportunity for the dramatic variety offered by the Canterbury pilgrimage. Lastly, and most important, the very nature of the plan involved inevitable monotony — all the stories were to be of true women, faithful though abandoned in love, and all were to be drawn from the realm of classical antiquity.

As Professor Lounsbury has pointed out, one can trace in the successive sections of the work the poet's growing tedium. Even as he wrote the last lines of the Prologue, he began to be oppressed with the magnitude of his undertaking. The god of love warns him : —

> 'I wot wel that thou mayst nat al hit ryme,
> That swiche lovers diden in hir tyme;

> It were to long to reden and to here;
> Suffyceth me, thou make in this manere,
> That thou reherce of al hir lyf the grete,
> After thise olde auctours listen to trete.
> For whoso shal so many a storie telle,
> Sey shortly, or he shal to longe dwelle.'

A similar note recurs in the first of the legends : —

> The wedding and the feste to devyse,
> To me, that have ytake swiche empryse
> Of so many a storie for to make,
> Hit were to long, lest that I sholde slake
> Of thing that bereth more effect and charge:
> For men may overlade a ship or barge;
> And forthy to th' effect than wol I skippe,
> And al the remenant, I wol lete hit slippe.

Other hints of weariness may be found frequently in the legends ; [1] but quite unmistakable are the following lines from the *Legend of Phyllis :* —

> But for I am agroted heerbiforn
> To wryte of hem that been in love forsworn,
> And eek to haste me in my legende,
> Which to performe god me grace sende,
> Therfor I passe shortly in this wyse.

With such a warning, one is not surprised to find the next legend broken off abruptly in the middle of a sentence. One curious slip on the poet's part gives further proof that his heart was not in the work. In the *Legend of Ariadne*, at line 2075, we are told that Theseus was but twenty years and three of age; only twenty lines farther on Ariadne suggests that her sister be wedded to Theseus's son.

On the basis of the lists of heroines given in the balade introduced into the Prologue, and in the Prologue to the *Man of Law's Tale*, Professor Skeat sur-

---

[1] See ll. 1002–1003, 1552–1553, 1565, 1679, 1692–1693, 1921, 2257–2258, 2470–2471, 2490–2491, 2513–2515.

mises that the remaining legends were to have dealt with
Penelope, Helen, Hero, Laodamia, Lavinia, Polyxena,
Deianira, Hermione, and Briseis: but since the two
lists are not in accord, we may well believe that Chaucer's mind was never clearly made up on the matter.

The peculiar charm of the Prologue to the *Legend
of Good Women* is in part the charm of spring-time
and out-of-doors, in part the charm of noble The Pro-
womanhood as figured in the fair Alceste, and logue.
even more the buoyant joyfulness of new-won freedom,
as of an Ariel set free. First we see the poet, Chaucer, himself in his daily life — in the study and in the
fields. Though he is no deep scholar, he modestly
confesses, it is his surpassing delight to read books, —

> And to hem yeve I feyth and ful credence,
> And in myn herte have hem in reverence
> So hertely, that ther is game noon
> That fro my bokes maketh me to goon,
> But hit be seldom, on the holyday.

Though a book-lover, Chaucer is no book-worm. There
is one attraction more potent than that of 'olde bokes'
— the beauty of nature in the fair spring-time.[1] But
when we speak of Chaucer's love of nature, we must
be careful not to confuse this with the love of nature
which marks more modern poets. Nowhere in his works
is there any suggestion that he cared for the wilder
beauty of mountains and rocks and surging sea. We
never hear that he spent a summer in Wales, or Corn-
wall, or the Scottish Highlands. In his journeys to
Italy he must surely have caught a glimpse of the Alps;
but never does he sing of cloud-capped peak or snowy

---

[1] Chaucer's picture of Maytide is, of course, largely influenced by
the conventionalities of the French love-allegories: but his poetry is so
spontaneous in its enthusiasm that we may safely assume that the convention chimed with his own natural feeling.

summit. In the *Franklin's Tale* the story demands a
description of the rocky coast of Brittany; but the
rocks are thought of as terrible and destructive rather
than as beautiful. They even cause Dorigen to doubt
the benevolence of their Creator : —

> Eterne god, that thurgh thy purveyaunce
> Ledest the world by certein governaunce,
> In ydel, as men seyn, ye nothing make ;
> But, lord, thise grisly feendly rokkes blake,
> That semen rather a foul confusioun
> Of werk than any fair creacioun
> Of swich a parfit wys god and a stable,
> Why han ye wroght this werk unresonable ? [1]

Once only does Chaucer give a sweeping view from
hill or mountain-side : —

> Ther is, at the west syde of Itaille,
> Doun at the rote of Vesulus the colde,
> A lusty playne, habundant of vitaille,
> Wher many a tour and toun thou mayst biholde,
> That founded were in tyme of fadres olde,
> And many another delitable sighte,
> And Saluces this noble contree highte.[2]

What appeals to Chaucer in the view is the fertility of
the plain, and the evidence of prosperous human life
furnished by 'many a tour and toun.' As for Mt. Ve-
sulus itself, he dismisses it with the single epithet
'colde.' The tale of Constance offers abundant opportunity for describing the beauty and grandeur of the
sea ; but the opportunity is not improved. It is merely
the 'wilde see,' or the 'salte see,' thought of as dangerous and cruelly malignant. What Chaucer, and the
men of the Middle Ages in general, loved in nature
was the peaceful and gentle, the beneficent to human
life. The beauty of a May dawning, the song of birds,
the fairness of the daisy, the gentle sweep of a green
meadow, the long avenues of a well-kept forest — these

[1] F 865-872.　　　　[2] E 57-63.

were the charms which could lure Chaucer from his books and make him happy for a long summer's day. It is hard for us, bred and born in the atmosphere of romanticism, to sympathize with such a choice, to understand why one of the most beautiful of Alpine passes should have received the name of Mala Via, the 'bad road;' and yet who shall say that love of the kindly and beneficent is not as sane and reasonable as romantic enthusiasm for the desolate and destructive?

Following on the description of Chaucer's daily life comes the dream-vision itself. In this charming vision one may notice the skill with which the poet paints a wide and crowded scene without any confusion or distraction of attention from its central figures. Though the long description of the beauty of a May meadow belongs to Chaucer's waking experience and not to the dream,[1] the memory of it is so fresh in the reader's mind that no further painting of background is necessary; and the dream begins at once with the entrance of the god of love, and of the queen whom he is leading by the hand. They, as the central figures of the scene, are described with all beauty of detail, the noble womanhood of Alcestis dominating all about her. Then, after the balade has been sung, our attention is diverted to a definite number of attendants, the nineteen ladies. They are in 'royal habit,' but beyond this single touch they are not described. From them we turn to a vast company without number, and the whole scene is filled with beauty and goodness. But suddenly the whole throng ceases its motion; all kneel and sing with one voice: —

> 'Hele and honour
> To trouthe of womanhede, and to this flour
> That berth our alder prys in figuringe!'

[1] We are speaking of the B version.

Once more our whole attention is brought back to the object of this adoration, and the action of the dream proceeds uninterrupted to the end.

Beyond all this beauty of nature and of fair vision, there is the spirit of health and free-hearted joy pervading the whole poem, which is too subtle for analysis, and fortunately needs no service of the critic.

Into the Prologue Chaucer threw all the enthusiasm of his art; but the legends which it introduces were The Nine Legends. written, as we have seen, half-heartedly. Though the tales are well and gracefully told, and much more than mere imitations of classical authors, many readers, I think, will fail to read them through. We are conscious of a 'hidden want,' the want of Chaucer's own participant enthusiasm. Anything which has been hastily and reluctantly written will be hastily and reluctantly read. There are a few passages of fine description, such as the highly animated account of the sea-fight at Actium in the *Legend of Cleopatra* (a description which suggests the tournament scene in the *Knight's Tale*), or the description of the hunt and ensuing thunder-storm in the *Legend of Dido;* there is true pathos in the story of Lucretia, and real lyric passion in the lament of forsaken Ariadne; and yet we feel that the legends are in the main creditable productions rather than inspired poems. Perhaps the *Legend of Thisbe* comes nearest to being real poetry.

CHAPTER IX

THE CANTERBURY TALES, GROUP A

EXCELLENT as is the quality of Chaucer's earlier work, —rich in characterization, in humor, in pathos, in essential poetry,—it is in the *Canterbury Tales*, and in them alone, that we find the full measure of Chaucer's greatness. In their endless variety of beauty and charm they themselves are Chaucer. To attempt any critical appreciation of the *Canterbury Tales* as a whole is to discuss the literary art of Chaucer, and that has already been attempted in an earlier chapter. Detailed estimates of the individual tales will be found in the pages which follow. All that remains for consideration here is the happy device by which the several tales are bound together into an artistic whole.

All the world loves a good story; and long before the days of Chaucer, collections of short tales in prose or verse were popular in Europe and in the Orient. Very often, too, an attempt was made to give to such compilations a sort of collective unity, either by community of theme, as in the *Legend of Good Women* and the *Monk's Tale*, or better by some framework story, as in the great collection known as the *Arabian Nights*. The *Confessio Amantis* of Gower is merely a vast treasure-house of stories bound together somewhat clumsily by the device of a lover's confession to the priest of Venus, the stories being told by the confessor as examples and admonitions to his penitent. Early in the fourteenth century we have in English a collection of fifteen tales

The Frame-work.

unified by an enveloping plot in the *Proces of the Sevyn Sages*. Most famous, perhaps, of such collections of stories is the *Decameron* of Boccaccio; and though, in all probability, Chaucer was unacquainted with this work, it is interesting to compare the way in which the two foremost of fourteenth century story-tellers gave unity to their work. In Boccaccio a company of ten young men and women of high social standing flee from plague-stricken Florence to a country estate, the property of one of them, and pass their days in telling stories. On each of ten days a story is told by each of the company, the stories of each day dealing with the same general theme. Connecting links describe the other diversions with which the days are filled.

Chaucer's device of a springtime pilgrimage to Canterbury has several advantages over that of Boccaccio. In the democracy of travel it was possible to bring together quite naturally persons of varied occupations and of diverse social rank, from the Knight to the Plowman, and in consequence to give to the stories a greater variety in theme and manner than is possible in the *Decameron*. Moreover, the motley complexion of the company and the adventures of a journey give rise to many humorous encounters, which add greatly to the realism of the whole. With constant change of scene, and with wide range of human characters, tedium is impossible; and the reader enters at once into the exhilarating spirit of travel and holiday.

Had Chaucer carried out his original plan for the *Canterbury Tales*, the Prologue describing the gathering at the Tabard Inn would have been followed by sixty tales, two by each of the pilgrims including Chaucer himself, each introduced by its own prologue. The connecting links between the tales would have kept us informed of the

The Nine Groups of Tales.

progress of the journey, where the nights were spent, where dinner was taken, of all the little happenings of the way. Then would have followed an account of the arrival in Canterbury and of the doings of the company while there. Sixty more tales, with their connecting links, would have brought us back to Southwark; and a concluding section would have described the supper given to him who should be judged the best *raconteur*. Of this grand scheme Chaucer completed less than a quarter. The plan was modified in the course of execution to *one* tale from each pilgrim on the way to Canterbury, and one on the return; but in the work as we have it, many of the pilgrims are never called upon, and the company never reaches Canterbury, though it gets within sight of its towers. Even the stories which we possess do not form an orderly sequence. We have the first tale told, the Knight's, and the last, the Parson's; but between the beginning and the end there are eight gaps which should have been filled with tales, or with connecting links; so that we have not a fragment of the whole, but nine separate fragments, the longest of which contains seven connected tales, and the shortest but one. These fragments are usually spoken of as groups, and are for convenience designated by the letters of the alphabet from A to I. Further confusion is caused by the fact that in the various manuscripts of the *Canterbury Tales* the order of the tales is different, even the integrity of the several groups or fragments not being always preserved. But the references in the link-poems enable us to constitute the groups; while the geographical references to the towns through which the pilgrims pass make it possible to determine with certainty the relative position of all but one of the nine groups. The group, of the position of which we are not certain, has been assigned by Mr. Furnivall to the third place in the series, and has therefore been denominated Group C. Its assignment to this position, though based on the slightest evidence, has been generally accepted as a convenient practical disposition of the case.

Fragmentary as is the work, we are none the less able to piece out its allusions to places and time with what we know independently of the usual proced- ure of pilgrims to the shrine of St. Thomas, and thus to reconstruct with some degree of probability the route followed by Chaucer's pilgrims, and the time taken by them upon their journey.

The Journey to Canterbury.

Though it was possible, when demanded by urgent business, to make the journey in much less time, it was the usual custom for pilgrims to spend four days in going from London to Canterbury, the recognized stopping-places for the night being Dartford, Roches- ter, and Ospringe, thus dividing the journey into three easy stages of about fifteen miles each, with a short stint of ten miles for the last day. Roads were rough and heavy, so bad that wheeled vehicles were usually impracticable; and progress was necessarily slow and fatiguing. In the case of the pilgrimage which Chaucer describes, there were many reasons why the ordinary rate of travel should not be exceeded. There were three women in the company, and several of the pilgrims, not- ably the Clerk and the Shipman, were but ill mounted; April, 'with his shoures sote,' had made the roads heavy with mud, as we know from the Host's assertion (B 3988) that he was so bored by the tale of the Monk that, save for the clinking of the bells on the Monk's bridle, he would certainly have fallen down for sleep,

Although the slough had never been so depe ;

lastly, the journey was being taken mainly for pleasure, and half the fun of a vacation is to take your time.

At the beginning of Group B, which, as we shall see, occupies the second day of the pilgrimage, we are told that the date is April 18. It is on the evening of April 16, then, that Chaucer enters the spacious hostelry of the Tabard, and finds the nine-and-twenty who are to be his fellow-voyagers. Allowing for the change in the calendar, April 16 corresponds to April 24 in our reckoning, and at that date, in southern England, the sun rises about quarter of five, and sets about quarter past seven. Early on the morning of April 17, at break of day, the Host awoke his guests, and gathering them into a flock, led them forth at an easy jog, ' a litel more than pas,' the Miller playing his bagpipes the while, till they came to the little brook which crossed the Canterbury way, called St. Thomas-a-Watering. Here the cuts are drawn, and the Knight begins his tale. By the time his tale is ended, the musical Miller is so drunk that ' unnethe upon his hors he sat.' Southwark ale, we are told, is responsible for his condition. He is not too drunk, however, to tell his churl's tale, at the conclusion of which the company has nearly reached Greenwich, and the hour is half past seven (half-way pryme). The *Reeve's Tale* next follows, and after that the fragment of the *Cook's Tale*, of which ' tale maked Chaucer na more.' Here ends Group A; and the rest of the tales of the first day are silence. The night is probably spent at Dartford, fifteen miles from London.

Either the start next day is delayed, or the story-telling postponed; for it is already ten o'clock of April 18, when the Host reminds his friends that a fourth part of the day is gone, and that they are wasting time. Group B is the longest consecutive series of tales, and since near the end of it, in the *Monk's Prologue*, the Host says, ' Lo! Rouchestre stant heer faste by!' and since Rochester was probably the stopping-place for the

second night, it may be that we have the full stint of
tales for the second day. Rochester is thirty miles from
London.

There is nothing to determine the place of Group C.
Mr. Furnivall thinks the Pardoner's desire for cakes
and ale more appropriate to the morning, and hence
assigns it conjecturally to the morning of the third day.

It was usual for pilgrims to dine on the third day at
Sittingbourne, ten miles from Rochester ; and since in
the *Wife of Bath's Prologue* the Summoner promises
to tell two or three tales about Friars before they come
to Sittingbourne, and at the end of his story says,
' My tale is doon, we been almost at toune,' it is reasonable to assign Group D to the morning of the third day.
Group E, which contains a playful allusion to the Wife
of Bath, is probably to be assigned to the afternoon of
the same day, during which the party rides six miles
to Ospringe, where the next night is spent.

Near the beginning of the *Squire's Tale*, which with
the *Franklin's* constitutes Group F, the Squire says
(F 73) : —

> ' I wol nat tarien yow, for it is pryme.'

Since, then, the time of day is nine of the morning, this
group has been assigned to the morning of the fourth
day. The position of Group G is clearly determined
by the opening lines of the *Canon's Yeoman's Prologue* : —

> Whan ended was the lyf of seint Cecyle,
> Er we had riden fully fyve myle,
> At Boghton under Blee us gan atake
> A man, that clothed was in clothes blake.

A little farther on we are told that the Yeoman had
seen the jolly company ride out of their hostelry in the
morning, and that he and his master had ridden fast
to overtake them. Measuring back five miles from the

little village of Boughton-under-Blean, we get Ospringe
as the town from which they had set out in the morning.
From Boughton the road leads through the Forest of
Blean, a favorable place for robbers, and unwillingness
to ride through so dangerous a place alone may account
for the Canon's desire to join the larger company.

It is at a little town, —

> Which that ycleped is Bob-up-and-doun, —

that Group H begins. Antiquarians are not agreed in
their identification of this village with the picturesque
name; but the village of Harbledown, just out of Canterbury, seems best to answer the requirements. It is
not yet noon, for the Cook, too drunk to tell the tale
demanded of him, is reproached for sleeping 'by the
morwe.' The Manciple offers himself as a substitute;
and it is his tale which constitutes Group H.

The *Parson's Tale* apparently follows immediately
on the Manciple's, for in the first lines of the *Parson's
Prologue* we read: —

> By that the maunciple hadde his tale al ended,
> The sonne fro the south lyne was descended
> So lowe, that he was nat, to my sighte,
> Degreës nyne and twenty as in highte.
> Foure of the clokke it was tho, as I gesse.

The difficulty, however, resides in the lapse of time. If
it was still morning when the Manciple began his tale,
how explain the fact that it is four o'clock at its conclusion? Because of this inconsistency in time, the
Parson's Tale has been separated from the Manciple's
and labeled Group I. When one remembers, though,
the way time is made to gallop in Shakespeare at the
demand of dramatic effectiveness, one wonders whether
the inconsistency may not have been deliberately
planned, so that the pilgrimage might end appropri-

ately as the shadows begin to lengthen. Personally I
see no sufficient reason for making the division which
Mr. Furnivall thinks necessary.[1]

What Chaucer would have done with his pilgrims
after their arrival in Canterbury we shall never know;
The Tale but a monk of Canterbury, nearly contempo-
of Beryn. rary with Chaucer, has given us a *Tale of
Beryn*, supposed to be the first tale of the journey back
to London, told by the Merchant, the Prologue to which
consists of a spirited account of the happenings in the
cathedral town. This tale was first printed by Urry
in his Chaucer edition of 1721, and has since been
reprinted in 1876 by the Chaucer Society from a manuscript belonging to the Duke of Northumberland.

On their arrival in Canterbury, the pilgrims go to
the 'Cheker of the Hope' Inn, where the Pardoner
at once makes friends with Kit the tapster, who gives
him false hopes of her favor. The cathedral is, of
course, the first attraction; and thither the company
goes to make its offerings at the shrine. The gentles,
after being sprinkled with holy water, pass directly to
the shrine back of the high altar; but the Pardoner,
the Miller, and other of the lewder sort, stare at the
painted windows, and try to guess out the figures depicted in them, and to interpret the armorial bearings.
One of them sees a man with a spear, which he takes for
a rake. After kneeling at the shrine, praying, and hearing service, all proceed to buy pilgrim's tokens to set
in their caps; but the Miller and Pardoner manage to
steal some Canterbury brooches for themselves. Dinner
passes by with much merry talk, and in the afternoon

[1] For the account of the journey to Canterbury and the time occupied therein, I have drawn on Furnivall's Temporary Preface to the Six-
Text edition of the *Canterbury Tales*, § 3, and on Littlehale's *Some Notes
on the Road from London to Canterbury in the Middle Ages*, Chaucer
Society, 1898.

each follows his inclinations; the Monk takes the Parson and Friar to call on one of his friends; the Knight and the Squire inspect the walls and fortifications; the Wife of Bath and the Prioress walk in the garden (one wonders what common interests they found to talk about); the Pardoner once more seeks out the tapster Kit.

Supper is eaten in grand style, the gentles treating the rest to wine, after which the more respectable go to bed, while the Miller and the Cook sit up to drink. Again the Pardoner makes advances to Kit, which develop into a broad farce, of which the Pardoner is the unhappy dupe. At daybreak the company starts on its journey home, and the Merchant is called on for the first tale.

This, of course, is not Chaucer; but it is written in Chaucer's spirit, and is interesting as the work of one who, living in Canterbury, knew well how pilgrims usually disported themselves.[1]

For a work so composite in its character as the *Canterbury Tales* it is impossible to set any definite dates. Several of the tales now incorporated in the collection, we know positively, had been written by Chaucer before the great work was planned; and the same may be true of other tales of which we have no definite information. The *Legend of Good Women* was pretty certainly begun in 1385 or 1386, and was probably left unfinished because of the poet's greater interest in his larger work. It is safe to say, then, that the idea of the *Canterbury Tales* was conceived not much before 1387, and that Chaucer continued to work at its execution intermittently until the time of his death. In the year 1387, April 16 fell on a

Date of the Canterbury Tales.

---

[1] Chaucer's disciple Lydgate also wrote a tale for the journey back, which is entitled *The Tale of Thebes.*

Tuesday, which would bring the pilgrims to Canterbury on Saturday, and since no mention is made of Sunday on the pilgrimage, it has been argued that Chaucer had the year 1387 in mind. But surely this is holding the poet down rather closely to the actual. If, however, we must have a precise date, 1387 has more in its favor than any other.

THE PROLOGUE

If we set aside the wonderful felicity of phrase and the sparkling humor which are common to nearly all of Chaucer's maturer compositions, the peculiar greatness of the *Prologue* may be said to reside in the vividness of its individual portraiture, and in the representative character of the whole series of portraits as a true picture of English life in the fourteenth century.

To the uncritical mind the value of a portrait depends on its likeness to the original, the fidelity with which it reproduces the peculiar traits of some individual man. Here, as in most things, the opinion of the man in the street is not to be lightly set at nought; if the portrait lacks fidelity to its original, it ceases to be a portrait at all. On the other hand, if it does no more than reproduce the individual, it falls short of true art. A photograph may be a perfect likeness, and at the same time supremely uninteresting to all but the friends of the sitter; the portraiture of a true artist is interesting to all people and to all ages. We look at Rembrandt's portrait of Dr. Tulp, and are immediately convinced of its lifelikeness. Though we never have seen the original, the marked individuality of the portrait, the peculiarities of feature and expression, convince us of its truth. But there is more in the portrait than the individual anatomist of long ago. The eager passion to learn and teach, the quick play of intelligence, the

unassuming authority of pose and gesture, betray the
scientist. We behold not only the individual, but the
type; the abstract type is made visible and real as
embodied in the individual. This, the end and aim of
true portrait-painting, is true in its measure of all high
art. The true ideal is to be sought in and through the
actual. However high we may tower into the region
of the universal, we must plant our feet firmly on the
actual; and the actual is of necessity individual.

It is by their successful blending of the individual
with the typical that the portraits of Chaucer's *Prologue*
attain to so high a degree of effectiveness. The Wife
of Bath is typical of certain of the primary instincts of
woman, but she is given local habitation 'bisyde Bathe,'
a definite occupation of cloth-making, and is still further
individualized by her partial deafness and the peculiar
setting of her teeth. A wholly different type of womanhood, the conventional as opposed to the natural, is furnished by the Prioress. The description of the gentle
lady abounds in minute personal, individual characteristics, physical and moral; yet all these individualizing
traits are at the same time suggestive of that type which
finds fullest realization in the head of a young lady's
school, who fulfills in our modern life precisely the function of the prioress of the Middle Ages. What is true
of these two is true of all the personages of the *Prologue*. The details enumerated nearly always *suggest*
at once the individual and the type, as in the splendid
line about the Shipman : —

> With many a tempest hadde his berd been shake.

It is the individual character of the several portraits
which gives to the *Canterbury Tales* its dramatic realism and lifelikeness. Their universal character makes
the *Prologue*, and indeed the whole body of the work,

a compendium of human life as it passed before the eyes
of Geoffrey Chaucer. It is as a representative assembly,
a parliament of social and industrial England, that we
may regard this Canterbury pilgrimage. Save for the
very highest stratum of society, the lords of the realm,
who are after all but the golden fringe of the garment,
every important phase of life is represented. We do
not, to be sure, see the artisan at his bench, the sailor
on his ship, the lawyer pleading his case; that is, of
course, dramatically impossible; but more than that,
it is artistically less desirable. Chaucer has shown his
personages away from their daily tasks, on a vacation;
and, though the marks of the profession are still plainly
discernible, it is their essential humanity which is
emphasized; each is measured by the absolute standards of manhood.

The life of the Middle Ages lent itself particularly
well to such a process of portraiture. Though the dawning of the Renaissance was beginning its emphasis of
the individual, society was still organized on a communistic basis; life was less complex. Members of
the various crafts were banded together in guilds and
mysteries, each with its peculiar livery. Each member
of a guild was conscious of himself as one of a body,
its representative and type. To-day things are very different. In the so-called learned professions, perhaps,
something of the old *esprit de corps* has survived. In
the essentially communistic life of our universities,
again, there may be found a strong, essentially mediæval feeling for the whole, and an approximation to
a common type, so that one may speak of a typical
Oxonian, a typical Yale undergraduate. But with the
majority of us, the typical is lost in the individual as
far as character goes, while in costume we dress, as far
as possible, alike.

Chaucer's west-country contemporary, in the Prologue to *Piers Plowman*, has also painted a wide picture of human life. In his fair field full of folk, all sorts and conditions are seen side by side, the mean and the rich, 'working and wandering as the world asketh.' It is instructive to compare this picture, which some have thought responsible for suggesting Chaucer's, with the picture furnished by the Prologue to the *Canterbury Tales*. Langland, with his allegorical imagery of the heaven and hell which bound our little life on this side and on that, gains much in grandeur and impressiveness. Chaucer, with his individualized types, gains infinitely in reality and in human sympathy.

THE KNIGHT'S TALE

Early on the morning of April 17, 'whan that day bigan to springe,' the Host calls his company together, and at an easy gait they ride out of Southwark to the music of the Miller's bagpipes. When two miles have been traveled, and St. Thomas-a-Watering has been reached, the Host suddenly stops his horse, and reminds his guests of the agreement made overnight: —

> If even-song and morwe-song acorde,
> Lat see now who shal telle the firste tale.

The cuts are drawn; and, either by fortune or overruling providence, or perhaps by the manipulation of the Host, the lot falls to the Knight, whom every one feels should be the first to tell his story; and the *Canterbury Tales* begin with a high-wrought tale of chivalry and old romance.

Though Chaucer is here and there indebted to the *Thebais* of Statius for a bit of description, his great obligation for the *Knight's Tale* is to the *Teseide* of Boccaccio, from which he drew **Source.** the whole outline of the story. Here, as in the case of *Troilus*, he has as his model a highly artistic poem by one of the foremost authors of Italy ; so that it becomes peculiarly interesting to see to what extent, and in what spirit, he has departed from his original.

Comparing Chaucer's version of the story with that of Boccaccio, the most striking fact is their disparity in length. Exclusive of the rimed *argomenti* which precede each of the twelve books, the *Teseide* comprises 9896 lines, or 1237 stanzas of *ottava rima*, while the *Knight's Tale* contains but 2250 lines — little more than a fifth the bulk of its original. Besides this ruthless use of the pruning-knife, one notices the abandonment by Chaucer of the division into twelve books, and with it of the conventional invocations of the Muses, of much of the mythological machinery, and, in short, of all the conventional ear-marks of the Virgilian epic. But more significant than these external changes are the modifications and omissions which Chaucer has made in the story itself. These can be best shown by giving a brief synopsis of Boccaccio's poem as it unfolds itself book by book.

Book I narrates in 1104 lines what Chaucer summarizes in a dozen : —

> How wonnen was the regne of Femenye
> By Theseus, and by his chivalrye.

Book II devotes 792 lines to the home-coming of Theseus, and to his expedition against Thebes, which results in the capture of Palemone and Arcita, and their condemnation to lifelong imprisonment. In the third book the real action of the story begins. After a year of imprisonment, the two kinsmen catch fatal sight of Emilia as she walks in her garden, but with Boccaccio it is Arcita who sees her first, not Palemone ; while the Emilia of the Italian is not, like Chaucer's Emily, so wholly unconscious that she has won the attention of the Theban captives. As Arcita, after his release, rides away from Athens, Emilia stands on a balcony and receives his impassioned farewell.

The whole of Book IV is devoted to Arcita, his love-longing in exile, his return to Theseus's court under the assumed name of Penteo. The sorrows of the love-lorn knight, which Chaucer passes over half humorously, are detailed by Boccaccio with all his native sentiment. Very characteristic is stanza 32, in which Arcita, who has come in his wanderings to Ægina, stands on the seashore all alone, and is comforted by the breeze which blows from Athens, the breeze which has been very near to Emilia. Book V, which brings the action up to the point of Theseus's intervention and the ordaining of the tournament, differs only slightly from Chaucer's story, save that the escape of Palemone is narrated in detail. In the following book the two kinsmen collect their champions; but instead of the two vivid descriptions of Emetrius and Lygurge, Boc-caccio devotes four hundred lines to a catalogue of the heroes who take part on the two sides. Book VII is given up to the prayers of Arcita, Palemone, and Emilia, and to the description of the amphitheatre. In the description of the tournament, which fills Book VIII, Chaucer's superiority to his original is again evident. Instead of his brief but vigorous picture of the *mêlée*, the Italian furnishes a series of single combats between the champions of the two sides, warriors in whom the reader has no direct interest whatever. Meanwhile Emilia looks on, and feels her love go out now to the one kinsman, now to the other, according as the fortunes of the battle sway now this way, now that. In Book IX the victor Arcita is hurt to death through the device of Venus and her hell-sent fury. In place of the brief, deeply pathetic speech in which Chaucer's Arcite takes leave of friend and loved one, Boccaccio, in Book X, draws a long death-bed scene, less effective because of its greater length. The 728 verses of Book XI are devoted to the funeral of Arcita, which is celebrated with elaborate games after Virgilian model. In the closing book, after an interval of only a few weeks, is solemnized the wedding of Palemone and Emilia.[1]

The *Teseide* is by no means a contemptible composition; but, considering the slightness of its plot, it is surely much too long. Nor is the essentially romantic, sentimental character of the tale in keeping with its elaborate epic machinery. In his great condensation, in his simplification, in all his changes of detail, Chaucer's superior literary discernment is plainly evident. What Chaucer has borrowed is the outline of the tale; the execution is mainly his own. Mr. Henry Ward has shown [2] that of Chaucer's 2250 lines, 270 are directly translated from Boccaccio, 374 are somewhat closely imitated, leaving three quarters of Chaucer's lines for which no parallel is found in Boccaccio.

The source of the *Teseide* has never been discovered. Boccaccio took many suggestions from the *Thebais* of Statius; but these are of minor importance. Scholars are inclined to believe that the ultimate source was a Greek prose romance of the Byzantine period, which may have reached Boccaccio in a Latin translation.

[1] In preparing this brief synopsis, I have made frequent use of the full outline of the poem given by Koerting in *Boccaccio's Leben und Werke*, pp. 594–615. The best edition of the *Teseide* is that given in vol. ix of *Opere Volgari di Giovanni Boccaccio*, ed. Moutier, Firenze, 1831.

[2] Temporary Preface to the Six-Text edition of the *Canterbury Tales*, p. 104.

That Chaucer had already written the story of Palamon and Arcite not later than 1386, we know from the
passage in the Prologue to the *Legend of Good*   Date of
Women where Queen Alcestis recites in   Composi-
Chaucer's defense a list of the poet's works   tion.
in which he had spoken nobly of woman and of love: —

> And al the love of Palamon and Arcyte
> Of Thebes, thogh the story is knowen lyte.

These lines can only refer to the story which we know
as the *Knight's Tale*.[1] If we can confidently date the
tale not later than 1386, we can also be pretty certain that it was not written earlier than 1382. Among
the ills visited upon the human race by power of Saturn
is mentioned (A 2459) 'the cherles rebelling.' This
seems to be an allusion to the Peasants' Revolt of 1381.
Similarly, the tempest at the home-coming of Queen
Hippolyta (A 884) was probably, as Professor Lowes
has pointed out, suggested by the violent disturbance
of the sea which took place just after Richard's young
queen, Lady Anne of Bohemia, had first set foot in England in December, 1381. Neither of these details is
found in the *Teseide*.[2]

The composition of the *Knight's Tale* falls, then, in
the same period as that of *Troilus and Criseyde;* and

---

[1] More recent investigations have rendered utterly improbable the
conjecture elaborated by Ten Brink (*Chaucer Studien*, pp. 39–70)
and Koch (*Englische Studien*, 1. 249–293, English translation in
Essays on Chaucer, pp. 357–415) and accepted by Skeat, that the reference is to an earlier 'Palamon and Arcite,' written in seven-line
stanzas and a close paraphrase of *Teseide*, and that Chaucer later
worked over this poem in a greatly abridged form for the *Knight's
Tale*. It is now believed that the poem referred to in the *Legend* was
in metre and in scope essentially what we know as the *Knight's Tale*.
See F. J. Mather in *Furnivall Miscellany*, pp. 301–313, and Tatlock,
Development and Chronology, pp. 45–70.

[2] On the date of the *Knight's Tale* see Tatlock, *op. cit.*, pp. 70–83.

the two poems have much in common. Each is a re-working of one of Boccaccio's youthful epics; in each we find the same blending of pathos and ironical humor; in each a tale of courtly love is philosophized by a copious infusion of Boethius, and made to point the moral that earthly felicity is transient and deceitful.[1] Which of the two was written first? The question cannot be answered finally; but the evidence points strongly, I think, to the conclusion that the *Knight's Tale* is later than *Troilus*.[2] In the Prologue to the *Legend of Good Women* it is clearly implied that *Troilus* is widely known, that it is notorious as a 'heresy' against the law of Dan Cupid; whereas it is explicitly stated that the story of Palamon and Arcite is 'knowen lyte' — it has exerted but narrow influence as a counteragent to the poison of *Troilus and Criseyde*. This suggests that it had only recently been finished, or at any rate that its circulation had not been wide. If composed as an independent poem earlier than *Troilus*, it is hard to see why the work should be 'little known.' It seems probable, then, that the poem was written about 1385. If so, it may, perhaps, have been intended from the first as one of the *Canterbury Tales*.

The Knight has wandered far and wide,[3] and has seen many cities of men, in Russia, in Asia, in Africa; but he has lived and traveled and fought in the fair dream of chivalry, —

The Knight's Tale.

---

[1] See Dr. B. L. Jefferson's dissertation, *Chaucer and the Consolation of Philosophy of Boethius* (Princeton, 1917), pp. 120–132.

[2] Professor Lowes argues for the priority of 'Palamon' in *Publications of the Modern Language Association*, 20. 841–854.

[3] See A. S. Cook on 'The Historical Background of Chaucer's Knight,' *Transactions of the Connecticut Academy*, 20. 161–240, and on 'Beginning the Board in Prussia,' *Journal of English and Germanic Philology*, 14. 375–388; and S. Robertson on 'Elements of Realism in the Knight's Tale,' *ibid*. 14. 226–255.

> Trouthe and honour, fredom and curteisye ;

he is as unworldly as his squire-son. As with Tennyson's Sir Percivale, —

> All men, to one so bound by such a vow,
> And women were as phantoms.

He tells no tale of his own wanderings, his own experience ; he hardly deals with real men and women at
all. His tale is of chivalrous ideals, of knightly encounters long ago, of men and women living as he has
lived, in dream and fancy. Even these shadow dreams
are hardly more than moving pictures in the rich and
varied pageantry which constitutes the world of the
knight-errant. The opening words of the tale, —

> Whylom, as olde stories tellen us, —

carry us far away from present-day realities, far from
the Tabard Inn and its varied company, into the land
of story and of long ago. It is to ancient Athens and
the days of Theseus that we are bidden go, but to
an Athens which the student of classical archæology
will hardly recognize. Though, in its simplicity and
restraint, the story is by no means un-Hellenic, the
manners and customs are for the most part those of
mediæval chivalry ; and we had best forget forthwith
all we know of ancient Greece. Neither Chaucer nor
his knight knew much, or recked much, of antiquarian
lore.

If we are to read the *Knight's Tale* in the spirit
in which Chaucer conceived it, we must give ourselves
up to the spirit of romance ; we must not look for
subtle characterization, nor for strict probability of
action ; we must delight in the fair shows of things,
and not ask too many questions. Chaucer can be realistic enough when he so elects ; but here he has chosen
otherwise.

Four characters only are brought before us with any prominence : Palamon, Arcite, Emily, and Theseus. Though not characterized subtly, as Troilus and Pandarus are characterized, Palamon and Arcite are more than mere lay-figures of the piece. Of necessity, the two kinsmen have much in common. They are sisters' sons ; they bear identical armor ; their lives have been spent in closest fellowship ; they have sworn a knightly vow of perpetual brotherhood. It is not until the fair ideal of friendship is shattered by the stern reality of love that they realize their disparity. Then it is clear, in the debate which they hold over Emily, and in their subsequent actions, that relatively to one another Palamon is the dreamer, Arcite the man of action. It is Palamon who insists on the inviolability of their vow of friendship, and Arcite who, after an attempt at unworthy quibbling, comes out with the plain statement that

> Love is a gretter lawe, by my pan,
> Than may be yeve to any erthly man,

and who recognizes that, since they are both condemned to prison perpetually, the question of prior claim to Emily is one of purely academic interest. Partly as a result of opportunity, partly as a result of character, it is Arcite who determines the destiny of the two ; while Palamon merely drifts with the current of circumstance. The same distinction is observed in Arcite's prayer to Mars for victory, the definite practical means to the attainment of his desires ; while Palamon prays Venus for success in his love, leaving the means of its attainment to the providence of the heavenly synod. But in prowess in arms, and in chivalric courtesy, there is not a jot of superiority in either ; and the reader of the tale, like Emily herself, is unable to decide on which he would wish the ultimate success to light. When

the action closes, and the dying Arcite betroths Emily
to his kinsman-rival, friendship wins its final triumph
over jealousy, and the two noble kinsmen remain in
our memory not as dissimilar rivals, but as eternal
friends, one and indivisible.

As for Emily, she is a fair vision of womanly beauty
and grace, and little more. Only once in the whole
story, and that when the story is more than half done,
in her prayer to Diana, do we hear Emily speak. We
think of her as she roams up and down in her garden
on the fatal spring morning, gathering flowers ' to make
a sotil gerland for hir hede,' singing like an angel of
heaven. We see her beauty and recognize her worth,
realizing that the love of her may well be strong enough
to break the friendship of a life; and yet we know
her not at all. She is the golden apple of strife, and
later the victor's prize; but, consciously and of her
own volition, she never affects the action of the tale;
she *does* nothing. When Fletcher in the *Two Noble
Kinsmen* tried to develop her into a dramatic character, her inaction and indecision rendered her contemptible or absurd. Chaucer wisely kept her a vision and a
name, letting us realize her character only in its effect
upon others.

Theseus, the brave warrior, the man of anger, who
is yet able to turn anger to justice when persuaded of
the right, who can good-naturedly see the absurdity of
Palamon and Arcite, yet tolerantly remember that

A man mot been a fool, or yong or old,

and that he too had been a lover in his youth, is the
most actual personage in the tale. He is, moreover,
the motive power of the plot; his acts and decisions
really determine the whole story.

It is not in the characterization, but in the descrip-

tion, that the greatness of the *Knight's Tale* resides.
The poem opens with the brilliant pageant of the victorious home-coming of Theseus, thrown into sharp
contrast by the band of black-clad widowed ladies who
meet him on the way.   A never-to-be-forgotten picture
is that of Emily roaming in her garden, while the
kinsmen look down upon her through thick prison-bars.
The meeting and silent encounter of the cousins in the
wood, the great theatre with its story-laden oratories,
the vivid portraits of Emetrius and Lygurge, all the
varied bustle of preparation, the vigorous description
of the tournament itself, — these, with occasional passages of noble reflection, form the flesh and blood of
the poem, of which the characters and the action are
merely the skeleton framework. The *Knight's Tale* is
preëminently a web of splendidly pictured tapestry, in
which the eye may take delight, and on which the
memory may fondly linger. In the dying words of
Arcite : —

> What is this world ? What asketh men to have ?
> Now with his love, now in his colde grave
> Allone, withouten any companye, —

the terrible reality of the mystery of life, its tragedy
and its pathos, are vividly suggested ; but it is only
suggested, as a great painting may touch on what is
most sacred and most deep.

It is this essentially pictorial character of the poem
which accounts for the slight success of Fletcher's attempt to translate it into drama, the poetry of action.
In the *Two Noble Kinsmen* the slenderness of the
plot, and the inconsistency of the characters, which we
have accepted without question in the *Knight's Tale*,
become painfully apparent. The splendid effectiveness
of silence, which Chaucer has utilized so artistically
in the first appearance of Emily, and in the encounter

in the wood, is necessarily sacrificed to dramatic exigencies. The tournament is transacted off the stage, and the descriptions of the three oratories drop out altogether. A reading of Fletcher's drama is of the greatest help in enabling one to recognize the distinctive poetic qualities of Chaucer's narration; just as a comparison with Dryden's brilliant modernization of the tale will help one to realize the peculiar charm of Chaucer's simple, unassuming diction.

THE TALES OF THE MILLER AND THE REEVE

The Knight's long tale of love and chivalry won, as it deserved, universal approbation : —

> In al the route nas ther yong ne old
> That he ne seyde it was a noble storie
> And worthy for to drawen to memorie.

The Host, chuckling with delight over the successful beginning of his story-telling scheme, turns to the Monk and courteously asks him to tell 'sumwhat to quyte with the Knightes tale.' The choice of the Monk was dictated, doubtless, by the Host's punctilious regard for social rank, the worthy ecclesiastic being after the Knight the most dignified personage of the company. But since the Monk must of necessity tell a serious tale, which could not offer a sufficiently effective contrast to the Knight's, the poet, as overruling providence of the pilgrimage, devises an interruption of the Host's less artistic scheme by the obstreperous intrusion of the Miller; who, though so drunk that 'unnethe upon his hors he sat,' insists that he knows a 'noble tale,' with which to repay the Knight. The Host, as complete tavern-keeper, knows not only the deference to be paid to men of rank, but also the more delicate diplomacy of dealing with a drunken man. When his soft-spoken words of deprecation fail to silence the unruly Miller, he recognizes that discretion is the better part of courtesy, and suffers him to proceed.

After making the quite unnecessary 'protestation' that he is drunk, — a fact of which he is convinced by the sound of his own voice, — he announces that his tale is to be of a carpenter and his wife, and of how a clerk made a fool of the carpenter. But this theme treads on the toes of another in the company. The General Prologue tells us of the Reeve that —

> In youthe he lerned hadde a good mister ;
> He was a wel good wrighte, a carpenter.

So we are prepared for the change from the 'noble tale' of the Knight to the ribald tale of the Miller by an altercation between drunken Robin and the white-haired Osewold, who thinks the tale directed against himself. And when the Miller's tale is done, the wounded professional pride of the Reeve furnishes us with a companion tale of how two Cambridge students got the better of a cheating miller.

The tales of the Miller and the Reeve are so closely linked by this dramatic interlude, and are moreover so similar in spirit, that it will be convenient to treat them together.

For neither of these tales do we possess Chaucer's immediate source ; but there exist stories sufficiently like them to indicate that in neither case did Chaucer draw wholly on his own imagination.

Sources.

In the *Miller's Tale* we have a combination of two stories originally distinct — the story of a man who is made to believe that the great day of reckoning is at hand, represented by a German tale of one Valentin Schumann, printed in 1559, and the story of Absolon and Nicholas, to which an analogue is found in a collection of *novelle* by Massuccio di Salerno, who flourished in the latter half of the fifteenth century. Other similar tales are found in German and in Latin.[1]

A tale similar to that of the Reeve is found in Boccaccio's *Decameron*, Day 9, Nov. 6 ; and still closer to Chaucer are two French *fabliaux* which are reprinted in the volume of *Originals and Analogues* published by the Chaucer Society.[2]

The point of strongest resemblance between the tales of the Miller and the Reeve is their extreme indecency, an indecency which cannot be wholly The Two explained away as due to the frankness of a Tales less delicate age. Chaucer, himself, was quite aware that to many of his readers these tales would be objectionable. Half seriously, half playfully, he prefaces them with an apology in which he warns away the squeamish, and at the same time disclaims any personal responsibility for the tales.

> What sholde I more seyn, but this Millere
> He nolde his wordes for no man forbere,
> But told his cherles tale in his manere ;
> Me thinketh that I shal reherce it here.
> And therfore every gentil wight I preye,
> For goddes love, demeth nat that I seye
> Of evel entente, but that I moot reherce
> Hir tales alle, be they bettre or werse,
> Or elles falsen som of my matere.
> And therfore, whoso list it nat yhere,
> Turne over the leef, and chese another tale ;
> .   .   .   .
> Avyseth yow and putte me out of blame ;
> And eek men shal nat make ernest of game.

---

[1] Those who wish to go farther with this not very profitable theme may consult the papers of R. Köhler, in *Anglia*, 1. 38–44, 186–188 ; 2. 135–136 ; of H. Varnhagen, in *Anglia*, 7. Anzeiger 81–85 ; of L. Fränkel, in *Anglia*, 16. 261–263 ; and of E. Kölbing, in *Zeitschrift für vergleichende Literaturgeschichte*, 12. 448–450 ; 13. 112. See also L. Proescholdt, in *Anglia*, 7. 117.

[2] Pp. 85–102. For a full discussion of the sources of the *Reeve's Tale*, see the paper by H. Varnhagen, in *Englische Studien*, 9. 240–266.

This is in effect a repetition of the disclaimer given in the General Prologue, ll. 725–742 ; what is its validity ? That he must rehearse all the tales of all his pilgrims precisely as they were told, whatever their character, or else ' falsen som of his matere,' is precisely the argument by which the followers of Zola defend their ultra-realism. The simple answer to all this is found in the fact that the great poets have never conceived of their function as that of a mere photographer or stenographer. They ' imitate nature,' to be sure, but with a difference. If it is their duty to observe, it is also their duty to select, to adapt, to idealize. It would have been perfectly possible to give a true picture of the varied humanity which made up the Canterbury pilgrimage, without suffering these churls to tell their ' cherles tales,' which no sophistry can elevate into true art.

I do not believe that Chaucer was in the least deceived by this argument. He deliberately chose to insert the tales, not as works of art, nor even as a necessary part of a great artistic whole, but merely as a diverting interlude. Making a rather considerable allowance for greater freedom of speech, they are tales of the sort which entirely moral men of vigorous nature have found diverting, and at which the less vigorous have always raised their eyebrows. Having chosen to insert the tales, he playfully answers the anticipated charges of the moralist, by assuring him that he wrote the tales unwillingly, compelled to do so by the higher moral consideration of strict truthfulness. Inasmuch as the *Canterbury Tales* are in the main truly great art, and as these tales are by their nature not true art, I think it unfortunate that Chaucer included them ; but I am very far from considering them as evidence of immoral character in their author.

What I take to be Chaucer's serious defense of these tales is contained in a single line, which concludes the passage quoted above : —

And eek men shal nat make ernest of game.

In other words, both these tales narrate practical jokes, and their comic interest depends on the clever working-out and complete success of the trick. In the *Miller's Tale*, for example, the attention is centred on the ludicrous gullibility of the jealous carpenter and the clever manœuvring of hende Nicholas, not on the immoral purpose for which the trick is devised. So in the *Reeve's Tale*, there is a sort of rough poetic justice in the complete discomfiture of the cheating miller; and on this, rather than on the immoral character of the retribution, the effectiveness of the story depends. It is not immorality for immorality's sake, but immorality for the joke's sake. Of course, this does not lessen the moral blame of the two Cambridge students, when seriously considered ; but it very materially lessens the immorality of the story. It is only when the reader reverses the emphasis, when, in Chaucer's words, he makes earnest of game, that the tales become actively immoral.

In the *Miller's Tale*, in particular, the attention is diverted from the lustful and nasty features of the story, to the brilliant characterizations, and to the consummate skill with which the narrative is transacted. In none of Chaucer's tales is there more convincing proof of his mastery of the technique of story-telling. The tale consists of two comic intrigues combined into a single unity. It will be worth while to notice with some particularity the steps by which this end is attained.

Since Nicholas is to be the prime mover of the action, without whose machinations neither plot could have matured, the first thirty-three lines of the tale are devoted to a vivid description of his person and personality. The carpenter, as passive centre of the plot, is next described more briefly. Nearly forty lines are then devoted to a description of Alisoun, whose attractiveness constitutes the *causa causans* for both intrigues. These portraits, and that of Absolon which follows a little later, are done with all the skill which marks the portraiture of the General Prologue. After another forty lines, in which the relations between Nicholas and Alisoun are established, the main action is fully launched, and the natural pause which ensues is utilized for the introduction of the second action. Absolon is described, and his persistent attentions to Alisoun are recorded, eighty-four lines sufficing to set the new intrigue afoot. Resuming the thread of the main argument, some two hundred and fifty lines are devoted to the clever scheme by which the carpenter is beguiled into believing that a second Noah's flood is toward, and the two lovers attain their end. Particularly rich in humor is the scene where Nicholas, in feigned trance, predicts the coming deluge, a prediction for which we have been artistically prepared by the earlier statement that all Nicholas's fancy 'was turned for to lerne astrologye.' Again there is a natural pause in the action, in which the story reverts to Absolon. Because the carpenter, in instant fear of the flood which is at hand, has kept all day to his house, Absolon is led to believe that he is from home, and consequently chooses this particular night to pay his addresses. He goes to Alisoun's window, where he is duped, and has his revenge. This section of the tale occupies about a hundred and sixty lines. Thirty-eight lines now suffice to end the tale. The frantic cry of 'Water!' uttered by Nicholas as a result of Absolon's revenge, wakes the sleeping carpenter, and, fitting in with his expectation of a flood, leads him to cut the ropes which suspend his ark of safety, thus bringing about the catastrophe of the main action.

It is certainly a pity that such excellent skill was expended on a story which many of Chaucer's readers will prefer to skip; and yet, as we have seen, it is this very skill which does most to minimize the objectionable character of the tale.

THE COOK'S TALE

Whoever may have been offended at the freedom of the *Reeve's Tale*, jolly Hodge of Ware was not of the strait-laced sect: —

> The Cook of London, whyl the Reve spak,
> For joye, him thoughte, he clawed him on the bak,
> 'Ha! ha!' quod he, 'for Cristes passioun,
> This miller hadde a sharp conclusioun
> Upon his argument of herbergage!'

Perhaps, in his vocation of cook, he has had to do with cheating millers, and consequently finds special relish in the tale. He volunteers a 'litel jape that fil in our citee,' which is to deal, saving the presence of mine host, with a London 'hostileer.' After some playful allusions to the tricks of the culinary profession, the Host bids him proceed.

The tale of the Cook is a mere fragment, extending only to fifty-eight lines, and though we have a fine piece of portraiture in the picture of Perkin Revellour, who is to be the hero, and a fairly complete *mise en scène*, we have not enough of the story to form any guess as to its plot. We can only surmise that it is to be a 'merry' tale of the same general type as those of the Miller and the Reeve. Perhaps it was a recognition of the fact that three tales of this sort on end would be too large a dose of 'mirth' that caused the poet to abandon it; for, as the old scribe says, 'Of this Cokes tale maked Chaucer na more.'

There is a spurious tale, certainly not by Chaucer, which some of the manuscripts, and the old editions, insert after this fragment under the title of *The Cokes Tale of Gamelyn;* but a discussion of this tale, which has some interest because of its relation to Shakespeare's *As You Like It*, is outside the scope of the present work.[1]

---

[1] The tale may be found in the appendix to vol. iv of Skeat's *Oxford Chaucer*. For a discussion of it, see the article by E. Lindner, in *Englische Studien*, 2. 94–114, 321–343.

CHAPTER X

THE CANTERBURY TALES, GROUP B

THE MAN OF LAW'S TALE

THE first day's journey had brought the band of pilgrims only fifteen miles on their way; and the night had been spent at the little town of Dartford in Kent.[1] Either the company had slept long and started late on the second day's ride, or the beauty of a sunny morning in mid-April had made the diversion of story-telling superfluous; for it is already ten o'clock when the Host suddenly turns his horse about, and reminds his fellow-voyagers that a fourth part of the day is already spent, and time is wasting. The Man of Law is called on to begin the entertainment of the day. As a lawyer, he is too well schooled in the law of contracts to refuse assent: —

> 'To breke forward is not myn entente.
> Bihest is dette, and I wol holde fayn
> Al my biheste ; I can no better seyn ;'

but since the tale he is minded to tell is in effect the legend of a good woman, he feels not unnatural hesitation in narrating it, when Chaucer, as all the pilgrims know, has written a whole volume of such legends.

> 'I can right now no thrifty tale seyn,
> But Chaucer, though he can but lewedly
> On metres and on ryming craftily,[2]

---

[1] Cf. p. 155.

[2] The depreciation of Chaucer's skill is to be considered a bit of the poet's half-humorous modesty, rather than as representing dramatically the opinion of the Man of Law.

> Hath seyd hem in swich English as he can
> Of olde tyme, as knoweth many a man.
> And if he have not seyd hem, leve brother,
> In o book, he hathe seyd hem in another.'

Hereupon follows a catalogue of women faithful in love whose stories Chaucer had narrated, or planned to narrate, in the *Legend of Good Women*, referred to here as the *Seintes Legende of Cupyde*. How shall he, the Man of Law, presume to rival such a master in this particular art? Ovid's story of the daughters of Pierus who dared contend with the Muses, and were for their presumption turned into chattering magpies, should give him pause : —

> 'But nathelees, I recche noght a bene
> Though I come after him with hawe-bake ;
> I speke in prose, and lat him rymes make.'
> And with that word he, with a sobre chere,
> Bigan his tale, as ye shal after here.

Though many of the incidents of the tale of Constance are found in other, earlier stories, Chaucer's immediate source was the *Anglo-Norman Chronicle* of the Englishman, Nicholas Trivet, a voluminous English scholar and historian, who flourished in the first half of the fourteenth century.[1] Trivet's chronicle, written in the Anglo-Norman French of the English court, devotes a long section to the history of 'la pucele Constaunce,'[2] the account agreeing in all important details with that given by Chaucer. Chaucer has very considerably condensed the story, has

Sources.

---

[1] The *Dictionary of National Biography*, following the early biographers, Leland and Bale, gives the date of his death as 1328; but since his chronicle includes the reign of Pope John XXII, who died in 1334, the date is certainly wrong.

[2] As reprinted in *Originals and Analogues*, the story occupies 25 pages. The text is provided with a running summary and a translation in English (pp. 1–53).

added many original passages of a reflective or lyrical
character, and has altered some of the minor details.[1]
Thus, for example, Trivet narrates in detail how King
Alla slew his mother with his own hands,[2] an episode
which Chaucer has preferred to soften down into a mere
vague statement. If the student will take the trouble
to pick out Chaucer's original additions to the tale, as
indicated in the foot-note, he will find that they comprise all the most beautiful passages in the tale. Thus,
when Constance and her child are put to sea in the rudderless boat, Trivet merely says: 'The mariners with
great grief commended her to God, praying that she
might again return to land.' It is Chaucer who has
added the sublimely beautiful lines (825–868) which
show her noble resignation, and supreme trust in God.
Of what wondrous pathos is the stanza : —

> Hir litel child lay weping in hir arm,
> And kneling, pitously to him she seyde,
> 'Pees, litel sone, I wol do thee non harm.'
> With that hir kerchef of hir heed she breyde,
> And over his litel yën she it leyde ;
> And in hir arm she lulleth it ful faste,
> And into heven hir yën up she caste.

Chaucer's less gifted contemporary, John Gower, has
also told the story of Constance in the second book
of his *Confessio Amantis ;* but that both poets went

[1] About 350 lines of the 1029 comprising the tale are not represented
in Trivet. Four of the added stanzas (ll. 421–427, 771–777, 925–931,
1135–1141) are translated from the *De Contemptu Mundi* of Pope Inno-
cent III, a work of which Chaucer tells us (Prologue to the *Legend of
Good Women,* A version, ll. 414–415) that he had made a translation (now lost). One stanza (ll. 813–819) is from Boethius. The rest is
Chaucer's own. Chaucer's additions comprise lines 190–203; 270–287;
295–315; 330–343; 351–371; 400–410; 421–427; 449–462; 470–504;
631–658; 701–714; 771–784; 811–819; 825–868; 925–945; 1037–1043;
1052–1078; 1132–1141.

[2] 'And with that he cut off her head and hewed her body all to pieces
as she lay naked in her bed ' (p. 38).

independently to Trivet is proved by the fact that each gives details found in Trivet, but not found in the other. But a few points of agreement between Chaucer and Gower as against Trivet make it probable that there is a relation closer than that of a common source, that one poet borrowed a touch here and there from the other's version. If so, the borrower was apparently Chaucer; for if Gower had had Chaucer's text before him as he wrote, it is hard to believe that he would not have appropriated some of the strikingly beautiful passages peculiar to that version.[1] As the *Confessio Amantis* was not published till 1390, we can with some confidence assign the composition of the *Man of Law's Tale* to the last ten years of Chaucer's life, a date which is in accord with other indications which we have as to the chronology of the *Canterbury Tales*.[2]

The Man of Law's statement that he learned the story from a merchant is not to be taken seriously;

[1] For a full discussion of the question, see the papers by E. Lücke, 'Das Leben der Constanze bei Trivet, Gower, und Chaucer,' in *Anglia*, 14. 77–122, 147–185.

[2] For the evidence which points to a date as late as 1390 (perhaps later than 1394) for the *Man of Law's Tale*, see J. S. P. Tatlock, *Development and Chronology*, pp. 172–188. Critics have been inclined to see in the Man of Law's statement (B. 77–89) that Chaucer would never write such 'unkinde abhominaciouns' as the stories of Canace and of Apollonius of Tyre, an implied allusion to the *Confessio Amantis*, which includes these tales. Though both stories must have been familiar quite independently of Gower's telling of them, this reference, if made shortly after the publication of the *Confessio*, may have been intended as a sly dig at a brother poet. There is no sufficient reason, however, for believing that these lines indicate a falling-out between the two friends. The only real basis for a supposed estrangement is the fact that in later recensions of the *Confessio* Gower omitted, along with his praise of King Richard, the passage of gracious compliment to Chaucer (8. 2941*–2959*) found in the first recension. It is at least hazardous to assume that this omission is to be explained only on the ground of lapsed cordiality. But see Tatlock, *op. cit*, p. 173, n. 2.

but it suggests, none the less, the way in which many mediæval tales were transplanted from one country to another.

Looked at merely as a narrative, the tale has but little claim to greatness. It consists of a series of improbable episodes, bound together merely by the accident that they all happen to the same heroine. Though in the fact that the fleet which eventually saves Constance, and brings her back to Rome, had been dispatched by the emperor on a punitive expedition against the 'cursed wikked Sowdanesse,' we see an attempt to link the beginning of the tale with its close, there is too much of accident, and too little of direct causal connection, in the events of the tale to leave it any organic unity. The episode of the steward of the 'hethen castel,' who comes down to Constance's ship and tries to violate her, is in no way connected with what precedes or follows. The tale has all the structural defects of the typical romance or saint's legend. *The Tale as a Work of Art.*

What raises this legend into the realm of true art, and even gives to it a high degree of spiritual unity, is the wonderfully beautiful personality of Constance. There is little to be said of this character by way of analysis ; there is no baffling problem of motives nor complexity of warring qualities to fascinate the intellect, no development of character under stress of circumstance ; from the first she is utterly transparent, utterly perfect. We see her in prosperity, we see her in bitterest adversity, in what she believes to be the hour of her death ; she is the same always, unmoved, unshaken. The great Christian virtues of humility, faith, hope, charity, sum up the whole of her nature ; by these stars she steers her rudderless boat as she sails in the salt sea ; by these she lives in the court of emperor and king. So little is she moved by outward circumstance, that the mere events of the story sink into insignificance ; we forget their improbability, or rather, in the presence of such superhuman perfection, the supernatural seems merely natural. Chaucer does not try to explain these miracles away ; he accepts them frankly, even gladly : —

> Men mighten asken why she was not slayn ?
> Eek at the feste who mighte hir body save ?
> And I answere to that demaunde agayn,
> Who saved Daniel in the horrible cave ?

Or again, ' Who kepte hir fro the drenching in the see?' Chaucer asks, and answers : —

> Who bad the foure spirits of tempest,
> That power han t'anoyen land and see,
> ' Bothe north and south, and also west and est,
> Anoyeth neither see, ne land, ne tree ? '
> Sothly, the comaundour of that was he,
> That fro the tempest ay this womman kepte
> As wel whan that she wook as whan she slepte.

When we see her set adrift again with her ' litel sone,' weeping piteously over his distress though not her own, we are inevitably reminded of another *Mater Dolorosa*, the ' Moder and mayde bright, Marye,' to whom she prays. We are quite ready to agree with Ten Brink when he says : ' The heroine here appears almost a personification of Christianity itself, such as it comes to heathen nations, is maligned and persecuted, yet, in the strength of its Founder, endures in patience and finally remains victorious.' [1] Be it remembered, how-ever, that she is more than a personification, a per-sonality.

I fancy that we are often inclined to underestimate the art which is requisite to the depiction of such a

---

[1] *Hist. Eng. Lit.* (Eng. trans.) 2. 156.

figure as that of Constance. It is precisely in its simplicity, its absence of all complexity, that the difficulty
of the portrayal resides. By 'character' we mean the
markings or traits which distinguish one individual
from another, or rather from our somewhat vaguely
conceived 'normal' man or woman. In bidding us
pattern our imperfect natures after the one perfect
nature, Christianity bids us shake off our personal
idiosyncrasies, the traits or markings — blemishes, if
you will — which distinguish us from our pattern. It follows logically that, if we were able to carry out this
Christian ideal, we should lose the distinguishing
traits which constitute our character as individuals.
Constance has attained the ideal; she is perfect; and
consequently her 'character' seems to us shadowy or
unreal. In a sense she has no character. To depict
such a nature as this in its ideal perfection, and yet
to make us feel the force of her personality, and love
her and sympathize with her, to accomplish this, is
a greater artistic triumph than to create a Criseyde.
Chaucer is here working in the spirit of the Christian
Middle Age, which loved the perfect, the universal; it
was the Renaissance which taught us to set such store
by the necessarily imperfect *individual*.

THE SHIPMAN'S TALE

The tale of Constance has given the lie to the Man
of Law's modest statement that he knows no 'thrifty'
tale. At its conclusion the Host rises in his stirrups
with the exclamation : —

> 'This was a thrifty tale for the nones ! '

He is apparently in the mood for 'thrifty' tales, for
he turns next to the parish priest, the 'povre persoun
of a toun,' and demands of him a tale. But he has

unfortunately larded his request with two of the oaths without which his tongue seldom wags ; and the good parson is scandalized : —

> The Persone him answerde, ' *ben'cite!*
> What eyleth the man so sinfully to swere ? '

Such unreasonable objection to the picturesque in language can come only from a follower of the new sect of Wiclif. The Host makes no great pretense to religion ; but he hates a heretic ; he ' smells a loller in the wind,' and dreads a ' predicacioun ' after the manner of Wiclif's itinerant preachers. There is another staunch upholder of orthodoxy in the person of the conscienceless Shipman.

> ' He shal no gospel glosen heer ne teche.
> We leve alle, in the grete god,' quod he.
> ' He wolde sowen som difficultee
> Or springen cokkel in our clene corn.' [1]

Such a calamity the Shipman stands ready to avert by telling a tale himself, which he promises shall be free from philosophy or other scientific lore. One need not dilate on the rich humor of this episode, wherein Chaucer chooses the Host and the Shipman as the bitterest opponents of heretical doctrine.

We do not know the immediate source of the *Shipman's Tale*. A similar story is found in the *Decameron*, Day 8, Nov. 1 ; but Chaucer's setting of the tale near Paris indicates that he derived it from a French *fabliau* now lost. Save for its general tone of loose morality, there is no special appropriateness in assigning the tale to the Shipman ;

Sources.

---

[1] The term ' loller ' or ' lollard,' derisively applied to the followers of Wiclif, probably means only a foolish talker ; but it was popularly associated with the Latin *lollium*, tares, with reference to the parable of the tares sown among the wheat.

and the use of the first person pronoun plural in the
passage beginning —

> He moot *us* clothe, and he moot *us* arraye,

shows that it was originally intended for one of the
female members of the company, who can have been
no other than the Wife of Bath. Apparently Chaucer
first wrote the tale for her, and then lighting on another
story which should more fully reveal his conception of
her character, utilized the rejected tale for the Shipman, forgetting to eliminate the inconsistent passage
referred to above.

Though much more delicate than the tales of the
Miller and the Reeve, the tale of the Shipman is essentially more immoral. Hende Nicholas receives a righteous retribution for his deeds;
and the two Cambridge students have at
least a certain provocation for theirs. The Monk, Dan
John, is false not only to his professions as a man of
God, but violates also the sacred laws of hospitality
and of common gratitude. He cultivates the friendship of the worthy merchant merely that he may live
on him, and, not content with that, deliberately plays
him false with his wife. With equal nonchalance he
leaves the woman he has corrupted to extricate herself
as best she can from an exceedingly embarrassing situation. The story ends with the laugh all on his side.
The moral of the tale seems to be, as Mr. Snell has
put it, ' that adultery is a very amusing and profitable
game, provided that it is not found out.' The intrigue
is, of course, a clever one, the actors are clearly characterized, and the narrative is well conducted ; but
neither the intrigue, nor the art of the tale, is brilliant
enough to blind us, even partially, to the disagreeable
picture of treachery and lust. The chief artistic merit

*The Ship-
man's
Tale.*

of the piece consists in the realistic picture it gives of a well-to-do *bourgeois* household, and of the business methods of a fourteenth-century merchant, such as Chaucer must have seen often at the London Custom House.

†THE PRIORESS'S TALE

Very different is the tale of the gentle Prioress which follows. With all courtesy, the usually rough-spoken Host turns to Madame Eglantine : —

> ' My lady Prioresse, by your leve,
> So that I wiste I sholde yow nat greve,
> I wolde demen that ye tellen sholde
> A tale next, if so were that ye wolde.
> Now wol ye vouchesauf, my lady dere ? '

And the courteous request meets with courteous assent.

As set forth in the General Prologue, Madame Eglantine's character is compounded of many affectations. Scrupulous in her dress and table manners, priding herself on her command of an antiquated Norman French which she supposes is still the French of fashionable society, in all things taking pains to ' countrefete chere of court,' she stands as the typical superior of a young ladies' school. Next to this quality of utter ' seemliness ' comes the good lady's tenderness of heart :

> She wolde wepe, if that she sawe a mous
> Caught in a trappe, if it were deed or bledde.

As seen superficially at the Tabard Inn, she is distinctly likeable, but also a little ridiculous. The true measure of her character is to be found in the fuller revelation of her tale. She might have been expected to tell a courtly tale, which should establish her reputation as an accomplished woman of the world ; but her affectations are only on the surface. Her legend of the ' litel clergeon ' breathes the spirit of earnest, heart-

felt religion, and shows that the tenderness of her
heart is not confined to the sufferings of a wounded
mouse or a favorite lap-dog, but makes her keenly
susceptible to the truest and deepest pathos. Instead
of the calm assurance and self-confidence of a lady
superior, we find in her invocation of the Blessed Virgin a sincere Christian humility : —

> 'My conning is so wayk, o blisful quene,
> For to declare thy grete worthinesse,
> That I ne may the weighte nat sustene,
> But as a child of twelf monthe old or lesse,
> That can unnethes any word expresse,
> Right so fare I, and therfor I yow preye,
> Gydeth my song that I shal of yow seye.'

To understand the spirit which gave rise to stories
such as that told by the Prioress, we must think ourselves back into a time when the antipathy
which some Christians now feel against the   Sources.
Jewish race on purely social grounds had all the force
of a religious passion. 'His blood be on us and on
our children,' shouted the multitude of Jerusalem ; and
the multitude of mediæval Europe felt it a sacred duty
that the blood-guiltiness should be brought home to
the self-cursed race. The pages of European history
are stained with many stories of senseless persecution,
which, though due doubtless in part to the fact that
the Jews were rich while the Christians among whom
they lived were poor, were possible only because of
this mistaken religious zeal.

It is entirely possible that, stung into fury by these
persecutions, the Jews may have sought revenge by the
treacherous murder of Christian children. So widespread a belief in such a murderous practice could
hardly have sprung up without some sort of foundation. But be that as it may, all Europe firmly believed

that, inspired by fierce hatred of Christ, the Jews, in Passion Week particularly, were in the habit of reën-acting the scenes of the crucifixion, taking as their victim any Christian child whom they were able to decoy into their houses. If the child was not crucified, he was murdered outright, and his blood was used in some gruesome religious ceremony.

The earliest story of a Christian child murdered by Jews comes from the first quarter of the fifth century, and is narrated in Greek by the Church historian Soc-rates. As translated by Dr. James of Cambridge,[1] the story runs as follows: 'Now a little after this the Jews paid the penalty for further lawless acts against the Christians. At Inmestar, a place so-called, which lies between Chalcis and Antioch in Syria, the Jews were in the habit of celebrating certain sports among them-selves: and, whereas they frequently did many foolish actions in the course of their sports, they were put beyond themselves (on this occasion) by drunkenness, and began deriding Christians and even Christ him-self in their games. They derided the Cross and those who hoped in the Crucified, and they hit upon this plan. They took a Christian child and bound him to a cross and hung him up; and to begin with they mocked and derided him for some time; but after a short space they lost control of themselves, and so ill-treated the child that they killed him. Hereupon ensued a bitter conflict between them and the Christians.'

There seems to have been no recurrence of this crime, either in fact or in fiction, until the year 1144, when occurred the famous 'martyrdom' of St. William of

---

[1] *The Life and Miracles of St. William of Norwich*, by Thomas of Monmouth, edited by Jessopp and James, Cambridge, 1896, p. lxiii. To the Introduction of this volume I am indebted for much valuable information about the legend.

Norwich. According to the life of St. William, written
a few years later by Thomas of Monmouth, a monk of
Norwich Priory, William, who had from the first been
distinguished for his sanctity, was at the age of twelve
decoyed on Tuesday of Holy Week into a Jew's house
in Norwich. Here on the following day he was crucified and pierced in the left side, a crown of thorns
upon his forehead. On Good Friday his body was put
in a sack and carried by the murderers to Thorpe
Wood, where it was hanged to a tree. It was finally
removed to the Monks' Cemetery in Norwich, where
many miracles were wrought by its agency. That a boy
named William was actually murdered in Norwich in
1144, and that his murder was attributed to the Jews,
we can assert without question; whether or not any
Jews were really concerned in the crime is open to
serious doubt. The fame of his martyrdom, however,
spread rapidly; and we begin to hear of similar boy-
martyrs in England and on the continent. Of these
the most famous is St. Hugh of Lincoln, alluded to by
the Prioress at line 1874 of her tale, who, according
to the chronicle of Matthew Paris, was murdered by
Jews in the year 1255.[1] The tomb of St. Hugh is still
pointed out to the curious visitor at Lincoln.

The number of such supposed martyrdoms is very
large. Adrian Kembter, in a book published at Inns-
bruck in 1745, enumerates fifty-two, the last of which
occurred in 1650. Even to-day a belief in such Jewish
atrocities has survived in Eastern Europe. The New
York *Sun* for April 4, 1904, published the following
statement under date of Vienna, April 3: ' *Die Zeit*
publishes an extraordinary anti-Jewish proclamation
issued by the Orthodox Association of Odessa, urging

[1] Three ballads on the murder of Hugh of Lincoln are found in Professor Child's *English and Scottish Ballads*.

right-minded Russians to follow the glorious example of their brethren who settled their accounts with the Jews at Kishineff last Easter. It declares that the victory is incomplete, for Satan has incarnated himself in the Jews. . . . The proclamation adds: "The Russians must aid the government to exterminate the Jews, who drink the blood of Russian children." ' [1]

A legend so widely current as this could not fail to find expression in literature, especially when it lent itself so readily to human pathos and religious enthusiasm. The Chaucer Society's volume of *Originals and Analogues* contains three stories similar to that of the Prioress: the legend of Alphonsus of Lincoln, from a volume entitled *Fortalitium Fidei*, written in Latin prose, and dating from the second half of the fifteenth century; a French poem of 756 lines from a collection of Miracles of the Blessed Virgin Mary by Gautier de Coincy (1177–1236), telling the legend of an English boy murdered by a Jew for singing *Gaude Maria ;* and an English poem of 152 lines of octosyllabic couplets from the *Miracles of Oure Lady*, which tells of a Paris beggar-boy killed by a Jew for singing *Alma Redemptoris Mater*.[2]

If we compare these three versions with the *Prioress's Tale*, we find that they exhibit several traits in common. In each instance the story is told to the greater glory of the Virgin Mary; it is the devotion of the boy-martyr to her, shown by the singing of a hymn in her honor, which leads to the murderous act of the Jew; it is by her agency that the miracle is wrought which betrays the murder. In each the child's

---

[1] My attention was called to this modern analogue by my friend and former pupil, Mr. S. B. Hemingway, of New Haven.

[2] *The Miracles of Oure Lady* have been published by Dr. Karl Horstmann, in Herrig's *Archiv für Neuere Sprachen*, 56. 223–236.

mother goes to seek him, and is advised of his where-
abouts by the miraculously continued singing of the
hymn. The first and third versions agree with Chaucer in specifying the *Alma Redemptoris Mater* as the
hymn which excited the wrath of the Jew; the first
and second agree in stating that the boy learned the
hymn at school; the first and third agree that the murdered body was thrown into a ' wardrobe ; ' the second
version differs from all the rest in that the murdered
boy is restored to life. Of the three versions the first
is, on the whole, nearest to Chaucer's; but its date
precludes the idea that it was Chaucer's source. Chaucer must have used some version of the story which has
not been preserved to us. For purposes of comparison,
however, a synopsis of the tale may be interesting.

In the city of Lincoln dwelt a poor widow, who had
a son ten years old named Alphonsus, whom she sent
to school. After he had learned to read, he was set to
study the rudiments of grammar and music. Hearing
often that splendid antiphon, *Alma Redemptoris*, sung
in church, he conceived such great devotion toward the
Blessed Virgin, and so deeply impressed the antiphon
upon his memory, that wherever he went, day or night,
he used to sing it most sweetly with a loud voice. Now
when he went to his mother's house, or back again to
school, his way led through the Jewry. One of the Jews
asked a Christian doctor what was the meaning of that
song that sounded so sweet. On learning that it was
a hymn sung to the praise and honor of the Blessed
Virgin Mary, he began to plot with his fellows how
they might slay the child who sang it. Waiting for a
favorable opportunity, they seized on the boy as he
was going through their quarter, singing the aforesaid
antiphon with a loud voice. Having cut out his tongue,
with which he praised the Blessed Virgin, and torn out

his heart, with which he pondered his song, they threw his body into their privy. But the Blessed Virgin, who is mother of mercy and pity, came to his aid, and placed a precious stone in his mouth to take the place of his tongue; and straightway he began to sing, as before, the aforesaid hymn, even better and louder than at first, nor did he cease day or night from his singing; and in this manner he continued for four days.

Now his mother, when she saw that he did not come home as usual, sought for him throughout the city; and finally, at the end of the four days, she went through the Jews' quarter, where her son had been slain, and, behold, the voice of her son, singing most sweetly that hymn of the Virgin which she had often heard from him, sounded in her ears. On hearing it, she shouted loudly; and her shouts gathered a crowd of people, who, with the judge of the city, broke into the house and took the body away; but never did he cease to sing that sweet song, even though he was dead. The body was placed on a couch and borne to the cathedral church of that town, where the bishop celebrated Mass, and bade the congregation pray earnestly that the secret might be revealed. When the sermon was finished, the little boy rose, and stood upon his couch, and took a precious stone from his mouth, and told all the people what had happened to him, and how the Virgin had come to him, and placed the stone in his mouth, that he should not cease, though dead, from her praise. Having finished, he gave the precious stone to the bishop, that it might be placed with the other relics on the altar, signed himself with the sign of the holy cross, and committed his spirit into the hands of the Saviour.

The version of the story which Chaucer used prob ably differed in some details from the foregoing. Chaucer's schoolboy lived in a great city of Asia, instead of in merry Lincoln ; but the more significant of the divergences may well be laid to Chaucer's artistic genius.

The art of the *Prioress's Tale* is shown chiefly in the increased emphasis laid on the human, as opposed to the supernatural aspects of the story. The main purpose of the other versions is to show the miraculous power of the Blessed Virgin and the black malignancy of the cursed Jews, the murdered boy himself being little more than a lay-figure, a necessary part of the machinery of the tale. Chaucer has slighted neither the glories of the Virgin nor the wickedness of the Jews ; but he has subordinated both to the deep and tender pathos which centres in his 'litel clergeon, seven yeer of age,' his 'martir, souded to virginitee.' Eight full stanzas are devoted to the setting forth of his sweetly simple child-nature, before the tragic murder is even hinted at. We see the little clerk on his daily walk to and from his school, bending the knee, and saying his *Ave Mary*, wherever he saw an image of the Mother of Christ. His learning of the hymn which is to prove his destruction is shown in detail. As he sits in school conning his 'litel book,' he hears the *Alma Redemptoris* sung by older children in another room, —

> And, as he dorste, he drough him ner and ner,
> And herkned ay the wordes and the note,
> Til he the firste vers coude al by rote.

Even the older schoolfellow who teaches him the rest of the song, and tells him what it means, is clearly, though briefly, characterized : —

> His felaw, which that elder was than he,
> Answerde him thus : 'this song, I have herd seye,
> Was maked of our blisful lady free,
> Hir to salue, and eek hir for to preye
> To been our help and socour when we deye.

> I can no more expounde in this matere ;
> I lerne song, I can but smal grammere.'

He is a likeable boy; but he lacks the divine spark of his younger comrade. To him the anthem is but part of his school task. Not so the 'litel clergeon:' —

> ' And is this song maked in reverence
>   Of Cristes moder ? ' seyde this innocent ;
> ' Now certes, I wol do my diligence
>   To conne it al, er Cristemasse is went ;
>   *Though that I for my prymer shal be shent,*
>   And shal be beten thryes in an houre,
>   I wol it conne, our lady for to honoure.'

If we wish to realize Chaucer's power in depicting these children, we have only to compare them with the utterly impossible children who occasionally appear in the plays of Shakespeare. If we wish to appreciate the difference between true pathos and mere sentiment in the portrayal of childhood, we may compare the *Prioress's Tale* with Tennyson's *In the Children's Hospital*.

After the murder is done, our attention is called for a while to the sorrowing mother, as she seeks her child, and to the tender love of the Virgin Mother who succors him in his death; but our ears ring through it all with the sweet, clear voice of the martyred boy as he sings : —

> Alma Redemptoris Mater, quæ pervia cœli
> Porta manes, et stella maris, succurre cadenti,
> Surgere qui curat, populo : tu quæ genuisti,
> Natura mirante, tuum sanctum Genitorem,
> Virgo prius ac posterius, Gabrielis ab ore
> Sumens illud Ave, peccatorum miserere.[1]

---

[1] This anthem is sung at Compline from the Saturday evening before the first Sunday in Advent until the feast of the Purification (*Breviarium Romanum*, Mechliniæ, 1866, *Pars Hiemalis*, p. 147). There is another Advent antiphon beginning with the same line (see Skeat's

SIR THOPAS AND THE TALE OF MELIBEUS

The Prioress's tale of the 'litel clergeon' has left the company, as well it might, in sober mood. It is the sort of story that one wants to ponder awhile in reverent silence. Even the rougher members of the party are deeply touched; and the Host himself, when, feeling his obligation to keep the journey a merry one, he begins to jest and jape again, pays subtle tribute to the potency of the spell by speaking in the seven-line stanza of the *Prioress's Tale.*

The Host begins to look about for the teller of the next tale. It must be a tale of mirth to restore the light-heartedness of the company; but not a 'mery' tale of the coarser sort — that would be too violent a shifting of tone. His glance lights on Chaucer, who is riding silently, his eyes upon the ground, 'in thoughtful or in pensive mood,' attentively listening to all that is said, but taking no part in the general conversation. He is just the man to tell 'som deyntee thing.' The poet is apparently traveling incognito;[1] the Host, at least, has no inkling as to the identity of the guest whom he is entertaining unawares. He begins by rallying him good-naturedly, though unceremoniously, on his retiring manners, and on the generous proportions of his figure : —

'He in the waast is shape as wel as I.'

There is something 'elvish' about his countenance, says the Host, as though he were a visitant from the land of faery, in the world, but not of it. Precisely the

Oxford Chaucer, 5. 177) ; but that the one given above is the one Chaucer had in mind is rendered probable by the direct translation from it given in the third of the three versions of the legend mentioned above.

[1] One wonders whether the Man of Law in his reference to Chaucer was equally ignorant of the poet's presence.

word, we agree, to describe the peculiar elusiveness of Chaucer's playful-serious nature.

If the Host is ignorant of Chaucer's identity, we are not ; and when Geoffrey agrees to tell a story, we prepare ourselves for a tale which shall be the masterpiece of the whole collection. But that is not Chaucer's way. It is much more modest, and vastly more humorous, that he should represent himself as telling a tale which should outwear the patience of his hearers before it was half told. Dramatically, too, his choice is entirely probable. Suppose a great master of the violin traveling incognito should be jocosely invited to ' favor the company with a tune;' what more likely, granting him a keen sense of humor, than that he should tune his fiddle and strike up Yankee Doodle or an Irish jig? His musical reputation is secure. And so with Chaucer; does not the reader know that all the tales are his? A keen observer would doubtless detect a master's touch even in the rendition of Yankee Doodle, and the veriest tyro in literature must recognize that the burlesque of *Sir Thopas* is executed with matchless poetical skill.

To appreciate fully the delicacy and point of this literary satire, one should know some of the weary romances which so vastly delighted our forefathers of long ago.[1] From morn to noon, from noon to dewy eve, one may read of Sir Degrevant and Sir Eglamour and Sir Guy of Warwick, of Lybeaus Disconus and of the mythical Alexander. These romances often have the charm of naïve simplicity, but they are terribly long-winded, full

The Rime of Sir Thopas.

---

[1] A readily accessible example of the species, though written long after Chaucer's death, is the *Squyr of Lowe Degre*, recently edited for the Athenæum Press Series by Professor W. E. Mead. It is by no means wholly devoid of interest, and is, as its editor remarks, ' mercifully brief.' The language will offer no difficulty to a reader of Chaucer.

of digression and minute description, and, of course, highly improbable.

With such works before him, Chaucer might very easily have given us a howling farce, after the manner of Shakespeare's 'Pyramus and Thisbe' or Butler's *Hudibras;* but this would not have been quite courteous to those of his contemporaries who were still writing such romances, and to the still larger number who still were glad to read them. Neither would it have been so effective; one may easily o'erleap himself in the matter of satire, and make his caricature so gross that it ceases to convince. Chaucer has performed the more delicate and much more difficult task of writing an imitation, so true to the original that one might easily read it through in a collection of romances without suspecting its good faith, while so subtly heightening the original traits of diffuseness and essential nonsense, that its absurdity becomes immediately patent to one who will look a second time. All the real charm of naïve simplicity Chaucer has reproduced intact. We are really disappointed when the tale is rudely stopped in the middle of a line. Nearly a hundred lines pass musically by before anything happens at all. At last the much belauded hero finds himself face to face with a 'greet geaunt,' and we look to see lively action. But no; Sir Thopas politely promises to meet the giant to-morrow, and makes his escape.

> And al it was thurgh goddes gras
> And thurgh his fair beringe.

We must hear to the minutest detail how he was armed, and how he appeared as he rode forth; and the tale is interrupted in its two hundred and seventh line, before there is any remote prospect of battle. The broad drift of the absurdity is obvious enough; it is in little touches of the deepest bathos, and in the continually recurring

tone of *petit-bourgeoisie*, that the subtler humor resides. We are to be impressed with the hero's surpassing comeliness of feature. His face is white as a lily?
No, as *payndemayn*, the choicest quality of wheat
bread. 'His rode is lyk scarlet in grayn,' i. e. it will
not come out in the wash. And to cap the stanza: —

> And I yow telle in good certayn,
> *He hadde a semely nose.*

The forest through which Childe Thopas rides is in-
fested with many wild beasts. We look to hear of the
lion and the pard; but the next verse explains: —

> Ye, bothe bukke and hare!

Or, again, we are to be told how the hero's very person
inspires fear: —

> For in that contree was ther noon
> That to him dorste ryde or goon,
> *Neither wyf ne childe.*

As examples of the *bourgeois* tone, as Professor Koelbing calls it,[1] one may notice that in the catalogue of
'herbes grete and smale' which spring in the forest is
mentioned

> Notemuge to putte in ale,
> Whether it be moyste or stale,
> Or for to leye in cofre.

So, too, when Sir Thopas wished to swear a mighty oath,

> He swoor on ale and breed,
> How that 'the geaunt shal be deed,
> Bityde what bityde!'

But to the Host, that sturdy dispenser of ale and wine,
the crowning absurdity, beyond which he cannot suffer
the tale to proceed a stanza, is the statement: —

> Himself drank water of the wel,
> As did the knight Sir Percivel.

Let him disdain the use of a roof, if he please, and

---

[1] 'Zu Chaucer's Sir Thopas,' *Englische Studien*, 11. 495–511.

'liggen in his hode;' but of deliberate choice to drink 'water of the wel' —

> ' No more of this, for goddes dignitee,'
> Quod oure hoste, ' for thou makest me
> So wery of thy verray lewednesse
> That, also wisly god my soule blesse,
> Myn eres aken of thy drasty speche.'

Under this rude interruption Chaucer shows an angelic sweetness of temper. It is the best rime he knows; but if it is not acceptable to the company, he will tell a little thing in prose. From the standpoint of the modern reader, at least, Chaucer more than revenges himself by inflicting his long ' moral tale vertuous' of Melibeus.

The *Tale of Melibeus* is a translation of a French work called *Le livre de Melibee et de dame Prudence*, which is in its turn based on the *Liber Consolationis et Consilii* of Albertano of Brescia, who died soon after the middle of the thirteenth century. Dame Prudence gives some excellent advice to her impulsive husband, Melibeus, and, to adopt the words of Tyrwhitt, the tale ' was probably much esteemed in its time; but in this age of levity, I doubt some readers will be apt to regret that he did not rather give us the remainder of Sire Thopas.' Here is a good opportunity to take Chaucer at his word, when he says of another tale : — ^{The Tale of Melibeus.}

> And therfore, whoso list it nat yhere,
> Turne over the leef, and chese another tale.

THE MONK'S TALE

The modern reader has doubtless been bored by the moralizing tale of Melibeus, if indeed he has not skipped it outright. Not so the honest Host. He has your true middle-class Englishman's love for moraliz-

ing, if not for morality. Moreover, the tale has for him
a special and personal interest: —

> Our hoste seyde, ' as I am faithful man,
> And by the precious *corpus Madrian,*
> I hadde lever than a barel ale
> That goode lief my wyf hadde herd this tale ! '

She is no Dame Prudence to restrain her husband's
wrath. On the contrary, she is a sort of *bourgeois* Lady
Macbeth, urging on her husband to acts of violence;
while in her ability to vilify the poor man, and force
him to do her will, she is own sister to the Wife of
Bath. She will make him slay one of the neighbors,
and bring him to a murderer's death, one of these days,
the Host predicts : —

> ' For I am perilous with knyf in honde,
> Al be it that I dar nat hir withstonde.'

After this bit of realism, which serves well as a buffer
between the rather ponderous ' tales ' which precede
and follow, the Host turns to my lord the Monk, and
begins to rally him on his general air of well-fed
prosperity and physical fitness. From such a sleek,
comfortable-looking gentleman, the Host confidently
expects a ' mery ' tale. But alas ! for mine Host's disappointed hopes ! The Monk is not, like the reckless
Pardoner, a man who can suffer his dignity to lie fallow
for a season. However far he may stray from the
' reule of Seint Maure or of Seint Beneit,' the dignity
of his person and his rank allow no unseemliness or
levity of speech. In his own cell, surrounded by his
fellow monks, with a plump swan and a good bottle
before him, his fat sides may have shaken often enough
with laughter at a merry jest; but no such relaxation
is convenient in the promiscuous company of the Canterbury Road. With unruffled patience he hears the
Host through to the end, suffering his free familiarity

and scarcely veiled innuendo to pass unanswered and
unnoticed.

> ' I wol doon al my diligence,
> As fer as souneth into honestee,
> To telle yow a tale, or two, or three.'

The tales he offers are a life of Edward the Confessor,
or a series of ' tragedies,' of which he has a hundred at
home in his cell. Condescendingly he explains to the
unlearned that —

> Tragedie is to seyn a certeyn storie,
> As olde bokes maken us memorie,
> Of him that stood in greet prosperitee
> And is yfallen out of heigh degree
> Into miserie, and endeth wrecchedly.

With true scholarly spirit he apologizes for the lack of
chronological order in what is to follow ; with a self-
depreciation worthy of Matthew Arnold he begs to be
excused for his ignorance ; and then, without waiting
to see whether the choice is going to be acceptable,
launches into his weary string of ' tragedies.'

One day, as the sprightly author of the *Decameron*
was sitting in his study, he was visited by a strange
monk, who told him of a death-bed vision, in
which a fellow monk had seen heaven and _Sources._
hell opened before him, and had clearly distinguished
Giovanni Boccaccio among those dwelling in the less desirable of these mansions. The impressionable, imagi-
native nature of Boccaccio was so deeply moved by this
gruesome prophecy that he was at first determined to
burn his books, and devote himself to a life of religion ;
but under the saner counsels of his friend Petrarch,
he decided instead to abandon his more frivolous compositions, and give himself to the study of classical
philology. Among the works which followed on this so-
called conversion is one entitled *De Casibus Virorum*

et Feminarum Illustrium, a sort of biographical dictionary, dealing with the lives of those who had stood in
great prosperity and had fallen from their high degree
into misery, and had come to a wretched end. Not a
very pleasant subject for a book, we are tempted to say;
but the subject was one which appealed to an age
intensely interested in biography, and eagerly craving
the excitement of tragic downfalls. During the period
when Chaucer was strongly under the influence of Boccaccio and other Italian models, — the exact year we
cannot determine, — he seems to have planned a similar
work in his own English, which was to have consisted
of a hundred 'tragedies,' beginning with Lucifer and
Adam and extending down to his own day — such a
work as his disciple Lydgate accomplished in his *Fall
of Princes,* a generation later. Fortunately, we think,
this work was one of the many which Chaucer planned
and started, but never brought to completion. He
either tired of it, or perhaps came soon to recognize
that the work was not worth doing. That he was conscious of its literary badness at the time he wrote the
Canterbury Tales is shown by the criticisms showered
upon it by such diverse characters as the Knight and
the Host. He had, however, written some dozen or
thirteen of the hundred tragedies, taking up his subjects
not chronologically, but according to his whim and
fancy; and when he came to construct the *Canterbury
Tales,* he saw a chance to utilize these discarded fragments, dramatically so appropriate to the ponderous dignity of the Monk, while at the same time indicating his
maturer critical judgment as to their literary worth.
He added four new paragraphs dealing with contemporary worthies,[1] purposely upset the chronological

[1] See Skeat's argument to prove that the tragedies of Pedro of Spain,
Pedro of Cyprus, Barnabo, and Ugolino are of later date, in the *Oxford*

order to conceal the incompleteness of the series and to give greater naturalness to the Monk's narration, and foisted the whole off upon the substantial shoulders of the defenseless Monk. Here is a thrifty way of disposing of one's literary bastards! In composing the several sections, Chaucer had recourse not only to his great model, Boccaccio, but to the Vulgate Bible, to Ovid, Boethius, Guido, and others, the tale of Ugolino being taken bodily from the thirty-third canto of Dante's *Inferno*.

A discussion of the literary merit of these ' tragedies ' must resemble the famous chapter on the snakes of Ireland. With few exceptions, they have no literary merit. Apart from the unspeakable monotony of the series, the dry epitomizing character of the individual narrations and the inevitably recurring moral make them intolerable. The one shining exception to this sweeping condemnation is the tale of Ugolino, a splendid bit of condensed narrative, rich in pathos and true tragic power ; but the excellence of this piece is due to the success with which the author has reproduced the matchless art of Dante.

The Seventeen Tragedies.

Before leaving the tale, one may pause a minute to notice the eight-line stanza in which it is written, a measure which Chaucer had used in his very early *A. B. C.* This stanza, when supplemented by an additional alexandrine, gives us the Spenserian stanza of the *Faerie Queene*.

THE NUN'S PRIEST'S TALE

Not only the Knight who interrupts courteously and the Host who seconds his objection more roughly,

Chaucer, vol. iii. pp. 428–429. The account of Barnabo deals with events which happened in 1385, which is the latest historical allusion contained in the *Canterbury Tales*.

but the whole company must have been bored to death
by the weary string of dismal 'tragedies' which
the Monk has thought fit to narrate on this sunny
eighteenth of April. The Knight objects that most
people care for but 'litel hevinesse;' it is pleasanter
to hear of men who from poor estate have attained to
great and lasting prosperity. The Host assures the
reverend gentleman that such talk as his is not worth
a butterfly: —

> ' For sikerly, nere clinking of your belles,
>   That on your brydel hange on every syde,
>   By heven king, that for us alle dyde,
>   I sholde er this han fallen doun for slepe,
>   Although the slough had never been so depe.'

We poor readers, who can hear this merry clinking
of the bridle bells but faintly with the inner ear of
imagination, are surely to be forgiven if we 'fallen
doun for slepe' before the 'tragedies' are half recounted.
However, we have, by way of compensation, a relief
which was not possible to the pilgrims — the blessed
relief of skipping; boldly turn three pages at once, and
we reach one of the merriest tales that ever graced
our English tongue.

Neither in the General Prologue nor in the links
which fit the tale into its framework has Chaucer taken
any pains to characterize the 'gentil Preest' who tells
this tale. So we may dismiss him without ceremony,
and imagine ourselves face to face with Chaucer; his
is the all-pervading geniality and sly elvish humor of
this sparkling tale, which seems part and parcel of
the April sunshine. There is no piece of all Chaucer's
writings that one would sooner choose to set before
the uninitiated and say, 'Here is the Chaucer whom
we love.' Dull must he be of soul who fails to become
a convert. Here is the vivid delineation of scene, the

subtle characterization, the infinite ease and grace of language and verse, the delicate play of humor, above all the fresh-hearted gayety and eminent sanity to which we gladly turn when wearied out with the more modern poets and story-tellers who insistently brood over the mystery of this unintelligible world, as the pilgrims turned from the weary 'tragedies' of the Monk.

Let no one suppose that our present-day fad for animal stories, wherein only too often an entirely respectable dumb beast is endowed with a degree of wishy-washy sentimentalism which even a *Sources.* moderately intelligent human being would be ashamed of, is at all a modern discovery. Far in the 'dark backward and abysm of time,' long centuries before the authors of the *Jungle Books* or the Brer Fox stories were dreamed of, our remote ancestors delighted in stories of beasts and birds who spoke and acted more or less like men and women, though keeping in the main the frolic wantonness and shrewd cunning of the beast. In those old days, I suppose, people were interested in animals as the daily companions of the field, and even of the hearth; to-day, in the crowded life of our cities, we are interested in beasts because we see so little of them. An honest, well-meaning clergyman spends a summer vacation in the country, and armed with opera-glass, note-book, and abundant sentiment, 'discovers' in the life of the forest a far-seeing wisdom, a pathos, a tragedy, with which he fills his books — or lecture-halls — for a year to come. From this so-called 'nature study' the step to the sentimental animal story is inevitable. I do not mean that all our animal stories are so written; I could name at least three writers of such tales who escape, or nearly escape, the charge of false sentimentality; it is the great army of their imitators — but enough of this.

Any one who will venture into the labyrinthine discussions of the folklorists will find abundant proof that stories not unlike the central episode of the cock and fox in Chaucer's tale have been told since the earliest times in all countries of the world, from darkest Africa to farthest Inde. Tales of the fireside soon find their way into literature, when literature has once appeared, and so it was with these popular stories of the beast and bird. There have been in the past two main forms of the animal story: the Æsopian fable, written by a moralizer who sought to give new effectiveness to a familiar bit of practical wisdom; and the animal epic, the great representative of which is *Reynard the Fox*, written, in its later form at least, by a satirist who wished to make fun of men and women under the convenient guise of animals, at whom any one may laugh without fear of the censor. Of these two literary forms, that of the fable is the simpler and apparently the earlier. I need not characterize it; every one knows his Æsop; but it is interesting to see how the germ of Chaucer's tale appears in fable setting. Here is a translation of a Latin fable from the early Middle Ages, one of a collection which goes under the name of Romulus: [1] —

A Cock was walking up and down on the dunghill, when a Fox, seeing him, came near, and sitting down before him, broke in with these words: ' I never saw a fowl equal to you in good looks, nor one who deserved more praise for the sweetness of his voice, save only your father. He, when he wanted to sing louder than usual, used to shut his eyes.' The Cock, who was a great lover of praise, did as the Fox suggested; he

[1] A verse translation of Marie de France's later but more artistic version of this fable is given by Professor Skeat in the *Oxford Chaucer*. vol. iii, p. 432.

shut his eyes, and began to sing with a loud voice. Immediately the Fox made a rush at him, and turned his song into sadness by hurrying off to the woods with the singer. There happened to be shepherds in the field, and they began to chase the Fox with dogs and with great outcry. Then the Cock said to the Fox: 'Tell them that I belong to you, and that this robbery is none of their business.' But when the Fox began to speak, the Cock dropped from his mouth, and by the aid of his wings soon found refuge in the top of a tree. Then the Fox said, 'Woe to him who speaks when he had better be silent.' And the Cock answered him from the tree, 'Woe to him who closes his eyes when he had better keep them open.' [1]

French and German scholars have not yet finished fighting out the question to which nationality belongs the honor of originating the great animal epic of the Middle Ages, in which King Noble the lion, Bruin the bear, Grimbald the wolf, and the other animals hold their parliaments, and issue their decrees for the suppression of Reynard the fox, hero of this ' vulpiad,' who manages by his cleverness to outwit them all. The epic of Reynard, as we have it in French and German, and in the other tongues into which it was translated,[2] is not the work of any single author or single age. Like the great cathedral buildings of England, the original fabric was freely added to and elaborated, any animal fable tending to get itself incorporated into this most popular of poems. The story of the cock and the fox is found both in the French *Roman de Renart* and in the German *Reinecke Fuchs ;* but neither can have been Chaucer's immediate source. Miss Kate Petersen,

---

[1] I have followed the Latin text given by Miss Petersen: *On the Sources of the Nonne Prestes Tale*, Boston, 1898, pp. 3–6.

[2] The first English translation was made by Caxton in 1481.

who has examined the matter most carefully, concludes that Chaucer follows a version of the epic now lost to us, which was nearer to the German *Reinecke* than to the French *Renart*. By comparing Chaucer's version with these two, and making allowances for what may have been Chaucer's independent changes and additions, she ingeniously reconstructs what must have been the main details of the version Chaucer used. This reconstructed version I shall reproduce here as a basis for comparison with the *Nun's Priest's Tale*.[1]

Beside a grove dwells a woman somewhat advanced in years, content with her property and with her provision of grain and bacon. Within her yard, protected by fence and hedge, she keeps a cock named Chantecler and a number of hens, the best of which is named Pinte. One day at sunrise the fox, full of tricks, comes after Chantecler, but finds the fence too strong for him. At last, however, he pulls out a slat with his teeth, and crawls through the hedge into a heap of cabbages, where he lies hidden. Pinte perceives his presence, and calling out to Chantecler, who is asleep, she and her companions fly up on a beam. Chantecler comes up proudly, assures the hens that they are quite safe in this yard, and bids them return to their former place. He then tells Pinte that he has had a bad dream in which he saw a reddish beast; is it any wonder that he is distressed and full of apprehension? May heaven interpret the dream aright! Here, perhaps, Pinte offers some interpretation of the dream. Chantecler makes a reply in which he scoffs at dreams and makes humorous

---

[1] *On the Sources of the Nonne Prestes Tale*, Radcliffe College Monographs, No. 10, Boston, 1898. (In reproducing her hypothetical version of the tale, I take some liberties with her language.) This study supersedes the discussion of sources given in *Originals and Analogues*, pp. 111–128, though the French texts there given are useful for consultation.

remarks about women. Summoning up his courage, he defies the dream.

A little before noon, Chantecler, unaware of the fox, flies nearer to the place where he is lurking, and on first seeing him, starts to flee. But the fox begs Chantecler not to flee from a friend. Have not their families always been on friendly terms? He praises the singing of Chantecler's father, who used to sing with closed eyes. Why should not Chantecler try to imitate him? Chantecler, too rash to perceive his folly, begins to beat his wings, and to sing with closed eyes. Upon this the fox seizes him by the throat and runs for the wood, while Pinte and the other hens lament their loss. The woman comes at the cry of the hens, and seeing the fox with Chantecler in his mouth cries, 'Harrow!' Every one pursues the fox. The dog is let loose. But Chantecler, in all his peril, prompts the fox to utter words of defiance to his pursuers. The fox opens his mouth, whereupon the cock escapes and flies into a tree. The cock assures the fox that the adventure shall not be repeated. The fox invokes shame upon the mouth that speaks out of season; and Chantecler says, 'Misfortune come upon him who shuts his eyes at the wrong time.'

Though the point of this tale is the same as that of the Latin fable, we find the characters supplied with definite habitation and with names, while the story is elaborated by the introduction of a new episode, that of the premonitory dream, and by some attempt at characterization. Chaucer, in utilizing this story, has made some changes in detail — the appearance of the fox is deferred until later in the story, when his part in the action is to be important, distinctly improving the structure of the narrative; he has greatly elaborated the discussion of the dream, giving the skeptical attitude to Pertelote rather than Chanticleer; and he has immensely heightened the description and characterization. In this way, what was originally a fireside story has become first a literary fable, then a developed narrative, and lastly a work of art.

Chaucer's first care in retelling the old story was to give heightened color and realism to his background.
Chaucer's Version. He goes out into the country and paints a peasant's cottage, such as must have been matter of common experience to the readers of his own day — the simple house of two rooms, with its sooty 'hall' serving as kitchen, living-room, hen-house, barn, and pig-sty, and the smaller 'bower' where slept the widow and her daughters. We are given a view of the every-day peasant life, its hard work and meagre fare, its narrowing interests; all this serving as a sharp contrast to the lordly elegance and wide intellectual scope of Chanticleer. Still, it is not an unhappy life that Chaucer shows; if the widow's board is but plainly furnished forth, she has as recompense a good digestion : —

> The goute lette hir nothing for to daunce,
> N' apoplexye shente nat hir heed.

Best of all, she has that 'hertes suffisaunce' which makes any life worth the living. Once again, later in the tale, the peasant life reasserts itself, when the widow, her daughters, the neighbors, and all the animals of the farm in wild bedlam join in the hue and cry after the marauding fox. Both these pictures have all the vividness and realism of a Dutch *genre* painting by Teniers or Gerard Dou.

A greater achievement than this is the creation of Chanticleer, a character which is real and interesting, while remaining still a rooster, at the same time human and galline. To accomplish this, Chaucer has seized on the trait of character which is in a rooster most human and in a man most galline, the quality which the two species share in common — egotism, personal vanity, in a word, the strut. This is the quality which mankind agrees in attributing to the rooster as a type; doubtless a rooster poet would attribute the same quality to man. This is the trait of character which in the old fable leads to Chanticleer's downfall, when the fox cozens him with his pretty obvious flattery; this is pre-eminently the quality of the domestic tyrant. So that it is without any sense of incongruity that we see the two types coalesce.

Chanticleer, as he is first described to us, is only a superlative rooster, superlative in his crowing, superlative in his galline beauty : —

> In al the land of crowing nas his peer.
> His vois was merier than the mery orgon
> On messe-dayes that in the chirche gon;
> Wel sikerer was his crowing in his logge,
> Than is a clokke, or an abbey orlogge.
> By nature knew he ech ascencioun
> Of equinoxial in thilke toun;
> For whan degrees fiftene were ascended,
> Thanne crew he, that it mighte nat ben amended.

From this it is an easy step to the singing of a song with words : —

> But such a joye was it to here hem singe,
> Whan that the brighte sonne gan to springe,
> In swete accord, 'my lief is faren in londe.'

This is followed up by an offhand statement : —

> For thilke tyme, as I have understonde,
> Bestes and briddes coude speke and singe.

We accept this statement readily enough, as a necessary condition of animal stories. But if animals can talk, they can also have dreams. So bit by bit we are led into the plausible impossibility of the conjugal

dispute, with all its display of erudition and dialec-
tics.

Dame Partlet becomes the typical housewife, kindly
solicitous of her husband's welfare, even though she
reproach him for his faint heart, —

'Have ye no mannes herte, and han a berd ? '

unwilling of course to accept his explanation of the
dream, confident in the superiority of her own wisdom
and in the efficacy of her own homely remedies. Was
there ever a wife who did not love to prescribe from
her medicine chest, or ever a husband who did not protest that medicine was quite unnecessary? She is even
ready to humor her husband's weakness for pedantry,
quotes to him from one of his own authors, enters at
length into a scientific explanation of dreams. She has
not lived with the learned Chanticleer for nothing. As
for the cock, he is your typical pedant and egotist. He
is proud of his voice, of his learning, and of his immense
superiority to his wives, whose company he enjoys because of his superiority. With what evident self-satis-
faction he quotes an uncomplimentary Latin proverb,
which he translates wrongly, deliciously conscious that
his playful fraud cannot be detected: —

'For also siker as *In principio*,
Mulier est hominis confusio; [1]
Madame, the sentence of this Latin is —
Womman is mannes joye and al his blis.'

His wife ventures to quote the authority of Cato
that dreams are not to be regarded. Very well, if she
wants authorities, she shall have them ; and he proceeds
to bury her volumes deep under his accumulated lore.
She ought to know that a woman can't argue. But if

[1] The phrase ' In principio ' begins the book of Genesis and the Gospel of St. John, in the Vulgate. ' It is as true as the Bible that woman
is man's confusion.'

Chanticleer is pedant and egotist, he is nevertheless a kindly soul, and we cannot but like him.

However learnedly Chanticleer may discourse, however human he may seem in his petty domestic tyrannies, Chaucer never suffers us quite to forget that he is but a rooster and that Dame Partlet is but a hen. Were we to forget, the delicious humor of the situation would be lost. This end Chaucer attains by constantly recurring to distinctly galline traits. After displaying her complete acquaintance with the *materia medica*, and assuring her husband that the herbs necessary

> ' To purgen yow binethe, and eek above '

are growing right there in the yard, she bids him

> ' *Pekke* hem up right as they growe, and ete hem in.'

So, too, when the long debate is ended, the rooster nature reasserts itself : —

> And with that word he fley doun fro the beem,
> For it was day, and eek his hennes alle ;
> And with a chuk he gan hem for to calle,
> For he had founde a corn, lay in the yerd.
> Royal he was, he was namore aferd.
>
> .   .   .   .
>
> He loketh as it were a grim leoun;
> And on his toos he rometh up and doun,
> Him deyned not to sette his foot to grounde.

The beautiful bubble of pride and lordliness is pricked to nothing by the clever stratagem of Daun Russel the fox, and his ignominious rape of Chanticleer. That the airy fabric of the tale may not fall too suddenly to ground, Chaucer has recourse to the mock heroic. The marauding fox is apostrophized as

> O newe Scariot, newe Genilon!
> False dissimilour, O Greek Sinon,
> That broghtest Troye al outrely to sorwe!

There is learned discussion of free-will and God's fore-knowledge, as one might debate the reason of a prince's fall. The outcry of the widowed hens is compared to the lamentations of the Trojan ladies when Ilion was won, to the shrieks of 'Hasdrubales wyf,' to the wailing of the senators' wives when Nero burned imperial Rome. It takes all the wild hubbub of shouting rustics, barking dogs, and quacking geese to bring us back again to the realization that all this mighty action has been transacted in a poor widow's barnyard, and that its protagonists are but a cock and a fox.

The rest of the story, which now follows the lines of the old fable, is disposed of quickly; the moral is pointed, and thus is ended Chaucer's tale of Chanticleer.

CHAPTER XI

THE CANTERBURY TALES, GROUPS C AND D

THE PHYSICIAN'S TALE

THE *Physician's Tale* begins a new group of tales, and Chaucer has provided it with no prologue by way of introduction. The portrait of this doctor of physic given in the General Prologue is allowed to stand as our sole information about the character which, judged from a modern standpoint, has in it more of the quack than of the reputable practitioner. Neither is the tale which Chaucer assigns to the man of medicine particularly appropriate to him. One cannot refrain a smile at Ten Brink's ingenious suggestion that its 'desperate, bloody ending' is 'appropriate to the character of the Doctor and his professional acquaintance with violent remedies.' One may notice, too, that Virginia's allusion to the daughter of Jephthah gives the lie to the statement of the General Prologue that

His studie was but litel on the bible.

Chaucer had apparently written the story with another purpose in view, perhaps with the intention of incorporating it into the *Legend of Good Women*, and finding it in his desk drawer, determined, with his accustomed literary thrift, to turn it to account in the *Canterbury Tales*. If not particularly appropriate, it is not markedly inappropriate. Possibly the digression on the proper bringing up of daughters may have been inserted as suitable to the Doctor in his capacity of family adviser.

One who was not familiar with Chaucer's literary
methods would immediately assume from the explicit
Sources. statement of the first line that the source of
the tale was Titus Livius. Livy's history is,
of course, the ultimate source; but the most hasty reading of the Latin story will show a wide divergence. In
Livy, Virginius, on hearing the unjust sentence, immediately snatches up a knife, and without any pause
buries it in his daughter's breast. This is more natural
and less revolting than the deliberate deed of Chaucer's
Virginius. The rather barbarous episode of the head
sent to Appius on a charger is also absent from Livy's
narrative. Chaucer did not make these changes himself; for in dealing with themes from antique history
he is usually chary of alteration. The tale explicitly
says : —

> This is no fable,
> But knowen for historial thing notable,
> The sentence of it sooth is, out of doute.

Moreover, though the change makes possible the affect-
ing dialogue between Virginia and her father, which is
the emotional climax of the tale, it involves, as we have
seen, a certain untruth to nature as compared with
Livy's treatment. The truth is that Chaucer did not
go to Livy at all. Indeed, we have no proof that Livy
was any more than a name to him. The outline of the
story, and the ascription of it to Livy, are taken directly
from that great storehouse of story, the *Roman de la
Rose*. Jean de Meun's narrative is not long, and since
a comparison of it with Chaucer's tale serves well to
show the latter's literary methods, I shall translate the
passage entire.[1]

---

[1] The story occupies lines 5613–5682 of Méon's edition of the *Roman
de la Rose*. Skeat has reprinted the passage in the *Oxford Chaucer*,
vol. 3. pp. 435–437. I have made my translation from his text.

Did not Appius well deserve to hang, who made his servant undertake, by means of false witnesses, a false quarrel against the maiden Virginia, who was daughter to Virginius, as saith Titus Livius, who knows well how to relate the case? This he did because he could not have mastery over the maiden, who cared not for him, nor for his lust. The false churl said in audience: 'Sir judge, give sentence for me, for the maid is mine; I will prove her for my slave against all men living: for soon after she was born, she was taken from my house and given in keeping to Virginius, where she has been brought up. Therefore I demand of you, Sir Appius, that you deliver me my slave, for it is right that she serve me, and not him who has brought her up; and if Virginius denies this, I am all ready to prove it, for I can find good witnesses of the fact.' Thus spake the false traitor, who was a retainer of the false judge; and when the plea had gone thus far, before Virginius, who was all ready to reply and confound his adversaries, had spoken, Appius gave hasty judgment that without delay the maiden should be returned to the churl. And when the good gentleman before named, good knight and well-renowned, that is to say, Virginius, heard this thing, and saw well that he could not defend his daughter against Appius, but that he would be forced to give her up and deliver her body over to shame, he chose injury rather than shame, by a wonderful determination, if Titus Livius lies not. For in love, and without malice, he straightway cut off the head of his beautiful daughter Virginia and presented it to the judge before all men in full consistory; and the judge, as the story says, straightway gave order that he be taken and led away to be slain or hanged. But he neither slew him nor hanged him, for the people defended him, being moved to great pity as soon as the deed was known; then, for this evil deed, Appius was put in prison, and there quickly slew himself before the day of his trial; and Claudius, who had challenged the maiden, was sentenced to death as a malefactor; but Virginius, taking pity on him, won a reprieve for him, making suit to the people that he should be sent into exile, and all were condemned and put to death who were witnesses in the case.

What Chaucer has done is to reproduce this narrative with substantial fidelity, heightening its effectiveness Chaucer's somewhat by a freer use of direct discourse, Version. while adding of his own fantasy two long original passages, which serve to change entirely the artistic emphasis of the tale. These passages are the charming description of Virginia's maidenly loveliness, with the digression on the bringing up of daughters, and the infinitely pathetic scene in which Virginia learns her father's purpose, and herself chooses death rather than shame. Beside the wonderful effectiveness of these two passages, the narrative portions sink into insignificance, or rather serve as a mere framework for the picture of Virginia's spotless purity. In the French it is the unjust judge and his righteous punishment that receive chief emphasis; with Chaucer, the personality of Virginia dominates the whole. The narrative is not slighted; it is merely subordinated; and the memory of the reader lingers fondly on the maid who

> Floured in virginitee
> With alle humilitee and abstinence.

⟨ THE PARDONER'S TALE

The Host has been so wrought upon by the pathos of the Physician's tale of Virginia, that he feels it absolutely essential to his physical well-being that he hear a

'mery tale.' With a delicate touch of satire, the author
makes him turn to the Pardoner as one most likely to
satisfy this need. The Pardoner is ready enough with
his assent; but the company has reached a wayside
tavern, whose 'ale-stake,' crowned with its garland,
projects far over the muddy road, and the physical
well-being of the Pardoner demands that he stop long
enough to drink a draught of corny ale and eat a cake.
The 'gentles' of the company, however, know only too
well what to expect when a pardoner undertakes to tell
a 'mery tale.' 'Let him tell us no ribaldry,' they cry.

> 'Tel us som moral thing, that we may lere
> Som wit, and thanne wol we gladly here.'

Ready complaisance is part of the Pardoner's stock in
trade.

> 'I graunte, ywis,' quod he, 'but I mot thinke
> Upon som honest thing, whyl that I drinke.'

Things honest and of good report proceed from a pardoner's lips only as the result of meditation.

The Pardoner is, of course, a dreadful hypocrite; but
his hypocrisy is a part of his profession merely, and he
is now on a vacation. He is an honest hypocrite, at least
in so far as he does not deceive himself, nor try to pass
himself for a holy man 'among friends.' As he sits
and quaffs his corny ale and surveys his fellow voy-
agers, his tongue is loosened, and in a spirit partly of
bravado, but more, I think, with an artist's natural
pride in his art, he begins to give away some of the
secrets of his trade. 'Here, in this company, you see, I
am a very unassuming, good-natured fellow; but when
I preach in church, I take pains to assume a haughty
manner of speech, and put in a word of Latin here
and there "to saffron with my predicacioun." I show
my relics — they are really only rags and bones — I

preach always on the sin of avarice, so that my hearers may give the larger offering. In this way I win a hundred marks [1] a year.'

The Pardoner's reason for giving this frank account of his own hypocrisies I take to have been something like this. 'I am not really a moral man,' he implies, 'and I do not intend to take the trouble of keeping up appearances on this journey; but it is my business to give moral discourses, and since you insist on having a moral tale, I will give you an example of my pulpit oratory.'

> ' For, though myself be a ful vicious man,
> A moral tale yet I yow telle can,
> Which I am wont to preche, for to winne.
> Now holde your pees, my tale I wol beginne.'

The sermon which follows on this preamble consists of a highly dramatic story, which is interrupted after a few lines by a long discussion on the sins of swearing, gluttony, dicing, and other of the deadly sins, and only continued after an interval of some hundred and sixty lines. This discussion contains several touches of humor; but our main attention must be occupied with the story itself.

The immediate source of the *Pardoner's Tale*, which may have been some *fabliau* now lost, is not known to us; but the story in its main features is one of great antiquity and wide dissemination. The earliest form of the tale which has been discovered is in an old Hindoo collection of tales, and bears the title *Vedabbha Játaka*. Other versions are found in Persian, Arabic, Kashmiri, and Tibetan. From the Orient the tale was brought to Europe, where versions are found in Italian, German, French, Portuguese, and Latin.[2]

Sources

---

[1] Equivalent to at least seven hundred pounds of modern money.

[2] See *Originals and Analogues of Some of Chaucer's Canterbury Tales,* pp. 129–134, 415–436.

The latest appearance of the story is found in the tale of *The King's Ankus,* in Kipling's *Second Jungle Book.* The version which bears closest resemblance to Chaucer's is found in the 1572 edition of the *Cento Novelle Antiche,* a collection of tales which probably antedates Boccaccio. This tale is in itself so well told, and furnishes so interesting a comparison with Chaucer, that I shall translate it entire.

Here is the story of a hermit, who as he was walking through a forest, found very great treasure.

Walking one day through a forest, a Hermit found a large cave which was well concealed, and betaking himself thither — for he was very weary — as he reached the cave, he beheld in a certain place a great gleaming; for there was much gold there. Now as soon as he saw what it was, incontinently he went away, and began to run through the desert as fast as he could go. As he was running thus, the Hermit came upon three great robbers, who had taken their stand in this forest to rob whosoever should pass there. But never as yet had they learned that this gold was there. Now as they stood concealed, and saw this man fleeing so, who had no one behind to pursue him, they were at first somewhat afeard; but, notwithstanding, they accosted him to know why he fled, for of this they marveled greatly. He answered and said: 'My brothers, I flee death, who comes after me, pursuing me.' They, seeing neither man nor beast that pursued him, said: 'Show us who pursues thee, and lead us where this death is.' Then the Hermit said to them, 'Come with me, and I will show you him;' but he begged them in every way that they should not seek death, forasmuch as he for his part was fleeing him. And they, wishing to find death, to see after what fashion he was made, asked him nothing else. The Hermit seeing that he could not do otherwise, and being in fear, conducted them to the cave whence he had departed, and said to them, 'Here is death which pursued me,' and showed them the gold that was there; and incontinently they knew what it was, and they began to be exceeding joyful, and to make great solace together. Then they dismissed this good man, and he went away about his own business; and they began to say to one another how he was a great simpleton. Remained all these three robbers together, to guard this treasure, and began to reason what they should do. One of them answered and said: 'It seems to me that since God has given us this high good fortune, we should not depart hence, until we carry away all this treasure.' And the other said: 'Let us not do so; let one of us take somewhat of it, and go to the city and sell it, and get bread and wine and whatsoever else we need, and on this errand let him use the best wit he has: let him so do, that he may furnish us forth.' To this agreed they all three together. Now the Devil, who is full of devices, and in his wickedness ordains as much evil as he can, put into the heart of him who went to the city for provisions, 'As soon as I am in the city (said he to himself), I will eat and drink as much as I need, and then provide myself with certain things for which I have use now at the present time; and then I will poison what I carry to my companions: so that when they shall both be dead, I shall be lord of all that treasure, and, as it seems to me, it is so great, that I shall be the richest man of all this country as regards my having;' and as it came to him in thought, so he did. He took meat for himself, as much as he needed, and then all the rest he poisoned, and so carried it to those his companions.

While he was going to the city, according as we have said, if he considered and devised evil to slay his companions, to the end that all might remain to him, they on their part thought no better of him than he of them, and they said to one another: 'As soon as this comrade of ours shall return with bread and wine and with the other things which we need, we will slay him, and then we will eat what we want, and then all this great treasure will be between us two. And as we shall be fewer that share it, so much greater part will each of us have.' Now comes he who was gone to the city to buy the things of which they had need. When he was returned to his companions, straightway when they saw him, they were upon him with lances and with knives, and slew him. As soon as they had him dead, they ate of what he had brought; and as soon as they were filled, both fell down dead. And thus they died all three; for the one slew the other as you have heard, and had not the treasure. And so our Lord God pays traitors; for they went to seek death, and in this manner they found it, and in such way as they were worthy of. And the wise man wisely fled from it, and the gold remained without a master as at first.

It is easy to see why this tale should have been a popular one; it is in its nature essentially tragic, the catastrophe coming as a direct result of evil character; in the eagerness with which death is sought and the ease with which it is found, we have a perfect example of dramatic irony.

The effectiveness of the *Pardoner's Tale* depends first on the effectiveness of its theme, as shown in the Italian *novella*, and in hardly less measure on the setting which Chaucer has given to it. In the background of the story looms that most terrible and mysterious force, the plague, death raised to its highest power. In our Western world of sanitary science, widespread pestilence has ceased to be a matter

The Pardoner's Version.

of national experience. To realize what it means, we must read in our newspapers of its ravages in India or China, or better still, read the accounts of Thucydides or Boccaccio or DeFoe. But to Chaucer and his readers the plague was a matter of personal experience. Four times during the reign of Edward III, in 1348–49, 1361–63, 1369, and 1375–76, England was swept by pestilence. In the first of these plagues, the same which Boccaccio describes in the Introduction of the *Decameron*, we are told that half the population of England perished.

A highly interesting feature of Boccaccio's description of the plague is the account he gives of its varying effect on the moral tone of Florentine society. Some gave themselves up to religious exercise ; others shut themselves up in their houses, ate the most nourishing food, and kept their minds occupied with pleasant topics ; but many, in the conviction that to-morrow they should die, spent to-day in eating, drinking, and making merry. It is to this last class that the three 'riotours' of the *Pardoner's Tale* belong. In the Flemish town where the scene of the story is laid, a thousand victims have already fallen ; but unchastened by the calamity, the three 'riotours' sit in drunken revelry at their tavern, though it is not yet nine of the day. Amid their laughter and oaths comes the solemn clink of the funeral bell. It is the corpse of one of their own friends, suddenly stricken as he sat drunk upon his bench. Though moved to no amendment of life, they are not sufficiently callous to continue their merry-making. In drunken rage they vow to seek out this false traitor Death and be revenged. The taverner has mentioned a great village a mile or more away, where not a human soul is left alive. Surely here victorious Death must keep his abode. The background darkens, as the three 'riotours,' after taking that ill-kept oath of mutual faith, with swords drawn and their mouths full of curses, rush madly towards the city of Death. We feel already that doom hangs over them. They are what a Scotchman calls 'fey,' marked out for death. All this, it will be noticed, is absent from the Italian *novella*.

Chaucer now provides a contrast of overwhelming power. An old, poor man, 'al forwrapped save his face,' meets them at a stile, which marks, perhaps, the confines of the village they are seeking. It is 'crabbed age and youth,' drunken excitement and calm philosophic meditation.

> 'Ne deeth, allas! ne wol nat han my lyf;
> Thus walke I, lyk a restelees caityf,
> And on the ground, which is my modres gate,
> I knokke with my staf, bothe erly and late,
> And seye, "leve moder, leet me in!
> Lo, how I vanish, flesh, and blood, and skin!
> Allas! whan shul my bones been at reste?
> Moder, with yow wolde I chaunge my cheste,
> That in my chambre longe tyme hath be,
> Ye! for an heyre clout to wrappe me!"
> But yet to me she wol nat do that grace,
> For which ful pale and welked is my face.'

He, too, it seems, is a seeker after death. But who is he, this mysterious passenger? Whence comes he? whither goes he? Whose is the treasure that lies beneath the oak? and how came it there? To none of these questions does Chaucer so much as hint an answer. We feel that the old man is something other than the hermit of the Italian *novella;* the hermit was fleeing death, this man is seeking it. One of the 'riotours' accuses him of being Death's spy; we are tempted to believe that he is rather very Death himself. But Chaucer does not say so; he wraps him in a mystery as deep as the mystery of death. The pale, withered face and heavily shrouded figure rise like a vapor, and fade as suddenly into thin air. Was he a reality or a vision? And the treasure, those eight bushels of gold florins, were they real and palpable, or only a dreadful mocking vision? Reality or vision, they have in them the power of deadly work.

The three doomed revelers run up the crooked way; but instead of grim, antic Death, they find what seems to them the very fullness of life. Here is provision for endless days and nights of dissipation. They are struck into silence by the vision. The clink of funeral bell, the mad quest of Death, the mysterious figure, all are forgotten. The fumes of drunkenness clear away. They are at once practical. No questions are asked; the money must be secured. Why care for Death? Here is life, and life in more abundance.

The cuts are drawn; the messenger is dispatched; the two plots are laid, and the poison is bought. A few brief strokes sketch in the triple murder.

> Thus ended been thise homicydes two,
> And eek the false empoysoner also.

Three dead bodies and a heap of worthless gold! They have found Death — the vanquisher. The strange old man totters on his way, tapping with his stick at the gates of our common grave, the earth, still seeking the death which these so readily have found. Will he ever find it? or is he doomed to a withering Tithonus-like immortality, deathless as Death itself?

This is the tale of the Pardoner, — full of tragic terror; dramatic in its structure, transacted as it is almost wholly in dialogue; never hurried, but marching forward with sure strides, unimpeded with a single superfluous detail, irresistible and inevitable as death and night.

As for the moral of it, one could draw morals enough if it were desirable. The miserable mountebank of a Pardoner sees in it only the exemplification of his favorite theme: *Radix malorum est cupiditas.*

One reads of the preacher Whitefield that, in addressing a seaman's mission in New York, he described a shipwreck with such vividness that a hardened old salt jumped to his feet and cried, 'Man the boats! she 'll sink!' And again that in Philadelphia the utilitarian skeptic Ben Franklin emptied his purse into the preacher's collection-box. With such a tale as this the Pardoner may well have passed off his spurious relics, and won the hundred marks a year which he boasts of as his income. The sublime audacity of the Pardoner, however, is reserved till the end of the tale, when in the glow of his oratory he offers his worthless relics to the very company to whom he has made an *exposé* of his lying methods. I hardly think he expected to win their silver; as we have seen, he is on a vacation. It is rather the conscious artist in hypocrisy, who wishes to give a crowning example of his art.

THE WIFE OF BATH'S PROLOGUE

The *Wife of Bath's Prologue* is a dramatic monologue in which a highly characterized, but at the same time a typical, woman of the middle class is made to reveal her own personality, narrate the events of her own life, and pronounce her opinions on the topic which is to her the most vital of our human life. At every step one is conscious of the new influences brought into our literature by the Italian Renaissance. The intense interest in all sorts and conditions of men, without which our great dramatic literature could never have been; the breaking down of class distinction, which makes a cloth-weaver 'of bisyde Bathe' fit subject for a poet's verse, and gives to her thoughts and experiences a value as real as those of a countess or queen; and lastly, the almost revolutionary daring with which the poet makes his creation demolish the cherished mediæval ideal of celibacy, — all these proclaim the author of the *Wife of Bath's Prologue* as the first modern man of England, with the virtues and faults of our modern world.

Though this composition is essentially one of Chaucer's most original productions, here as elsewhere he is indebted to 'olde bokes.' The original con-

Sources.

ception of the Wife of Bath is due, apparently, to an allegorical personage in the *Roman de la Rose* named La Vieille, a personage who, though first introduced in the earlier part of the poem by Guillaume de Lorris, is elaborated in Jean de Meun's satirical continuation of the work. But though the points of similarity are numerous, La Vieille remains, as her name indicates, an abstraction, or at most a type; while the Wife of Bath is a living, breathing woman. Other hints for the elaboration of the character Chaucer seems to have drawn from Jean de Meun's description of Le Jaloux, an old married man, who attributes to woman many of the qualities which the Wife of Bath eagerly claims for herself.[1] For the long discussion of celibacy, however, Chaucer has gone directly to a work of St. Jerome, used also by the author of the *Roman de la Rose*, known as *Hieronymus contra Jovinianum*, in which the holy father demolishes with much acerbity the argument of one Jovinian, who had ventured to write against the practice of celibacy. In the course of this argument Jerome inserts a long extract from a lost work of a Greek named Theophrastus, entitled

[1] See W. E. Mead, 'The Prologue of the Wife of Bath's Tale,' *Publications of the Modern Language Association of America*, 16. 388–404.

Liber Aureolus de Nuptiis. A further source is the
Epistola Valerii ad Rufinum de non Ducenda Uxore,
printed among the works of Jerome, though written
much later. These three works, it will be observed,
were all contained in the favorite volume of the Wife
of Bath's fifth husband, the volume which the irate
lady forces him to burn. The delicious humor of Chaucer's procedure consists in suffering the serious arguments of a father of the church to be quoted and
refuted by such a one as the Wife of Bath. Bitter
attacks on the frailty of woman were a commonplace
of the old monastic literature ; but Chaucer is engaged
in no moral diatribe. Neither does he feel called upon
to espouse the cause of woman vilified ; in the spirit
of the dramatist he creates a woman who not only
exemplifies all that had been charged against woman,
but who even glories openly in the possession of these
qualities, and by his art forces us to take her point of
view, and all but sympathize with her.

It is hard to say how far Chaucer himself was in
sympathy with the views which the Wife of Bath pro-
pounds on the subject of marriage and vir- The Argu-
ginity. That he was no mere glorifier of the ment
against
sensual may go without saying ; but that he Celibacy.
recognized the fallacy of the prevailing ideal of celibacy, and that besides his merely dramatic interest in
the Wife of Bath he was also interested in breaking
down a false idol, is quite probable. Professor Lounsbury has called attention to the fact that Chaucer has
twice put into the mouth of the Host, in his words
to the Monk (B 3133–3154) and to the Nun's Priest
(B 4637–4646), opinions of a similar character, and on
the basis of these facts he calls the Wife's Prologue a
'revolutionary document,' in which the poet, shielding
himself behind the ample figure of this clothmaker of

Bath, has spoken out with playful exaggeration his opinion on one of the questions of the day.

Whether Chaucer's or not, the opinions are revolutionary enough even at the present day. This fourteenth-century advocate of a return to nature is, however, so prolix in her speech, and so given to digression, that it is not wholly a work of supererogation to sum up briefly the argument she advances.

A little while ago she had been told that since Christ went to but one wedding, she too, the much-married, should have confined herself to a single husband. Then, too, what a sharp word Christ spoke to the woman of Samaria anent her five husbands, — precisely the number which the Wife has reached herself! But the good woman frankly confesses that the significance of that rebuke she has never been able to understand. There is another 'gentil text,' though, the meaning of which she can easily grasp, — the command to be fruitful and multiply. God never defined the number of husbands which might be taken.

> But of no nombre mencioun made he,
> Of bigamye or of octogamye.

(Notice the delicious coinage of a new word, necessary to contain the new wine of her advanced opinions.) Solomon had many wives at once. 'Would that similar liberty were allowed to me!' sighs the Wife of Bath.

So far, it will be noticed, the argument has dealt with second marriage; but there are those who recommend the avoidance of marriage altogether, and praise perpetual virginity. Yet God has never expressly commanded virginity, and the apostle, though he counsels it, does not enjoin it. Up to this point the discussion has consisted of an appeal to the authority of holy writ; the Wife now descends boldly to the ground of common sense. If every one should practice virginity,

who, pray, is to beget virgins and bring them forth?
It may be that virginity is more excellent than the
married state; very well, wooden vessels are needed
in the household as well as golden. The Wife of Bath
is quite contented with the humbler lot. Once more
there is a bold appeal to common sense: it is the
obvious intention of nature that man should marry
and bring forth issue. Having established her point,
she can afford to be generous to her opponents; they
may follow virginity if they please: —

> I nil envye no virginitee;
> Lat hem be breed of pured whete-seed,
> And lat us wyves hoten barly-breed;
> And yet with barly-breed, Mark telle can,
> Our lord Jesu refresshed many a man.
> In swich estaat as god hath cleped us
> I wol persevere, I nam nat precious.

Despite its playful tone, the argument is a good one,
and it may well be believed that Chaucer is at least
half in earnest.

The chief interest of this Prologue lies not in its
character as a controversial pamphlet, but in The Wife
its portrayal of a human type. It is a great of Bath.
human document.

Looked at superficially, the Wife of Bath is a thoroughly healthy animal, somewhat over forty, of
substantial figure, dressed conspicuously, exceedingly
coarse in her speech, but withal a friendly, good-natured
woman, and by no means lacking in shrewd, practical
wisdom. Though she has picked up many odds and
ends of knowledge from her scholar-husband, Jankin,
her manner of speech shows her to be essentially illit-
erate. Her whole theory of life is one of frank animalism. This is what one takes in at first glance,
and this, probably, is all that her companions on the

Canterbury journey saw in her; but Chaucer saw more. He saw that with all her apparent gayety, she was not happy.

She begins her long preamble with mention of 'wo that is in mariage.' She argues at length to prove that marriage is the *summum bonum* of life, and she has had the singular good fortune to enter five times into this blessed state; surely she should know the quintessence of bliss. But none of her marriages has been fortunate; of her husbands she says: 'Three of hem were gode and two were badde;' but with none of them was she happy. The first three she had married for their money. They were too old to satisfy her lust; they chided and harangued her; they would not even give her money enough to satisfy her love of finery. The fourth husband was a reveler, who made her as jealous as she had made his predecessors. The fifth, clerk Jankin, tried to lord it over her, and told her uncomplimentary stories from his books. When she had at last won the mastery, he disobligingly died. Is not this 'tribulacioun in mariage'?

She is haunted, moreover, with a vague suspicion that, argue as she may to the contrary, her way of life is not the right one, a subconscious conviction that reaches masterful expression in the single exclamation:

Allas! allas! that ever love was sinne!

A further proof of her failure to attain happiness is found in her restlessness. As the souls of the lustful in the first circle of the *Inferno* are blown about continually by the whirlwind, so she has been driven by her restlessness to seek strange lands. She has been to Rome, to Santiago in Spain, to Boulogne, to Cologne. Thrice she has made the long journey to Jerusalem. When we meet her, she is on the road to Canterbury.

It is the same insatiable lust for travel which marks the restlessness of our modern life.

Worst of all, the Wife of Bath is growing old. Married first at the age of twelve, she is already forty when she marries her fifth husband. She must now be nearing fifty. Her good days are done. If, as Horace tells us, no piety can give pause to wrinkles and sure-advancing age, neither can the impiety of rank animalism. It is not only 'indomitable death' whose approach she has to dread, but the dulling of the sharp edge of pleasure on which her fancied happiness depends.

> 'But age, allas ! that al wol envenyme,
> Hath me biraft my beautee and my pith;
> Lat go, fare-wel, the devel go therwith !
> The flour is goon, ther is na-more to telle,
> The bren, as I best can, now moste I selle;
> But yet to be right mery wol I fonde.'

The spirit of reckless bravado in these lines cannot blind us to the terrible truth they contain. The last line in particular tells us that the gayety of her character is a forced gayety:—

> 'But yet to be right mery *wol I fonde.*'

There is, as Professor Lounsbury has said, a profound 'undertone of melancholy' running through all the apparent gayety of the piece.

It is this deeper significance of the character which we must urge against those who are tempted to quarrel with the Prologue on the score of morality. Chaucer has indeed chosen to depict an immoral woman, and he has allowed her to reveal herself with a coarse plainness of language which is sure to shock the fastidious of a more prudish age, and which may well have shocked the more fastidious of Chaucer's contemporaries; but we must remember that Chaucer has not apologized for her immorality, nor attempted to represent it as other than it is. Some readers may find the poem disgusting; but no one can call it seductive. Chaucer has, moreover, preserved the moral balance by his clear appreciation of the fact that unstinted gratification of sense is not the road to happiness.

THE WIFE OF BATH'S TALE

It was Chaucer's first intention, as we have seen above,[1] to put in the mouth of the Wife of Bath the 'merry' *fabliau* of the Parisian merchant and his unfaithful wife which we know as the *Shipman's Tale.* The general tenor of this tale is thoroughly appropriate to the Wife of Bath; but Chaucer conceived a new and better idea. The good woman's prologue has dealt with the 'wo that is in mariage.' She has proposed a problem — how to be happy though married; and in her own tale and in those of the Clerk, the Merchant, and the Franklin which follow are presented various answers to the problem or contributions towards its solution. Recent critics have called this set of tales the 'marriage group.'

In the Wife's own tale the knight, confronted with the choice whether he would have his wife old and foul but faithful and devoted, or young and fair but skittish, leaves the decision to the lady herself, giving her the mastery and sovereignty over him. As a reward for his submission, she promises to be both fair and good.

> And thus they live, unto hir lyves ende,
> In parfit joye.

The recipe for marital happiness is to let your wife have her own way in everything.

[1] See page 189.

After the quarrelsome interlude of Friar and Summoner is concluded, the Clerk of Oxford returns to the theme of marriage with a tale addressed directly to the Wife of Bath, which offers exactly the opposite answer. Marquis Walter rules his ever-patient wife with the most autocratic sovereignty. To all his commands, however outrageous, she gives unquestioning, uncomplaining obedience; and, her twelve years of trial over —

> Ful many a yeer in heigh prosperitee
> Liven thise two in concord and in reste.

The Clerk's playful recipe for happiness is complete wifely submission.

The *Merchant's Tale* offers no recipe for happiness, but elaborates further the woe that is in marriage, particularly in such an ill-assorted union as that of January and May, perhaps in any marriage entered into with the sole idea of 'fol delit.' Chaucer had been reading the *Miroir de Mariage* of Deschamps, and from it he draws in considerable measure the long satirical discussion of marriage which occupies the earlier part of the *Merchant's Tale*.[1]

The final contribution to the debate is found in the *Franklin's Tale*. Dorigen and her husband Arviragus have found the solution in mutual forbearance. The husband swears that he will 'take no maistrye agayn hir wil'; and she in return promises that there shall never be dispute between them, that she will be his 'humble trewe wyf.' This, says the Franklin, is the only way to married happiness: —

> For o thing, sires, saufly dar I seye,
> That frendes everich other moot obeye,

---

[1] See the article by J. L. Lowes on 'Chaucer and the Miroir de Mariage,' *Modern Philology*, 8. 165–186, 305–334.

If they wol longe holden companye.
Love wol nat ben constreyned by maistrye;
Whan maistrie comth, the god of love anon
Beteth hise winges, and farewel! he is gon! [1]

Stories closely akin to that told by the Wife of Bath
are found elsewhere in English literature. Gower tells
essentially the same story, though in much
less artistic form, in the first book of the *Confessio Amantis*. In Bishop Percy's folio manuscript
there are two ballads — the *Wedding of Sir Gawain
and Dame Ragnell* and the *Marriage of Sir Gawaine*
— which develop the same theme. Still another instance of the tale is the border ballad of *King Hen-
rie* in Scott's *Minstrelsy of the Scottish Border*. Similar stories of a loathly lady who becomes beautiful in
her marriage-bed are found in Icelandic, Gaelic, French,
German, and in the Orient. Indeed, the idea of dis-
enchantment by a kiss is a common theme of fairy
tales, as in the well-known nursery story of the Sleeping Beauty.[2]

Sources.

Though Gower's version and Chaucer's are nearer
akin to one another than to any other of the tales known
to us, neither seems to have been direct source for
the other. Dr. G. H. Maynadier,[3] who has gone most
thoroughly into the question, believes that the tales
of Chaucer and Gower go back ultimately to an Old

---

[1] Through these tales of the 'marriage group' there runs another
thread of common interest, the discussion of 'gentillesse.' The doctrine that 'gentillesse' depends not on birth but on excellence of
character, promulgated by the loathly lady in the Wife's tale, is exemplified by the perfect bearing of the lowly-born Griselda. The
Franklin is impressed by the 'gentillesse' of the Squire and his tale of
Canace. He wishes that his own son 'mighte lerne gentillesse aright.'
The *Franklin's Tale* shows that a clerk can 'doon a gentil dede' as well
as a knight or squire.

[2] See *Originals and Analogues*, pp. 481–524.

[3] *The Wife of Bath's Tale, its Sources and Analogues*, London, 1901.

Irish original; but his argument, though interesting, is so involved that one fails to be convinced by it.

The Friar, always ready, as the Summoner declares, to intermeddle in matters that do not concern him, has laughed at the undue length of the Wife's preamble to her tale. She does not immedi- The Tale Itself. ately answer him; indeed, the loud-voiced Summoner gives her no chance; but when the Host has called the Friar and Summoner to order, she takes occasion, in the opening paragraph of her tale, to pay back her critic with a clever dig. Her tale is to be a fairy tale, and so she begins with the remark that

> In th' olde dayes of the king Arthour,
> Of which that Britons speken greet honour,
> Al was this land fulfild of fayerye.
> The elf-queen, with hir joly companye,
> Daunced ful ofte in many a grene mede;

but now their place has been taken by these limiters and other holy friars: —

> For ther as wont to walken was an elf,
> Ther walketh now the limitour himself.

As a result of this change, —

> Wommen may go saufly up and doun,
> In every bush, or under every tree;
> Ther is noon other incubus but he,
> And he ne wol doon hem but dishonour.[1]

The Wife of Bath has introduced her tale and paid back the Friar at the same time; while the combination of delicate imagination with coarse insinuation serves admirably as a transition from the Prologue to the tale itself.

[1] I. e., 'He will not carry them off to fairy-land; he will only dishonor them.' This is the reading of Skeat's text and of the best MSS. The Globe Edition, following the Cambridge MS., reads: 'And he ne wol doon hem *non dishonour*,' which must, of course, be taken as sarcasm.

The story proceeds smoothly for a while, till the knight begins to collect answers to the riddle, 'What thing is it that wommen most desyren?' The Wife finds herself face to face again with the question she has debated in her Prologue; and fifty-seven lines are devoted to a discussion of the various answers suggested, and to the tale of Midas's wife (learned doubtless from husband number five). One may notice that she here returns for a while from the land of fiction to the problems of reality. This is suggested subtly by a change of tense, and by the introduction of the pronoun 'we,' which indicates her lively personal participation in the matter. Compare, for example, the

> Somme seyde, wommen loven best richesse

of line 925 with

> Somme seyde, that *our* hertes been most esed,
> When that *we* been yflatered and yplesed

of lines 929, 930, and with change to the present tense:

> And somme *seyn*, how that *we* loven best
> For to be free, and do right as *us* lest.

The story is resumed with the charmingly poetical vision of the four and twenty ladies dancing under a forest side, who vanish as the knight approaches. The picture is not elaborated as Spenser would have treated it; [1] it is merely suggested to the imagination. It is sufficient, however, to furnish us with the hint that the loathly lady is not of human kind. One may notice in passing how Chaucer has managed to introduce an element of surprise into the story. The hag does not, as in Gower, specify the condition on which she will extricate the knight from his difficulty, she merely demands the granting of her first request; not till after the knight's triumphant answer to the queen, is

---

[1] Cf. *Faerie Queene*, 6. 10. 10–18.

marriage mentioned. Nor does the reader learn the answer to the riddle till the knight speaks it out in full court.

Brought to the fulfillment of his pledge, the knight ungenerously, though not unnaturally, objects that his wife is loathly and old and come of low kind. This gives occasion for the long and excellent sermon on the nature of true nobility which occupies the last quarter of the tale : —

> Loke who that is most vertuous alway,
> Privee and apert, and most entendeth ay
> To do the gentil dedes that he can,
> And tak him for the grettest gentil man.

The noble ideas nobly expressed in this speech, which suggest familiar words of Burns and of Tennyson, though part of Chaucer's personal creed, as shown by their reappearance in his balade of *Gentilesse*, are not his original discovery. A similar strain of democracy may be found in Dante, in Petrarch, in Boccaccio, and in the *Roman de la Rose*. Some exception has been taken, however, to the dramatic appropriateness of such sentiments to the character of the Wife of Bath. Ten Brink says, for example : ' The thoroughly sound moral of the long sermon given by the wise old woman, before her metamorphosis, to her young, unwilling husband, comes more from the heart of the poet than from the Wife of Bath.' [1] But is not the Wife of Bath, as a prosperous member of the middle class, precisely the person to assert that true gentility is not the peculiar possession of the nobly born? If the poet has lent to these lines a tone of higher poetry than the Wife can be conceived capable of, he has done only what Shakespeare does continually. The function of the dramatist is not that of the mere reporter.

[1] *History of English Literature* (English trans.), 2. 163.

Another possible objection that may be urged against this passage is that so long a digression interrupts too seriously the progress of the tale. On the contrary, it is an artistic device of the highest skill. A loathly hag is to be transformed suddenly into a beautiful lady. Such a process makes a large draught on our powers of belief. The high poetry of the long discourse serves to bridge over the change; our minds are for the time being diverted from what is going on. We are held captive by the spell of her poetry, and at the conclusion of the speech are not surprised to find that the speaker is of wondrous beauty. As a further instance of Chaucer's art in the management of the metamorphosis, we may notice that he refrains from any *detailed* description either of her ugliness or of her beauty. Our minds are less startled by the change from ugliness in general to beauty in general than by that of a definite type of ugliness into a definite type of beauty.

The tale is one of Chaucer's poetic triumphs.

✕ THE FRIAR'S TALE

At the conclusion of the Wife of Bath's long preamble, it will be remembered, the Friar had 'intermeddled' with a derisive laugh at the good woman's long-windedness, and had been promptly called to order by the Summoner. Each promised to tell a tale which should not be complimentary to the other's profession; and only with difficulty could the Host calm them down, and win a hearing for the Wife of Bath. All through this enforced silence, the quarrel has been smouldering; and the Friar has cast dark looks upon his natural foe. When Dame Alice has ended, the Friar hastens to seize the opportunity to strike the first blow. His tale is ably paid back by the Summoner; and each reader must decide for himself which comes

out better in this war of tales. The enmity of the
Friar and the Summoner is not come of new; their
quarrel is the quarrel of their professions. The Summoner belongs to the organization of the so-called secular clergy, which includes the parish priests, the arch-
deacons, and the bishops. The Friar, as a member of
a mendicant order, belongs to the so-called religious
clergy — those who had taken definite religious vows,
and belonged to world-wide organizations, which held
authority directly from the Pope, and were independent of the jurisdiction of the national church. Such
a co-existence of separate ecclesiastical organizations
within the same realm gave rise, of course, to endless
jars; for the religious clergy were continually en-
croaching on the privileges of their secular brethren,
and the latter not unnaturally tried to curb their
power. Thus the Friar boasts that he and his order
are outside the Summoner's jurisdiction; to which the
Summoner gives countercheck quarrelsome by the
answer that so are 'the wommen of the styves.' Since
we know that the Friar could rage 'as it were right
a whelpe,' and since the 'fyr-reed cherubines face' of
the Summoner portends a choleric disposition, their
quarrel was a foregone conclusion. As it was apparently Chaucer's purpose to show up both professions
impartially, he chose the clever device of 'making
each of these rascals demolish the other,' a device
which serves also to heighten the dramatic realism of
the Canterbury pilgrimage.

The *Friar's Tale* is merely an application to the
profession of the Summoner of a popular anecdote, previously told at the expense of a bailiff or a
lawyer, but equally appropriate to any other   Sources.
unpopular functionary. Two analogues to Chaucer's
tale are given in the Chaucer Society's volume of

Originals and Analogues. The first of these, and the one which illustrates most clearly what the poet had to build on, is found in a volume, printed probably about 1480, written by a Dominican friar named John Herolt, which is intended as a help to sermon-writers. The second section of the work contains a series of short anecdotes which a preacher might find useful as examples to point his moral. Among them is the story just referred to. Of course this volume appeared nearly a century later than the *Canterbury Tales ;* but the anecdote may well have been in circulation long before. If Chaucer found it in some similar work on sermon-writing, its appropriateness to the preaching Friar is very obvious. The heightened effectiveness of Chaucer's tale, which, in the absence of any evidence to the contrary, we may suppose due to his own genius, is clearly shown by a comparison with this Latin *Narrative of a certain Wicked Seneschal* which I shall give here in translation.

There was a certain man, a seneschal and lawyer, a calumniator of the poor, and a despoiler of goods of every sort. One day he went to court to bring a suit, and to enrich himself. A certain man met him in the way and said to him, ' Where are you going? and what is your business ? ' The first man answered, ' I am going to make money.' And the second said, ' I am just such a one as you. Let 's go together.' When the first man consented to this, the second said to him, ' How do you make your money ? ' And he answered, ' The substance of the poor, as long as they have anything, which I get by law-suits and prosecutions, either justly or unjustly. Now I have told you how I make my money, tell me, prithee, how do you make yours ? ' The second answered him and said, ' I put down to my profit everything that is given to the devil in curses.'

The first man laughed, and made fun of the second, not knowing that he was the devil. After a little, as they were going through a town, they heard a poor man curse a calf, which he was leading to market, because it would not go straight; and they also heard a similar curse from a woman who was beating her boy. Then said the first to the second, 'Here's a chance for you to make money if you wish. Take the boy and the calf.' The second answered, 'I can't, because they are not cursing from their hearts.' Now when they had gone a little further, a band of poor men came along, going to the law-court, and seeing the seneschal, they all began to hurl curses at him with one accord. And the second said to the first, 'Do you hear what they say?' 'I hear,' said he, 'but it makes no difference to me.' And the second said, 'They are cursing from their hearts, and giving you over to the devil, and so you shall be mine.' And straightway he snatched him up and disappeared with him.[1]

This is a clever and diverting anecdote; but Chaucer's tale is something more. We may notice first of all the heightened realism given by the detailed description of the Summoner and his methods, and of the fiend, as he rides in his gay disguise of yeoman's green; by the vivid picture of the carter urging his horses, Brok and Scot, through the heavy slough, whacking them and cursing them while the wagon sticks, calling down all the blessings of heaven upon them when the wheels begin to turn; and by the half-humorous, half-pathetic figure of old Mabely indignantly repelling the Summoner's persecution, wishing him and the new pan, which he covets, both to the devil together. The dialogue between the

Chaucer's Tale.

---

[1] Still another analogue, from the Zürich poet, Usteri (1763–1827), is given by F. Vetter in *Anglia, Beiblatt,* 13. 180, 181.

two travelers is, as Ten Brink calls it, a little masterpiece. Though he is entertaining him unawares, the
Summoner finds the fiend such eminently congenial
company, that he immediately pledges him a life-long
friendship. Shameless as he is, he none the less tries
to hide the fact of his detested calling : —

> He dorste nat, for verray filthe and shame,
> Seye that he was a somnour, for the name.

Deliciously humorous is the series of hints by which
the fiend gradually reveals his true identity. He, too,
is a sort of bailiff, who must gather in his lord's rents.
As for his dwelling-place, it is ' fer in the north contree ' (the region where Lucifer set up his power) ; [1]
the yeoman hopes to see his new friend there some
day ; he will give him such clear directions before they
part, that he cannot possibly miss it. The fiend's account of his own unscrupulous methods draws from
the Summoner a frank confession that he makes off
with everything that he can find, ' but-if it be to
hevy or to hoot.' The Summoner must know the name
of this stranger so completely after his own heart.

> This yeman gan a litel for to smyle.
> ' Brother,' quod he, ' wiltow that I thee telle ?
> I am a feend, my dwelling is in helle.'

The Summoner is naturally a little startled at the
revelation, but not for long ; he is not the man to give
up so charming an acquaintance for a trifling circumstance. One may be a little taken aback on discovering that a chance acquaintance is a rabid anarchist or
violent atheist. If he is well dressed, and a gentleman,
we can pardon him some eccentricities of belief ; and

---

[1] The hell of Teutonic mythology was located in the north, as the
region of darkness. A false interpretation of Isaiah 14. 12–14 may
have helped to incorporate the same idea into Christian myth. Cf.
Milton, *Paradise Lost*, 5. 755.

then, too, a man of revolutionary tendencies is so interesting. The Summoner begins immediately to question him on the 'privitees' of a fiend's existence. The fiend, who, we may notice, has a supreme contempt for the speculations of theologians —

I do no fors of your divinitee —

obligingly satisfies his curiosity, so far as these things can be explained to a mere mortal. Hereafter, he promises, the Summoner shall come where he needs no further teaching : —

> For thou shalt by thyn owene experience
> Conne in a chayer rede of this sentence
> Bet than Virgyle, whyl he was on lyve,
> Or Dant also.

The Summoner may be professor of demonology, if he wishes, and lecture from a professional chair draped in the red, not of a doctor of divinity, but the red glare of hell-fire.

There is one moment of suspense, just before the tale reaches its catastrophe. Old Mabely wishes the Summoner to the devil with all her heart, but with one proviso, ' but he wol him repente.' The Summoner, who has surely had warning enough of what he is to expect, who was quick enough to suggest to his diabolic friend that the carter's horses were legitimate prey, is fatally blind. Proudly he asserts that he has no intention of repenting, and the fiend bears him off body and soul to hell,

> Wher-as that somnours han hir heritage.

THE SUMMONER'S TALE

Once, near the beginning of the Friar's tale, the Summoner could not refrain an interruption; but, on the whole, he kept himself very well in hand, knowing that the hour of his revenge was near. At the end

of the tale, however, he is quaking like an aspen leaf
for wrath, and, unable to wait for the slower revenge
of his tale, serves an *hors d'œuvre* in the shape of a
not very savory anecdote, which describes the particular place in hell reserved for these cursed friars. If
the Friar has been able to tell much of the true nature
of fiends, it is no wonder, for

> Freres and feendes been but lyte a-sonder.

The tale of the Summoner is, as far as our present
knowledge suffers us to say, mainly original. The central idea of it, to be sure, may very well have
been suggested by an old French story, the
Tale of the Priest's Bladder, versified by one Jakes
de Basiu.[1] This story tells of a priest near Antwerp,
who is visited on his death-bed by two Jacobin friars,
who beg an offering. He has already made his will,
and at first refuses them outright; but when they are
importunate, he bids them come next day with their
prior, and he will give them a jewel which he would
not part with for a thousand silver marks. The jewel
turns out to be his own bladder, which they may
cleanse and use for a pepper-box; and the friars go
home, laughed at of all. Quite possibly Chaucer knew
some variant of this tale, now lost to us. The definite
localization of the incident at Holderness in Yorkshire makes this probable. If such a variant existed,
it probably contained the change in the nature of the
bequest, and the germ, at least, of the closing scene
in the hall of the lord, where the young squire wins
a new gown by his clever resolution of the problem
which the churl had set. We may assume, with some

Sources.

---

[1] The tale is given by Legrand d'Aussy in his collection of *Fabliaux
ou Contes, Fables et Romans du XIIe et du XIIIe Siècle* (1829). It is
reprinted in *Originals and Analogues of Some of Chaucer's Canterbury
Tales*, pp. 137–144.

confidence, that the long hypocritical prediction with which Friar John favors the bed-rid churl, and the perfect life-likeness of the scene, are Chaucer's original addition.

Some readers, I suppose, will be offended at the coarseness of the *Summoner's Tale*. Coarse it certainly is in its closing portion, but not in the least vicious. So callous is the wretched friar of the tale in his miserable hypocrisies, that he needs a coarse insult by way of discipline. Indeed, the outspoken frankness of the conclusion comes as a positive relief after the sanctimonious pretenses of the friar. As for the coarseness of old Thomas, we may dismiss that as does the lady in the castle, whither the irate friar has betaken himself for redress : —

The Summoner's Tale.

> I seye, a cherl hath doon a cherles dede;

as for the coarseness of the squire, that is so ingenious that it is surely forgivable.

But the real literary value of the *Summoner's Tale* lies not in the plot of it, however artistically conducted, so much as in the masterful portrait of the dissembling friar. James Russell Lowell has called attention to the rich suggestiveness of the line : —

> And fro the bench he droof awey the cat.

'We know without need of more words that he has chosen the snuggest corner.' Admirable, too, is the picture of the good-wife with her kindly hospitality, her openness to flattery, and her ample faith in the efficacy of Friar John's prayers, contrasting sharply with the companion picture of her churlish husband and his rough incredulity.

At the shameless hypocrisy of the friar, one knows not whether to laugh or to weep. So complete a master is he of the art of shamming that, even in his trans-

port of rage, he remembers to protest at the title of
' master ' which the lord bestows on him : —

> 'No maister, sire,' quod he, 'but servitour,
> Thogh I have had in scole swich honour.
> God lyketh nat that " Raby " men us calle,
> Neither in market ne in your large halle;'

a disclaimer which is careful to specify that the title is
not at all inappropriate. The only thing he forgets is,
that for a preacher who has so ably denounced the sin
of wrath, it is hardly consistent to give such an eminent example of the sin in his own person : —

> He looked as it were a wilde boor;
> He grinte with his teeth, so was he wrooth.

All this is humorous enough on the surface of things;
but to one who knows something of the high ideals
which St. Francis and St. Dominic set before their
orders of mendicants, and something of the great work
for humanity, and for true religion, which these orders
achieved in the early days of their purity, this picture
of degradation has more of tragedy than of comedy.
It is precisely the greatest tragedy and the most
inexplicable mystery of our little life, that the great
institutions founded by our wisest and best for the
attainment of the noblest aims should, almost without
exception, develop, sooner or later, into instruments
of positive evil. The friar does not sin in ignorance;
his long sermon shows that he had all the precepts of
his pious founder at the tip of his oily tongue; but
these precepts have become a hollow mockery, and
worse. Unfortunately, the testimony of Chaucer does
not stand alone. Boccaccio, Gower, Langland, and
Wiclif, men of very diverse temperaments and preju-
dices, all agree with Chaucer in painting the mendicant orders as hopelessly corrupt — a thinly whited
sepulchre filled with dead men's bones.

CHAPTER XII

THE CANTERBURY TALES, GROUPS E, F, G, H, I

THE CLERK'S TALE

APPARENTLY the university students of the fourteenth
century were as diverse a lot as those of the present
day. Clerk Nicholas of the *Miller's Tale*, with his
gay sautrye,' and the two Cambridge students who
take their mischievous revenge on the Miller of Trump-
ington, represent one species of the genus; while the
poor clerk of the Canterbury pilgrimage belongs to
the class which we thoughtlessly dismiss with the word
'grind.' Lean he is of figure, sober of his bearing,
threadbare as to his coat : —

> For him was lever have at his beddes heed
> Twenty bokes, clad in blak or reed,
> Of Aristotle and his philosophye,
> Than robes riche, or fithele, or gay sautrye.
>
> .   .   .   .
>
> Of studie took he most cure and most hede.

Sharply contrasted with the ready assurance of 'hende
Nicholas ' is the bashful reserve of this nameless Clerk
of Oxenford : —

> ' Sir clerk of Oxenford,' our hoste sayde,
> ' Ye ryde as coy and stille as dooth a mayde,
> Were newe spoused, sitting at the bord;
> This day ne herde I of your tonge a word.
> I trow ye studie aboute som sophyme.'

So academic is his bearing, that the Host feels it necessary to request that he refrain from preaching, and from
too scholarly a manner of speech. But the Clerk is no

mere mechanical 'grind.' We discover the eager play
of an active and original mind in his very way of speaking, 'short and quik, and ful of hy sentence.' It is a
delight to see the sudden flash of enthusiasm with which
he refers to the great and worthy clerk, Fraunceys
Petrark. That he is by no means lacking in a healthy
vein of roguish humor, the closing stanzas of his tale
show clearly enough. That the Host's warning against
too lofty and pedantic a style was superfluous, the tale
itself may bear witness. It is written in 'an honest
method, as wholesome as sweet, and by very much more
handsome than fine.'

Sources.   In response to the Host's command to tell a
tale, the Clerk says : —

> I wol yow telle a tale which that I
> Lerned at Padowe of a worthy clerk,
> As preved by his wordes and his werk.
> He is now deed and nayled in his cheste,
> I prey to god so yeve his soule reste!
> Fraunceys Petrark, the laureat poete,
> Highte this clerk.

Chaucer's tale of Griselda is, indeed, only a close translation of Petrarch's *Fable of Obedience and Wifely
Faith*, which is in its turn a somewhat freer Latin rendering of the tenth *novella* of the tenth day in Boccaccio's *Decameron*. Prefixed to Petrarch's rendering of
the tale is a Latin letter to Boccaccio telling how the
translation came to be made. Though Petrarch and
Boccaccio were close friends, and though the *Decameron*
had been written at least twenty years earlier, Petrarch
seems not to have read it till a year or two before his
death, which occurred in 1374. Even then Petrarch
found the book too big to read through. He merely
glanced over the greater part of it, reading carefully
only the introductory description of the plague and

the concluding tale of Griselda. The latter impressed
him so deeply that he committed it to memory, and was
in the habit of repeating it to his friends. Wishing to
make it current among those who knew no Italian, he
found leisure to turn it into Latin, retelling it in his
own words, adding and changing a little here and there.
That Chaucer used Petrarch's version rather than
Boccaccio's original we know from the Clerk's explicit
statement. Independently of that, a comparison of the
three versions establishes the fact beyond shadow of
doubt. Great as is Chaucer's debt to Boccaccio, we have
no evidence that he ever read a line of the work on
which Boccaccio's fame now chiefly rests. The problem
of Boccaccio's sources for the tale is a puzzling one, and
fortunately is of no immediate concern to the student
of Chaucer. We may notice, however, that the tale is
found in a collection of French *Fabliaux, ou Contes
du XIIIe et du XIIIIe Siècle*, edited by Le Grand
(1781).[1]

If the question of Chaucer's source for the *Clerk's
Tale* is a simple one, very complicated is the question
as to the exact way in which Petrarch's fable
reached him. The Clerk of Oxenford is made   The Sup-
to say that he learned the tale at Padua from   posed Meet-
                                                 ing of
the worthy clerk, Fraunceys Petrark; and this   Chaucer
has been taken to mean that Chaucer himself   and
                                                 Petrarch.
heard the story from Petrarch's lips. At first blush there
is much to lend probability to this interpretation. Petrarch's version of the tale was made in 1373, while the
'laureat poete' was actually living at Arqua, a suburb
of Padua; and 1373 is the date of Chaucer's first visit
to Italy. What more likely than that Chaucer should
have sought out the chief man of letters in all Italy,

---

[1] An abstract of the *fabliau* is given in *Originals and Analogues to
Some of Chaucer's Canterbury Tales*, pp. 527–537.

and that Petrarch, who, we know, was in the habit of reciting the tale to his friends, should have entertained his guest with the fable of Griselda? If it is objected that Chaucer's version follows Petrarch's so closely that he must have had the Latin text before him as he wrote, it is plausibly suggested that Petrarch presented his visitor with a manuscript of the tale as a parting gift. Professor Skeat is so sure of the interpretation that he insists that any one who doubts it must accuse Chaucer of deliberate falsehood. Chaucer's romantic biographer, Godwin, even tells us just how the two poets felt on meeting, and what each said to the other.

Nevertheless, there have long been skeptics to doubt this pleasing theory. Professor Lounsbury, after calling attention to the fact that the *Canterbury Tales* is a dramatic composition, and that it is the Clerk of Oxenford and not Chaucer who says he learned the tale from Petrarch at Padua, sums up with the sentence: ' We can creditably and honestly try hard to think that the two poets met; but with the knowledge we at present possess, we have no right to assert it.' [1] Much as we should like to believe a story which appeals so strongly to our sense of what ought to have been, I fear that in view of recent investigations, even the cautious position of Professor Lounsbury is no longer tenable. Mr. F. J. Mather, after carefully investigating the exact date of Petrarch's composition of the fable, and the chronology of Chaucer's Italian journey, and looking into the conditions of traveling in the fourteenth century, has come to the following conclusions.[2] For Petrarch's translation of the Griselda story ' any date in the early months of 1373 is possible, any date earlier

[1] *Studies in Chaucer*, 1. 68.
[2] ' On the asserted meeting of Chaucer and Petrarca,' *Modern Language Notes*, 12. 1–11.

than April is improbable.' The mission of which
Chaucer was a member was sent primarily to conduct
business at Genoa. Leaving England on December 1,
1372, it could not have reached Genoa much before
February 1, 1373.[1] On reaching Genoa, Chaucer was
detached from his associates and sent on special business to Florence. Supposing that he made no stay in
Genoa, he may have been in Florence about February
10. He was apparently back in Genoa by March 23.
The length of his possible stay in Florence is thus seen
to be only a few weeks; and diplomatic business is usually not very quickly dispatched. Moreover, a journey
from Florence to Padua, easy enough in the day of rail-
ways, was then to be accomplished only by a long and
dangerous ride over mountain roads, still made difficult by the winter's snow. It seems improbable that
Chaucer made this wide détour, but if he did, he could
not have been in Padua later than March 15, a date too
early for the probable composition of Petrarch's Latin
version.

We cannot assert positively that Petrarch and Chaucer
did not meet; but in the absence of any positive evidence of their meeting, we must admit that the probabilities are strongly against it. As for Chaucer's actual
possession of the tale, Mr. Mather has shown that it
speedily became popular, and that manuscripts of it
were early multiplied. That Petrarch was dwelling near
Padua, Chaucer might easily have learned without
coming within two hundred miles of the place.

What we shall think of the *Clerk's Tale* will be
largely determined by what we think of the   Griselda
woman about whose personality the whole   the Patient.

---

[1] An allowance of two months for the journey to Genoa is probably
excessive. On his second Italian voyage of 1378, Chaucer was absent
from England less than four months. The second journey, however, was
made in the summer, when traveling was doubtless easier.

action centres. ⌊We are shown a young peasant-girl of
blameless life, who is suddenly taken from her daily
round of unremitting toil and frugal simplicity to be
made first lady of a great domain.   The sweet nobility
of her character is raised far above the play of outward
circumstance. She fills her new station as naturally and
simply as she had tended sheep or turned her spinning-
wheel; she gives to her husband the same unfeigned,
unstinted love and devotion that she had given to her
old and feeble father. With a character such as this,
and with great beauty of person as its fitting shrine, it
is no wonder that Marquis Walter loved her, and that
his people came to look upon her as the brightest star
of all their land. A character which can stand sudden
prosperity without receiving a flaw can also stand adversity. With unquestioning obedience she suffers her
children to be snatched from her, and herself to be sup-
planted by an unknown rival. The crowning instance
of her wonderful patience is her prayer to Walter to
spare his new-found lady: —

> ' O thing biseke I yow and warne also,
>   That ye ne prikke with no tormentinge
>   This tendre mayden, as ye han don mo;
>   For she is fostred in hir norishinge
>   More tendrely, and, to my supposinge,
>   She coude nat adversitee endure
>   As coude a povre fostred creature.')

Here is no word of reproach; though the reproach inevitably implied is heavy enough. Notice the carefully
guarded phrase, 'as ye han don mo,' where *mo* means
not *me* but *more*, 'as you have done to others.'[1]

---

[1] Petrarch's Latin reads: 'Unum bona fide te precor ac moneo, ne
hanc illis aculeis agites, quibus alteram agitasti.' Boccaccio is a little
more definite: 'Ma quanto posso vi priego, che quelle punture, le quali
all' altra, che vostra fu, gia deste, non diate a questa.' (But I beg you
with all my might that you give not to this woman those pricks which
you gave to the other who was yours.)

What are we to think of this matchless patience? Most modern readers, particularly women readers, I suppose, will think it ridiculous, if not positively criminal. Imagine a convention of woman's rights advocates debating the conduct of Griselda! 'Miserable, weak-spirited creature!' one hears them shriek. But those were the days when women still promised at the altar to obey their lords, and considered the promise as something more than a meaningless phrase. Moreover, Griselda was not only her husband's wife, but his subject as well; and the obligation of the vassal to obey the lord was only less sacred than man's obligation to obey his God. Griselda merely lives up strictly to the letter and spirit of her obligation, and, one may add, to the letter and spirit of the command that we 'resist not evil,' a command which our modern world has agreed to ignore. But, some one exclaims, is not a woman's first duty to protect her offspring, and is not Griselda virtually an accomplice before the act to what she supposes to be the murder of her children? A duty, doubtless, and a sacred one; but by what authority do we call it her 'first duty'? Mothers have been known to urge their sons on to almost certain death in battle; and the deed has been called one of noble patriotism. There is an old story, not yet quite forgotten, of a father who stood ready to sacrifice an only son, at what he believed to be the command of his God. He may have been mistaken; Griselda may have been mistaken; perhaps we shall one day be so civilized that the Spartan mother will no longer be held up as a model. The question of precedence in moral duties is a more troublesome one than any that has vexed the master of ceremonies at a court levée; and each age must be left to settle the matter for itself. Griselda merely put in practice what all her contemporaries held in theory. Petrarch was a man of

enlightened views, far in advance of his age; yet it did
not occur to him to question the rightness of her conduct.
He tells, in one of his letters, how he once gave the tale
to a friend, and asked him to read it aloud. The friend
broke down in the middle of the reading, and could not
continue for his tears. I am not arguing the question
on its merits; I merely insist that he who would read
the tale aright must imaginatively think himself into
the spirit of a time long past, in which men held principles quite other than ours, but in which, as in our own,
there were found those who would answer unflinchingly
to the stern voice of duty. Unquestioning obedience
to duty is a quality too noble and too rare in any age to
suffer us to question too nicely the occasion which calls
it forth. The tale is, as Ten Brink calls it, 'the Song
of Songs of true and tender womanhood.'

Just what Chaucer himself thought of Griselda is
not entirely clear to me. At the conclusion of the tale
he makes the teller say: —

> This storie is seyd, nat for that wyves sholde
> Folwen Grisilde as in humilitee,
> For it were importable, though they wolde;
> But for that every wight, in his degree,
> Sholde be constant in adversitee
> As was Grisilde.

The difficulty of interpretation lies in the word 'importable,' which means 'unbearable.'[1] Does it mean that such
conduct would be unbearable to others, or that a woman
who should strive to follow Griselda would be unable
to bear the strain? The context seems to me to favor
the latter interpretation, in which case we shall conclude
that Chaucer considered Griselda's humility entirely
right, but for the majority of women an unattainable
ideal. The roguish reference to the Wife of Bath, and

---

[1] Cf. *Canterbury Tales*, B 3792 : 'His peynes weren importable.'

the humorous envoy which follow are merely intended
to restore the playful tone which Chaucer wished
should dominate the *Canterbury Tales*.

One dramatic problem of peculiar difficulty is presented by the character of the Marquis, Griselda's
husband. The plot of the story demands that
he shall act with wanton cruelty, and cause his
wife twelve years of needless sorrow. Yet it
was not possible to paint him as a heartless villain; for
Griselda must not only obey him, but love him. This
fundamental inconsistency cannot be removed; but
the art of the story is shown in the extent to which it
is concealed.

The Marquis
Walter.

The opening sections of the tale present him in a
distinctly favorable light. He is young, handsome, and
good-natured : —

> A fair persone, and strong, and yong of age,
> And ful of honour and of curteisye,
> Discreet ynogh his contree for to gye.

All his people love him, both lords and commons. He
has no vices; in light-hearted carelessness he spends his
time a-hawking and a-hunting. Though he was

> To speke as of linage,
> The gentilleste yborn of Lumbardye,

he is quick to discern the true nobility of a peasant girl;
and, far from entertaining any dishonorable designs
upon her, is ready to make her his wife, and treat her
as his equal. It is easy to see the grounds of his general popularity.

Yet, withal, there is an unlovely side to his nature;
he is essentially selfish, a spoiled child. He neglects
affairs of state, thinking only of his own pleasure. It
is obviously his duty to marry and beget an heir; yet
he prefers bachelor freedom, and has to be reminded
of his duty by a delegation of his subjects. He is too

good-natured to refuse the request; but willfully declines
the offer of his lords to choose a fitting consort for him,
and asserts his liberty of action by flying in the face of
conventionality and wedding a peasant. There is surely
as much of pride as of generosity in his action; and one
is tempted, too, to think that he foresees less interfer-
ence to his liberty from a wife who is his inferior.

He has his way, weds Griselda, and is proud to find
his eccentric choice justified by Griselda's popularity,
and by her dignity in her new position. He is fond of
her as a spoiled boy is fond of a favorite horse, and in
mere pride of possession proceeds to put her through
her paces. As the reckless horseman is not contented
that his mare can take an ordinary hedge or ditch, but
keeps trying her at harder barriers to test the limits
of her excellence, so Walter devises still harder tests of
his wife's patience and obedience. He does not mean to
be cruel; he believes in his wife, and intends to set all
right in the end; he loves her after a selfish fashion.
Even when all is over, he feels no particle of remorse; he
has restored to her her children and the incomparable
blessing of his own love. But those twelve years!

THE MERCHANT'S TALE

Whatever Chaucer may have thought of Griselda as
an ideal of womanhood, he was quite aware that actual
realizations of the ideal are not over-numerous. The
fabulous Chichevache, who feeds only on patient wives,
is never in danger of a surfeit. Having depicted a wife
of the type of Griselda, the poet restores the balance of
actuality by telling, in the person of the Merchant, the
not very edifying tale of January and May.

As seen at the Tabard Inn, on the eve of the Canterbury pilgrimage, no one would have suspected the skeleton in the prosperous merchant's domestic closet. His

forked beard, his Flemish beaver hat, his 'botes clasped
faire and fetisly,' his self-satisfied manner of speech, —

> Souninge alway th'encrees of his winning,

suggest no hidden tragedy. But he has listened with
strange feelings to the Clerk's story of Griselda, who
suffered twelve long years without a murmur. He, poor
man, has been married but two months, —

> ' And yet, I trowe, he that al his lyve
> Wyflees hath been, though that men wolde him **ryve**
> Unto the herte, ne coude in no manere
> Tellen so muchel sorwe, as I now here
> Coude tellen of my wyves cursednesse ! '

The Host, it will be remembered, has some experience
in conjugal infelicity, and readily enough gives the
Merchant leave to tell his tale.

The greater part of the *Merchant's Tale* is, as far as
we know, Chaucer's original creation; only the climax
of the tale, the scene in the garden, where the
blind husband recovers his sight just in time   Sources.
to witness his wife's infidelity, and is persuaded that all
was done for his own good, can be traced to an earlier
original. The particular version of this 'pear-tree story'
which Chaucer used is not known to us; but several
analogous tales, European and Oriental, are given in
the Chaucer Society's volume of *Originals and Analogues*,[1] which may be read and compared by those who
think it worth while to trace the genesis of a tale which
was hardly worth telling in the first place. Of these
analogues, the best known is the ninth *novella* of the
seventh day in Boccaccio's *Decameron*. This, though
obviously a related tale, differs materially from the version Chaucer must have followed, the element of the
husband's blindness being entirely lacking. Even in
the portion of the tale which is borrowed, Chaucer's

----

[1] Pp. 177–188, 341–364.

originality may be seen. As Tyrwhitt says: 'Whatever was the real origin of this tale, the machinery of the faeries which Chaucer has used so happily, was probably added by himself; and indeed, I cannot help thinking that his Pluto and Proserpina were the true progenitors of Oberon and Titania, or rather, that they themselves have, once at least, deigned to revisit our poetical system under the latter names.'

Chaucer's tale has been retold by Pope under the title of *January and May.*[1]

Whatever one may think of the merits of the *Merchant's Tale*, it will not do to dismiss it, as does a recent writer on Chaucer, as a mere 'tale of harlotry;' for the poet's chief interest in the story centres not in its adulterous *dénouement*, but in the humorous character-sketch of old January. The doting gray-beard has spent his godless life in unbridled wantonness; and now that he is sixty years and more, and the spark of desire is burning low, he decides that the comfort and happiness of his declining years, and incidentally the salvation of his soul, will be furthered by a tardy entrance into 'that holy bond with which that first God man and womman bond.' Only a young and beautiful wife will answer the purpose; and with such a one old January foresees a life of unmixed bliss:—

> For wedlok is so esy and so clene,
> That in this world it is a paradys.

The sage counsels of Justinus, who urges objections manifold, avail as much as good advice usually avails a man who is already decided:—

> For whan that he himself concluded hadde,
> Him thoughte ech other mannes wit so badde,

---

[1] For a comparison of Pope's version with the original, see the article by A. Schade, in *Englische Studien*, 25. 1–130, 26. 161–228.

> That inpossible it were to replye
> Agayn his chois, this was his fantasye.

The sycophant, Placebo, who is clever enough to argue on the popular side, bears away the palm for wisdom. Exceedingly delicate is the irony with which Chaucer manages this debate, and proclaims the unending happiness of the married state, while making it quite apparent all the while that for January the roseate vision is to be but mockery. So plausible is the sarcastic praise of marriage that the passage beginning : —

> For who can be so buxom as a wyf ?
> Who is so trewe, and eek so ententyf
> To kepe him, syk and hool, as is his make ?

has actually been quoted, in all seriousness, to show Chaucer's ' perception of a sacred bond, spiritual and indestructible, in true marriage between man and woman ' ! [1]

Foredoomed inevitably to failure, this senseless union of ' crabbed age and youth ' is rendered yet more absurd by the elaborate marriage-feast, which Chaucer, contrary to his usual custom, has described at length, but described with an irony all the more biting because of its apparent good faith : —

> Whan tendre youthe hath wedded stouping age,
> Ther is swich mirthe that it may nat be writen.

When, in the sequel, the entirely natural happens, and ' faire fresshe May ' plays false with her marriage vows, she carries our sympathies with her. Not that we approve of her conduct exactly, but our attention is diverted from the merely lascivious in the tale, and from the moral questions involved, to the eminent poetic justice of old January's cuckoldom. An immoral tale is made to subserve a sort of crude morality.

[1] *The Prologue, Knight's Tale*, etc., edited by Richard Morris, Oxford, 1895, p. xviii, and Morley, *English Writers*, 2. 135, 256, 286.

Even when the faithless wife occupies the centre of attention, it is the cleverness of her intrigue, and the sublime audacity of her inspired self-vindication, rather than her sensual desires which interest us; while the delicate conceit of an overruling providence in the persons of Pluto and Proserpine, king and queen of faery, who sagely debate the wisdom of King Solomon and of Jesus *filius Syrak*, relieves the essential coarseness of the tale. Even in the realm of faery, a wife will have her way: Pluto may espouse the cause of the injured husband, but the queen knows a subtler magic than his own.

It would have been easy, had Chaucer so wished, to give the tale a tragic ending; but it is conceived from beginning to end in the spirit of a 'humor' comedy of Ben Jonson. The tragedy is there, to be sure, but it is concealed so successfully from its victim that he ends his days, for aught we know, in the paradise of fools whose bliss is their ignorance.

The *Merchant's Tale* was written when Chaucer was at the height of his power, after he had already achieved one masterpiece of the same general character in the *Wife of Bath's Prologue*.[1] Immoral the tale certainly is; but its immorality is not insidious, and the spirit of broad comedy which pervades the piece is all but sufficient to sweeten the unwholesomeness of it.

THE SQUIRE'S TALE

When Milton in *Il Penseroso* wished to summon up the memory of Chaucer, he did so by an allusion to the *Squire's Tale*: —

> Or call up him that left half-told
> The story of Cambuscan bold,
> Of Camball, and of Algarsife,

---

[1] That the *Merchant's Tale* is later than the *Wife of Bath's Prologue* is shown by the direct allusion to the latter at line 1685.

And who had Canace to wife,
That owned the virtuous ring and glass,
And of the wondrous horse of brass
On which the Tartar King did ride.

Another of England's greater poets, the author of the *Faerie Queene*, took upon himself the task of completing the half-told story, after addressing 'Dan Chaucer' in terms of deepest reverence and love.[1] A lesser poet, Leigh Hunt, who made a modernization of the *Squire's Tale*, entertained the idea of writing a conclusion to it, but wisely refrained.[2] The critic, Warton, placed the tale next after that of the Knight as 'written in the higher strain of poetry.'

A considerable part of the attention which this tale has received is due, I fancy, to the very fact that it was left half told. I am inclined to suspect that Chaucer abandoned the work because he did not know how to conclude it; and if this is so, any attempt on our part to guess its conclusion must be futile. The Tartar King is provided with a wondrous horse of brass, on which he can fly 'as hye in the air as doth an egle,' and in the space of four and twenty hours arrive in whatsoever land he will. To his daughter, Canace, is given a magic ring, whose virtue is such that with it on her finger she shall understand the voices of all the birds of heaven and converse with them in their own tongue, and a mirror in which all the deeds of men are revealed as if face to face. There is a magic sword, too, which will pierce the strongest armor, and like Achilles' spear 'is able with the change to kill and cure.' In the second part, Canace, by virtue of her

[1] *Faerie Queene*, Book 4, Cantos 2 and 3.

[2] See Lounsbury, *Studies in Chaucer*, 3. 211–212. One John Lane, a friend of Milton's father, produced in 1630 a long continuation of the tale, which has been published by the Chaucer Society. It is miserable nonsense.

ring, learns a tale of unhappy love from a falcon, who is, we must suppose, some princess laboring under an enchanter's spell. There are great wars toward. With such a beginning, what is not possible? The imagination roams through limitless fields of pleasing conjecture. The very name of magic has its fascination for our poor race of mortals, shut in as we are by the relentless barrier of the possible and the actual. Any conclusion which Chaucer, or any other poet, could have written would be barren and commonplace compared with our vague imaginings. And this is inevitable in the very nature of the case. Let the magic horse, the ring, the sword, and mirror be put to practical use, let their use result in any definite achievements or events, and they are immediately vulgarized. Once more the tyranny of the actual, if not the possible, shuts us in; and the boundless scope of the imagination is narrowed to nothing. An exactly similar case is presented by Coleridge's wonderful fragment, *Kubla Khan*, which deals, be it noticed, with the same Oriental dynasty as Chaucer's tale, Kubla Khan being a grandson of Gengis Khan, whose name becomes the Cambinskan of Chaucer. This poem is unfinished for the good reason that it could not be finished; it is essentially a fragment; and so great is Coleridge's art that the fragment may be said to constitute a distinct literary form. Much might be said of the beauty of the incomplete, of the desirability of leaving things half finished. The beauty of a spring day is in large measure the promise of summer days to come, which, when they come, fall often below our expectation. The unequaled charm of a noble youth rests on the unlimited possibility of noble action which lies before him. The early death of Keats has served to magnify fourfold the estimate set upon his work. We have no proof

that he would ever have surpassed the actual achievements he has left to us. Indeed, there are indications
that he would not have done so. Yet such is the power
of the incomplete, that we hear critics speak of him as
one who might have been a second Shakespeare. Or, to
take an example from what might have been, suppose
that Milton had been cut off after he had completed
only the first two books of *Paradise Lost*. What
should we not have expected of the ten remaining
books of a poem which opens so magnificently? But
we have the poem entire, and know that the level of
the first two books was higher than Milton could consistently maintain. The more one considers the keen-
ness of Chaucer's critical insight and the strange
'elvishness' of his character, the more strongly one suspects that Chaucer recognized this power of the incomplete, and deliberately left his tale half told.

In no case has Chaucer more happily suited the tale to
the character of the teller than in the case of the Squire.
As the Knight, his father, tells a noble tale of tournament and knightly love, so his son, the Squire, turns
naturally to a theme of chivalry. But there is a difference. Warton says that 'the imagination of this story
consists in Arabian fiction engrafted on Gothic chivalry.'
It is in the days of our youth that the fiction of the *Arabian Nights* appeals most strongly to us. Before the
'shadows of our prison house' close about us, we are
all impatient of the actual, and dream of the infinite
possibilities that might follow on the impossible. The
Knight has lived his life and worked his work, and so
his story, however ideal in its spirit, is of things accomplished, of deeds already done. The Squire, though

> He had been somtyme in chivachye,
> In Flaundres, in Artoys, and Picardye,
> And born him wel, as of so litel space,

is living mainly in the infinite future, where all things are possible. All that his father has accomplished is as nothing beside what he intends to do. His charm, like that of the tale he tells, is in large measure the charm of incompleteness.

There is hardly a feature of the *Squire's Tale* which does not find its parallel in the Oriental literature of magic. A reader whose acquaintance with this literature is confined to the *Arabian Nights* will find such parallels in abundance.[1] But no single narrative which Chaucer might have used has yet been discovered. Whether any such narrative existed, or whether Chaucer merely allowed his imagination to play freely with the familiar themes of Arabian magic, filling in his background with such scraps of knowledge about Tartary and the Far East as he had picked up in reading or conversation, we cannot say. The general character of the tale, and in particular its unfinished state, would favor the latter theory.

Professor Skeat tried hard to prove that Chaucer's acquaintance with Gengis Khan, and with such features of local color as his story presents, was derived from the famous book of the travels of Marco Polo; but this theory has been shown to be absolutely without foundation.[2] Such are Chaucer's mistakes and confusions that it is hard to believe that he could have had any connected account of the Tartars before him.[3]

[1] The whole subject has been investigated with great thoroughness by Mr. W. A. Clouston, in an article entitled *On the Magical Elements in Chaucer's Squire's Tale*, appended to the Chaucer Society's edition of John Lane's continuation of the *Squire's Tale*.

[2] J. M. Manley, 'Marco Polo and the Squire's Tale,' *Publications of the Modern Language Association of America*, 11. 349–362.

[3] Perhaps this is the best place to notice another exploded theory, that of Professor Brandl, who with characteristic German ingenuity has found in the *Squire's Tale* an elaborate allegory of the English court, Cambinskan representing Edward III, and Canace his daughter-

THE FRANKLIN'S TALE

The portrait of the Franklin in the General Prologue, though an attractive one, hardly does full justice to this ' worthy vavasour.' We are shown a prosperous country land-holder, a man of sixty or over, we may suppose, with beard as white as the daisies which stud his spacious meadows, and with countenance as ruddy as the wine which lies in his well-stocked cellar. It takes no extraordinary power of clairvoyance to know that his table must be loaded with ' alle deyntees that men coude thinke,' while the general kindliness and good-nature of his bearing tell us that there is always room at his board for another guest. We like the good man, and should be glad enough to receive an invitation to spend a week-end in a house where it ' snows meat and drink.' But we dismiss him from our thought as ' Epicurus owne sone ' for his good living, and as the Saint Julian of his country for generous hospitality. It is only after we have traveled a day or two with him on the Canterbury road, and heard him tell his noble tale, that we see more intimately into his life and aspirations.

The Franklin has much in common with the better type of the 'self-made man.' He has at his disposal all that money can buy, and he has held office in his own county; but he is uncomfortably conscious of a certain lack of ' gentility,' — betrayed by his fondness for the words ' gentil ' and ' gentilesse,' — and of the full education which would adorn his prosperous estate.

> ' But, sires, bycause I am a burel man,
> At my biginning first I yow biseche
> Have me excused of my rude speche ;
> I learned never rethoryk certeyn.'

in-law Constance, second wife of John of Gaunt (*Englische Studien*, 12. 161). This fanciful theory has been demolished by Professor Kittredge, in *Englische Studien*, 13. 1–25.

That he has made up in some way or other for the lack
of early advantages, is shown by the excellence of his
tale, and by the more or less learned discussions which
he rather needlessly introduces, such as the historical-
mythological catalogue of women who died rather than
sully their honor, which occupies lines 1366–1456. His
enlightened views and sound good sense are shown in
the opinion he expresses of astrology : —

> And swich folye,
> As in our dayes is nat worth a flye.

Once he indulges in one of the figures of rhetoric of
which he has professed his ignorance : —

> But sodeinly bigonne revel newe
> Til that the brighte sonne loste his hewe ;
> For th'orisonte hath reft the sonne his light ;

but his good sense and native honesty bring him down
to earth again in the line which follows: —

> This is as muche to seye as it was night.

Conscious that, with all that he has acquired and attained, he can never be quite the complete gentleman, he
would fain be the father of a gentleman; but his hopes
are disappointed by the unfortunate vulgar procliv-
ities of his son and heir. To the gallant young squire he
says : —

> ' I have a sone, and, by the Trinitee,
> I hadde lever than twenty pound worth lond,
> Though it right now were fallen in myn hond,
> He were a man of swich discrecioun
> As that ye been ! fy on possessioun
> But-if a man be vertuous withal.
> I have my sone snibbed, and yet shal,
> For he to vertu listeth nat entende;
> But for to pleye at dees, and to despende,
> And lese al that he hath, is his usage.
> And he hath lever talken with a page
> Than to commune with any gentil wight
> Ther he mighte lerne gentillesse aright.'

So might a Toledo oil-magnate bewail the vicious tendencies of the son whom he is lavishly maintaining at
Yale or Harvard. Considering this, there is something
of pathos as well as fine generosity, in the enthusiastic praise which the Franklin bestows on the Squire
for his noble tale, which we, alas! can never hear to its
end: —

> ' In feith, Squier, thou hast thee wel yquit,
>   And gentilly; I preise wel thy wit.'

This outburst of praise calls the Host's attention
to the Franklin; and, though he disposes of the good
man's most cherished aspiration with a contemptuous
'straw for your gentillesse!' he nevertheless singles
him out as the teller of the next tale.

Were it not that in other instances we find Chaucer
assigning a fanciful, rather than the actual, source for
his compositions, the opening lines of the
Franklin's Tale would seem sufficient evi-   Sources.
dence that its source was a courtly Breton lay, such as
those that have come down to us in French dress from
the hand of Marie de France.

> Thise olde gentil Britons in hir dayes
> Of diverse aventures maden layes,
> Rymeyed in hir firste Briton tonge;
> Which layes with hir instruments they songe,
> Or elles redden hem for hir plesaunce;
> And oon of hem have I in remembraunce,
> Which I shal seyn with good wil as I can.

But no such lay has been preserved to us.[1] Tales similar

---

[1] Dr. W. H. Schofield has attempted to prove from an account of a
Briton chieftain, Arviragus, in Geoffrey of Monmouth's *Historia*, that
such a legend actually existed in South Wales, whence it was carried
to Brittany, and written up, perhaps with accretions from another source
ultimately Oriental, by a poet of the school of Marie de France. (*Publications of the Modern Language Association of America*, 16. 405–449.)
The argument is ingenious, and one would be glad to accept it; but it
consists of hypotheses rather than of evidence. An elaborate refutation

to that of the Franklin have been found in Sanskrit, Burmese, Persian, and other Oriental tongues; and a still closer parallel is offered in a tale told by Boccaccio in his early prose work the *Filocolo*, and again, with slight variations, in the *Decameron*, Day 10, Nov. 5.[1] In Boccaccio's version, a faithful wife promises an importunate lover, of whom she wishes to be rid, that she will give him her love, if he can make a garden bloom and bear fruit in mid-January. The lover accomplishes this by the help of a magician; and the story concludes as does the Franklin's. Of the two parallel tales of Boccaccio, that in the *Filocolo* is somewhat nearer to Chaucer's; and it is possible that Chaucer may have drawn his material thence, changing the scene to Brittany, altering the names in accordance with this change, and considerably modifying the story itself; but it is more probable that his source was a French *fabliau*, closely related to the source whence Boccaccio's tale was drawn. The fact that the scene was laid in Brittany would be sufficient to explain the fanciful attribution to a Breton *lai*. The history of the tale, as it traveled from the distant east to Chaucer's study, was probably similar to that of the story which we have in the *Pardoner's Tale*.[2] It is interesting to notice that Beaumont and Fletcher have utilized the plot of the *Franklin's Tale* for a one-act play entitled *The Triumph of Honour*.

The chief beauty of this tale resides in the noble

of Dr. Schofield's contention is given by P. Rajna in *Romania*, 32. 204–267. ('Le Origini della Novella narrata dal Frankeleyn nei *Canterbury Tales* del Chaucer.')

[1] The story also appears in the twelfth canto of Boiardo's *Orlando Innamorato*. See *Originals and Analogues to Some of Chaucer's Canterbury Tales*, pp. 289–340, where several Oriental versions and the *Decameron novella* are given in translation. For the relation of Chaucer's version to Boccaccio's, see the article by P. Rajna, in *Romania*, 32, 204–267. Rajna's conclusions in this matter the present writer cannot accept.

[2] Cf. above, p. 224.

spirit which pervades it.   The unswerving fidelity of
Dorigen, who cannot make merry when her husband is
overseas, and who unhesitatingly rejects the Literary
advances of her lover Aurelius ; the utmost Qualities.
loyalty to the spoken pledge, which impels Arviragus
to send his wife to keep a promise, though spoken in
jest — are so potent in their power for good that not
only the passionate lover, but the poor scholar in far-
off Orleans, are compelled to an equal nobility.   Ten
Brink says of the poem : ' The contagious influence of
good, proceeding from a common as well as from a
noble disposition, and the wondrous power of love, are
beautifully symbolized in this fable.   And throughout
all his story Chaucer gives special prominence to the
idea by which the whole receives its internal completion, viz., the idea that love and force mutually exclude
each other, while patience and forbearance belong to
the very essence of love.' [1]

Beautiful as is this picture of married love, Chaucer
has taken care that it shall not become sentimental, by
touching it here and there with his own peculiar humor.
Thus with sly ambiguity he asks, after describing the
bliss of Arviragus and Dorigen, —

> Who coude telle, but he had wedded be,
> The joye, the ese, and the prosperitee
> That is betwixe an housbonde and his wyf ?

And again in describing the grief of Dorigen at her
husband's departure for Britain : —

> For his absence wepeth she and syketh,
> As doon thise noble wyves *whan hem lyketh*.

After giving us the passionate 'complaint ' uttered by
Aurelius in his love-longing, there is on the author's
part a playful assurance of his own unconcern : —

[1] *History of English Literature* (English trans.), 2. 169.

> Dispeyred in this torment and this thoght
> Lete I this woful creature lye ;
> Chese he, for me, whether he wol live or dye.

The poem ends in the manner of the *débat* literature so popular in mediæval France, with a question addressed to the judicious reader, or rather to the members of the pilgrimage : —

> Lordinges, this question wolde I aske now,
> Which was the moste free, as thinketh yow?

Which of the three — Arviragus, who sacrifices his wife to his sense of honor, Aurelius, who foregoes his coveted opportunity, or the clerk of Orleans, who in remitting his promised fee, showed that he too ' coude doon a gentil dede ' — shows the greatest freedom, i. e., generosity ? One would be glad to hear the discussion which must have arisen among the company when this question was propounded ; but one of the several gaps in the unfinished framework of the *Canterbury Tales* follows the *Franklin's Tale*, and the reader is left to imagine the debate, and to settle the burning question by himself. In attempting the question, one must decide whether or not the terrible sacrifice of Arviragus was necessary, or even justifiable. Probably most modern readers will decide that it was neither. A jesting promise is made on condition that the seemingly impossible be performed. By calling in the aid of magic, the condition is fulfilled. Surely it is a hyperquixotic sense of honor which shall insist on the fulfillment of a pledge so circumstanced. But the Middle Age apparently admired such extreme conceptions of honor,[1] and I, for one, am not willing to say that they were wrong. It would not hurt our modern world to be a little more quixotic in its sense of honor. I am quite ready to grant that in this in-

---

[1] Cf. The tale of Nathan and Mithridanes, in Boccaccio's *Decameron*, Day 10, Nov. 3.

stance Arviragus was mistaken, that truth did not demand the sacrifice ; even, if you will, that the sacrifice should not have been made; and yet his act is none the less a noble act. I cannot see that its spirit is very different from the spirit of the equally quixotic command, ' If any man will sue thee at the law, and take away thy coat, let him have thy cloke also.' In the event, at least, Arviragus is justified ; his noble deed begets nobility in others ; and we are shown once more that it is indeed possible to overcome evil with good.

THE SECOND NUN'S TALE

Of the Second Nun, to whom the manuscript rubrics assign the legend of St. Cecilia, we know nothing beyond the mere fact of her presence in the pilgrim-company as attendant on the Prioress. At the end of the description of Madam Eglantine in the General Prologue we read : —

> Another Nonne with hir hadde she,
> That was hir chapeleyne.

Chaucer has provided no introductory prologue to the tale itself to inform us further of the good lady's personality, nor of the circumstance of her narration. The appropriateness of tale to teller is, however, obvious at a glance. Like the tale of the Prioress, the story breathes that spirit of peculiar religious exaltation which we associate with all that is most beautiful in the monastic life.

That the legend of St. Cecilia was not originally intended for its present place as one of the *Canterbury Tales* might be shown from the internal evidence of the tale itself. In open contradiction to the idea of oral narration on the pilgrimage is line 78 : — *Date of Composition.*

> Yet preye I yow that *reden that I wryte*.

Equally inconsistent is line 62, in which the speaker refers to herself as ' unworthy *sone* of Eve.' We have, however, a piece of external evidence on the question which is even more convincing. In the *Legend of Good Women* Dan Cupid says of the poet: —

> He hath in prose translated Boëce,
> And mad the Lyf also of seynt Cecyle.

This evidence taken together may be held to prove that the tale was written before 1385, and was not revised for its present position.

That the legend was written after Chaucer's Italian journey of 1373 is rendered probable by the fact that lines 36–51 are translated from the last canto of Dante's *Paradiso*. From its general stylistic qualities, and in particular from the closeness with which it follows its original, critics have been inclined to ascribe it, with Ten Brink, to the very beginning of Chaucer's so-called Italian period, that is, to the years 1373–74. Probability favors this ascription; but it must be remembered that we have no positive evidence in its support.[1]

The source of the *Second Nun's Tale* is suggested by the rubric which precedes line 85: *Interpretacio nominis Cecilie, quam ponit frater Iacobus Ianuensis in Legenda Aurea.* This Jacobus Januensis, better known as Jacobus a Voragine, was a Dominican friar, who in 1292 was consecrated archbishop of Genoa; and his *Golden Legend*, 'a collection of the legendary lives of the greater saints of the mediæval church,' was one of the most popular books of the Middle Ages. Professor Koelbing has shown, however, that Chaucer's original was a Latin life of St. Cecilia, which, though closely related to that in the *Golden Legend*, is in some particulars nearer to the

Source.

---

[1] Dr. Koeppel, in *Anglia*, 14. 227–233, favors a date later than that of *Troilus and Criseyde*.

life of the saint written by Simeon Metaphrastes,[1]
printed in a collection of saints' lives by Aloysius
Lipomanus, Louvain, 1571. There is no proof that
Chaucer used the French translation of the *Golden
Legend* by Jehan de Vignay, nor any of the earlier
English accounts of St. Cecilia.[2]

Though we do not possess Chaucer's exact original,
we know from the extant Latin versions, from which it
probably differed only in minute details, that his translation is exceedingly literal. The following extract
from the version of Metaphrastes may be compared with
Chaucer's corresponding lines : ' Dixit Almacius præ-
fectus : Elige tu unum ex duobus, aut sacrifica aut
nega te esse cristianam, ut delicti tibi detur venia.
Tunc dixit ridens sancta Cæcilia : O judicem pudore
necessario affectum ! Vult me negare et esse me inno-
centem, ut ipse me faciat crimini obnoxiam.' [3]

In Chaucer's English this becomes : —

> Almache answerde, 'chees oon of thise two,
> Do sacrifyce, or Cristendom reneye,
> That thou mowe now escapen by that weye.'
> At which the holy blisful fayre mayde
> Gan for to laughe, and to the juge seyde,
> 'O juge, confus in thy nycetee,
> Woltow that I reneye innocence,
> To make me a wikked wight ? ' quod she.

This passage is typical of Chaucer's procedure throughout, so that we may agree with Professor Koelbing's
assertion that 'apart from the charming versification,
which seems splendidly suited to the subject, Chaucer's
proprietorship in the composition consists only in single
words or half lines, which he used to fill out his verse.'
Any criticism of the tale, then, must be a criticism of

---

[1] *Englische Studien*, 1. 215–248.
[2] See *Originals and Analogues*, pp. 189–219.
[3] From Koelbing's article cited above, p. 223.

the original saint's legend rather than of Chaucer. It is a story of a type to which our modern world is The Tale inclined to do small justice. Full as it is of Itself. the supernatural and the impossible, it lends itself readily enough to the laugh of the mocker; while even the human motives of the saintly heroine are far from the comprehension of to-day. Yet for its pathos, its noble spirit of high religion, above all for the irresistible force of Cecilia's sweet personality, the tale may still be read and loved by all whose hearts are not completely hardened. Chaucer, apparently, took the tale quite seriously; the genuineness of its religious feeling cannot be questioned. So that his deliberate choice of theme, not in the first place for the Second Nun, but for himself, is a valuable piece of testimony as to his deeper and more serious life.

Of the historical Cecilia little is known beyond what can be inferred from the developed legend. Her martyrdom is usually assigned to the reign of the Emperor Alexander Severus (A. D. 222–235); but even this is not certain. St. Cecilia's present fame as patroness of music and inventor of the organ is a later development, of which Chaucer probably never heard. The Cecilia of the legend sang to God in her heart 'whyl the organs maden melodye,' and she received an angel visitant; but the two facts are unconnected, and the mention of the organ is only a passing one.

THE CANON'S YEOMAN'S TALE

When the Second Nun has finished her tale of St. Cecilia, and the company have reached the little village of Boghton under Blee, they are joined by two newcomers, the Canon and his Yeoman, who have ridden furiously to overtake them, fearing perhaps to travel alone through the robber-haunted Forest of Blean.

The black-clothed Canon speaks but little; but his
silence is more than atoned for by the garrulous lo-
quacity of his Yeoman. Little by little it transpires
that the Canon is a practicer of alchemy. The Yeoman
will not be silenced : —

> And whan this chanon saugh it wolde nat be,
> But his yeman wolde telle his privetee,
> He fledde awey for verray sorwe and shame.

Chaucer had little, if any, of the reformer's spirit
in his make-up; but with his temperamental tendency
to see the comic in human life, he had a keen interest
in hypocrisy and clever imposture, an interest which
at times almost extends to an intellectual admiration.
With lively intellectual interest, but with no trace of
bitterness, he shows up the lying devices of his Pardoner. With less detail, but with rich humor, Clerk
Nicholas in the *Miller's Tale* is made to exemplify the
tricks of the false astrologer. The *Canon's Yeoman's
Tale* is a complete *exposé* of alchemy made by one of
its victims, and consequently made with a personal bitterness that has led many critics to the unwarranted
supposition that Chaucer himself had fallen prey to the
imposture. Chaucer may have believed, as did all the
most learned of his time, in the theoretical possibility
of transmuting the baser metals into gold. The fullness
and accuracy of his acquaintance with the subject, as
shown in the tale itself, prove that his intellectual
curiosity had led him to explore the mysteries of the
science. Even the *Canon's Yeoman's Tale* itself indicates no active disbelief in the theory of alchemy.
But his sound common sense told him that in actual
experience the search for the philosopher's stone had
been but a pursuit of will-o'-the-wisp, when it had not
been downright fraud and imposture. We can be sure,
I think, that the only use Chaucer made of alchemy was

in transmuting the base metal of human greed and folly into the finer gold of humor. The bitterness of the *Canon's Yeoman's Tale* is the dramatic indignation of the Yeoman, who at last discovers that he has been made a gull. Needless to say, it gives the highest realism and color to the tale.

When his master takes to flight, and the Yeoman finds himself free of the incubus that has for seven long years possessed him, robbing him of money and of health, his pent-up scorn finds vent in a long rambling exposition of alchemical mysteries. He has learned his lesson well; and the 'terms' of the 'elvish craft,' 'so clergial and so queynte,' flow freely from his loosened tongue. There is no order in his speech; and the majority of his terms are, of course, meaningless to us. The total effect is one of bewildering confusion, precisely the effect which Chaucer wished to produce. Deliciously humorous is his description of the sudden bursting of the pot which contained the mixture which was to bring great wealth. Some said this, and some said that, but the bitter fact remained that months of labor had gone for nothing.

The first part of the tale deals with the futile attempts of serious alchemy, in which the deceivers are themselves deceived, and all alike share in the common failure. The second part, which is the more interesting, tells of the clever trick of legerdemain by which another canon, less scrupulous than the one we have met, convinces a gullible priest that he actually possesses the elixir, and disposes of his worthless receipt for the considerable sum of forty pounds.

No source for the tale is known, and probably none is to be sought. Very likely the anecdote of the second part is founded on an actual occurrence. A trick closely similar to this was actually perpetrated in New York

in the summer of 1890.[1] After all, the chief interest
of the tale lies not so much in its substance as in the
personality of the Yeoman who relates it.

THE MANCIPLE'S TALE

The journey to Canterbury is nearly ended, and
already the company is in sight of a little town, —

> Which that ycleped is Bob-up-and-doun,
> Under the Blee, in Caunterbury weye.

Meanwhile honest Hodge of Ware, the Cook of London, has been taking advantage of his vacation days to
sample the wine or ale of every wayside tavern, until he
has got himself disgracefully drunk. He talks through
his nose, breathes heavily, and finally falls from his
horse into the mire, whence he is raised into the saddle
again only after much shoving and lifting. Obviously,
he is in no condition to tell the tale which mine Host
demands of him ; so that the Manciple's ready offer to
serve in his stead is gladly accepted. On the first day
of the pilgrimage, it will be remembered, the Cook had
been called on for a tale, and had responded with the
story of Perkin Revelour, which Chaucer left unfinished after the fifty-eighth line. That he should be
called on a second time is proof that, when the Manciple's Prologue was written, Chaucer had not abandoned his original plan, as announced in the General
Prologue, that each of the pilgrims should tell *two*
tales on the road to Canterbury, and other two on the
journey home.

The tale which the Manciple tells is a short and simple one, and needs no long exposition here. It is merely

---

[1] See Dr. C. M. Hathaway's edition of Ben Jonson's *Alchemist*, New
York, 1903, pp. 87, 88. The introduction of this volume contains an
interesting history of alchemy, its theory and practice, down to the
present day.

a clever retelling of the fable of Apollo and Coronis in Ovid's *Metamorphoses*, 2. 531-632. Chaucer has somewhat simplified the tale, and has added some moral reflections on the futility of trying to restrain a wife, and on the undesirability of repeating scandal, the latter taken from Albertano of Brescia's treatise on the *Art of Speaking and of Keeping Silence*.[1] The same tale is told by Gower in *Confessio Amantis*, 3. 783–830. Mr. Clouston has shown [2] that the tale is ultimately of Oriental origin, and that a version of the story, independent of that given by Ovid, was brought to Europe in the Middle Ages, and incorporated into the popular collection of tales entitled *Li Romans des Sept Sages*. But Chaucer's tale was probably drawn directly from Ovid, and certainly has no connection with this version last named.

THE PARSON'S TALE

In the life of the fourteenth century the Church played, for good and for evil, a part of the first importance, so that one need not be surprised that of the nine and twenty gathered together at the inn in Southwark, eleven are connected in one way or another with the ecclesiastical organization. Surveying this delegation as a whole, one is forced to the conclusion that the English Church had fallen on evil days ; and this conclusion is strengthened by the appearance of other churchmen quite as unworthy as these in the tales themselves. Unfortunately, the concurrent testimony of such diverse observers as Gower, Langland, and Wiclif proves that Chaucer's picture is not overdrawn. Against such a background of corruption and unworthiness, the poor parson of a town stands out with singular beauty, and the sympathetic portrait of him given

---

[1] See the article by Koeppel, in Herrig's *Archiv*, 86. 44.

[2] *Originals and Analogues*, 437–480.

in the General Prologue is justly regarded as one of the loveliest bits of Chaucer's poetry.

Often enough on the road to Canterbury the good priest must have been shocked by the words he had to hear; but he knew how to keep his peace. He 'ne maked him a spyced conscience.' Only once does he protest, when on the second day of the journey the Host turns to him and with an oath demands a tale. The Parson's mild rebuke calls forth from the Host a scornful answer : —

> 'I smelle a loller in the wind,' quod he.
> 'How ! good men,' quod our hoste, 'herkneth me;
>   Abydeth for goddes digne passioun,
>   For we shall han a predicacioun;
>   This loller heer wil prechen us somwhat.'

But the Shipman, that stout defender of the established faith, throws himself into the breach; the danger of a 'predicacioun' is for the present averted; and the unpleasantness blows over. Not, however, till all the other pilgrims have told their tales, late in the afternoon of the last day's ride, does the Host again make requisition for the Parson's tale. This time the Parson suffers his profanity to pass without rebuke. The Host's earlier fears of a 'predicacioun,' however, are fully realized. The Parson will tell no fable, either in rime or alliteration; his tale is to be 'moralitee and vertuous matere,'

> To shewe yow the wey, in this viage,
> Of thilke parfit glorious pilgrimage
> That highte Jerusalem celestial.

The whole company sees the appropriatness of ending 'in som vertuous sentence,' and the Parson is given free audience.

Much as we may admire the beauty of the Parson's character as parish priest, we are heartily glad that we do not have to sit under his preaching of a Sunday. His sermon, or meditation, as he calls it, is interminably long, and for our modern taste at least, intolerably dull. It is full of excellent teaching, often expressed in trenchant language; but for effectiveness as a whole, it is immeasurably inferior to the brilliant sermon of the miserable Pardoner. The theme of the discourse is Penitence; but into its midst is introduced a digression on the seven deadly sins and their remedies, longer than all the rest of the sermon, which hopelessly destroys the unity and proportion of the whole.

Of the source of the *Parson's Tale* Professor Skeat says:[1] 'It is now known that this Tale is little else than an adaptation (with alterations, omissions, and additions, as usual with Chaucer) of a French treatise by Frère Lorens, entitled *La Somme des Vices et des Vertus*, written in 1279.'[2] Until quite recently this statement was universally accepted; but we now know that the *Parson's Tale* and *La Somme des Vices et des Vertus* both go back to an earlier common original, the *Summa seu Tractatus de Viciis* of Guilielmus Peraldus, a Dominican Friar of the thirteenth century, while the main body of the tale which deals with penitence is from the *Summa Casuum Pœnitentiæ* of another Dominican of the same century, Raymund of Pennaforte.[3] In just what versions these treatises reached Chaucer we do not yet know; but,

(margin: Sources and Authenticity)

---

[1] *Oxford Chaucer*, 3. 502.

[2] In the Chaucer Society's volume of *Essays on Chaucer*, pp. 503–610, may be found a minute comparison of the *Parson's Tale* and the *Somme*, by W. Eilers.

[3] *The Sources of the Parson's Tale*, by Miss Kate O. Petersen, Radcliffe College Monographs, 12. Boston, 1901. Favorably reviewed by E. Koeppel, in *Englische Studien*, 30. 464–467. Professor Liddell's 'A New Source of the Parson's Tale,' in the *Furnivall Miscellany*, 255–277, is no longer important.

though the *Somme* of Frère Lorens may have been
consulted, it cannot have been his direct or even indirect source. Nor do we know whether the unfortunate
piecing together of two distinct treatises is due to
Chaucer, or to his immediate original.

So inartistic is this combination, that many critics,
among them Ten Brink, have been unwilling to believe
that the tale as preserved to us is Chaucer's authentic
work. The whole digression on the seven deadly sins,
and other lesser sections of the work, they regard as
interpolations by another hand. But this method of
higher criticism, by which everything offensive to the
æsthetic taste of the critic is conveniently branded as
interpolation, is fortunately going out of fashion ; and
in this particular case there is no adequate ground for
supposing that the tale is not in all essentials as Chaucer wrote it.[1]

It will be remembered that the Host accused the
Parson of being a ' loller,' i. e. a lollard, a follower of
Wiclif. Superficially, the portrait of the Parson in the
General Prologue suggests the ' poor preachers ' who
spread the reformer's teachings through the country-
side ; and a serious attempt has been made to prove
that he was intended as a Wiclifite, and that Chaucer
himself was in sympathy with the movement. Of course
the Parson's ' meditation,' with its insistence on the
necessity of auricular confession, is eminently orthodox ;
and if we accept it as genuine, we must at once dismiss the theory of his Wiclifite sympathies. Apart
from this objection, the theory never had any adequate
evidence in its favor. As for the Host's playful charge,
one may readily enough answer that it is quite in

[1] Professer Koeppel, in Herrig's *Archiv*, 87. 33–54, has shown that
many quotations from the section on the seven deadly sins occur in
Chaucer's other works, just as we find similar quotations from Boethius and from the *Tale of Melibeus*.

accord with Chaucer's characteristic humor to have it
suggested that the one thoroughly worthy ecclesiastic
in the company is a heretic.[1]

In the last paragraph of the *Parson's Tale*, under
the caption ' Here taketh the makere of this book his
The Re- leve,' is found a strange and sad leave-taking,
tractation. in which the poet beseeches ' mekely for the
mercy of god, that ye preye for me, that Crist have
mercy on me and foryeve me my giltes : — and namely,
of my translacions and endytinges of worldly vanitees,
the whiche I revoke in my retracciouns : as is the book
of Troilus ; The book also of Fame ; The book of the
nynetene Ladies ; The book of the Duchesse ; The
book of seint Valentynes day of the Parlement of
Briddes ; The tales of Caunterbury, thilke that sounen
into sinne.' The only works that he does not regret
are the translation of Boethius, ' and other bokes of
Legendes of seintes, and omelies, and moralitee, and
devocioun.' All for which we prize Chaucer he would
rather not have writ! We should be glad to believe
that these words are not authentic ; but, remembering
Tolstoi and Ruskin, we dare not. The sincerity of the
passage cannot be questioned. We must believe that
in the sadness of his latter days the poet's conscience
was seized upon by the tenets of a narrow creed, which
in the days of his strength he had known how to trans-
mute into something better and truer. But into the
sacredness of his soul we had better not pry too curiously.

' So here is ended the book of the Tales of Caunterbury, compiled by Geffrey Chaucer, of whos soule Jesu
Crist have mercy. Amen.'

---

[1] Those who wish to pursue this Wiclifite theory may read the essay
on ' Chaucer a Wicliffite,' in *Essays on Chaucer*, 227–292, by H. Simon.

APPENDIX

SUGGESTIONS FOR THE STUDY OF CHAUCER

THE first question that presents itself to the student of Chaucer is that of editions of the poet's works. The more advanced student must have access to Skeat's edition in six volumes,[1] commonly known as *The Oxford Chaucer,* published in 1894. Though somewhat deficient in scholarly method, this edition contains the most satisfactory text of Chaucer's works in their entirety which has yet appeared, and in notes and introductions a vast store of valuable information. The introductions, however, are already in many particulars antiquated. Skeat's text, with condensed glossary, and brief general introduction, but without explanatory notes, is also published in a single volume, called *The Student's Chaucer* (Oxford University Press, 1900). This is the most satisfactory edition of Chaucer now available for the average reader. It is, everything considered, preferable to the Globe edition, edited by Pollard, Heath, Liddell, and McCormick (Macmillan, 1903). Professor F. N. Robinson of Harvard has now (1921) in preparation and nearly completed a single volume edition of Chaucer to be published in the Cambridge Poets Series (Houghton Mifflin Company), which will undoubtedly supersede both the Globe edition and the *Student's Chaucer* of Skeat. The older editions of Chaucer have no value save to the book-collector or the special student of textual criticism, and should be avoided.

For the student of Chaucer's language and verse the standard work is Ten Brink's *The Language and Metre of Chaucer* (English translation of the second German edition by M.

---

[1] A seventh volume contains all the pieces which have in the past been erroneously included among Chaucer's works.

Bentinck Smith, Macmillan, 1901).[1] The less advanced student will find all that he needs clearly presented in Professor Samuel Moore's *Historical Outlines of English Philology and Middle English Grammar* (George Wahr, Ann Arbor, Michigan, 1919). This small volume contains an excellent account of Chaucerian pronunciation, with phonetic transcriptions. The best existing glossary is that in the *Oxford Chaucer*. Under the auspices of the Carnegie Institution, Professor J. S. P. Tatlock of Leland Stanford University is now completing a concordance to Chaucer originally undertaken by the late Professor Flügel. This work, when published, will be indispensable to serious students.

For the life of Chaucer, about which we have but few significant details, the student may best use the article by J. W. Hales in the *Dictionary of National Biography*. The fullest presentation of the little we know is given in the Chaucer Society volume of *Life Records of Chaucer* (1900). Interesting light is thrown on one phase of the poet's career in Dr. J. R. Hulbert's University of Chicago dissertation, *Chaucer's Official Life* (1912). The most comprehensive study of the chronology of the poet's literary career is Professor Tatlock's Chaucer Society volume, *The Development and Chronology of Chaucer's Works* (1907). The author's conclusions have not, however, been accepted in their entirety by other scholars. Miss Caroline F. E. Spurgeon's Chaucer Society volumes, *Five Hundred Years of Chaucer Criticism and Allusion* (1914 and 1918), and her earlier book, *Chaucer devant la Critique en Angleterre et en France* (Paris, 1911), form the starting-point for any study of Chaucer's influence on later literature.

The great mass of Chaucerian scholarship is contained in the voluminous publications of the Chaucer Society (London), in the various scholarly journals, English, American, and German, and in various university series of doctoral dissertations. This material has been made accessible by the admir-

---

[1] A third edition of the German work, revised by Eduard Eckhardt has just appeared (Leipzig, Tauchnitz, 1920). The advanced student will also consult *Die Sprachlichen Eigentümlichkeiten der wichtigeren Chaucer-Handschriften und die Sprache Chaucers*, by Dr. Friedrich Wild (*Wiener Beitrage*, xliv, Vienna and Leipzig, 1915).

able bibliography compiled by Miss E. P. Hammond, *Chaucer, a Bibliographical Manual* (Macmillan, 1908). This volume is indispensable to advanced students. It is supplemented, particularly in the case of matter published since 1907, by Professor J. E. Wells's *Manual of the Writings in Middle English* (Yale University Press, 1916), and the 'First Supplement' to this work (1919).

Among more popular discussions of Chaucer and his poetry may be mentioned the study by Professor E. Legouis of the Sorbonne, *Geoffroy Chaucer* (Paris, 1910; English translation, London and New York, 1913), and Professor Kittredge's delightful and illuminating volume of lectures entitled *Chaucer and his Poetry* (Harvard University Press, 1915). Mr. G. G. Coulton's *Chaucer and his England* (Putnam's, 1908) contains interesting matter on the daily life of Chaucer's England. Professor T. R. Lounsbury's three volumes of *Studies in Chaucer* (Harper's, 1892) and the pages devoted to Chaucer in Ten Brink's *History of English Literature*, Vol. ii, Part I, (Holt, 1893), contain much that is still of value.

NOTES AND REVISIONS

(IN this appendix will be found references to important books and articles which have been published since the first edition of this book appeared in 1906, and a few corrections and additions to its text, which could not conveniently be incorporated in the body of the volume. It is not intended that the bibliography of recent books and articles should be complete. For example, no notice is taken of such unfounded conjectures as those contained in Mr. Victor Langhans's extensive volume, *Untersuchungen zu Chaucer*, Halle, 1918.)

Page 59. Professor W. O. Sypherd has pointed out interesting similarities between the *Book of the Duchess* and the anonymous fourteenth-century French poem, *Le Songe Vert: Modern Language Notes*, 24. 46–47 (1909). See also Professor Kittredge's article on 'Guillaume de Machaut and the Book of the Duchess,' *Publications of the Modern Language Association*, 30. 1–24 (1915).

Page 64. It was formerly believed that the two eagles 'of lower kinde' in the *Parliament of Fowls* stood for William of Bavaria and Frederick of Meissen; but Professor O. F. Emerson, *Modern Philology*, 8. 45–62 (1910), and Professor Samuel Moore, *Modern Language Notes*, 26. 8–12 (1911), have shown that it is more probable that the third eagle represents Charles VI of France, and the second, Frederick of Meissen. In 1913 Professor J. M. Manly, *Studien zur englischen Philologie*, ed. Morsbach, 50. 279–290, argued that the poem is merely a variation of the conventional *demande d'amours*, where a hypothetical case of love-casuistry is propounded and left for solution to the wits of readers or auditors. He declines to see in it any allusion to the marriage of Richard and Anne, or to admit the necessity of any personal allegory. In the following year Professor Emerson, *Journal of English and Germanic Philology*, 13. 566–582, replied with new evidence in support of his position. In 1920 Miss Edith Rickert, *Modern Philology*, 18. 1–29, argued that the *demande d'amours* of Chaucer's poem was intended to compliment not Queen Anne, but the Lady Philippa of Lancaster, eldest daughter of John of Gaunt. In this interpretation the three suitor eagles become the lady's cousin, King Richard II, whom, as Froissart declares, Duke John wished to annex as son-in-law, William of Bavaria, and John of Blois, all of whom were possible suitors for the lady in the year 1381.

The arguments are too complex for summary and criticism here. The present writer can only state his opinion that the *demande d'amours* of the *Parliament of Fowls* seems clearly intended as an allegory of some actual courtship, and that Miss Rickert's interpretation involves more serious inconsistencies than those which she and Professor Manly have pointed out in the theory which identifies the 'formel egle' with the Lady Anne of Bohemia.

Page 66, line 1. The present writer now believes that the composition of the *Knight's Tale* falls two or three years later than that of the *Parliament of Fowls*. Cf. p. 168.

Page 66, line 8. The *De Planctu Naturæ* may be read in the English translation of D. M. Moffat, *Yale Studies in English*, vol. 36 (1908).

Page 68. Dr. Edgar F. Shannon, *Publications of the Modern Language Association*, 27. 461–485 (1912), has pointed out resemblances of a general character between *Anelida and Arcite* and the *Heroides* of Ovid. In the same article he has shown that the *Amores* of Ovid were sometimes referred to by mediæval scholars under the title 'Corinna' — the name of Ovid's mistress in whose honor they are written. He suggests that this is the explanation of Chaucer's mysterious 'Corinne.' Unfortunately, Dr. Shannon has been able to find but one possible parallel between *Anelida* and the *Amores*, and that of a sort that might easily be fortuitous.

In *Publications of the Modern Language Association*, 36. 186–222 (1921), Professor Frederick Tupper has argued that the story of Anelida and Arcite was intended to shadow forth the events of an unhappy marriage in one of the noble families of

Ireland. Anelida, the 'quene of Ermony,' he identifies with the young countess of Ormonde. The name Ormonde was commonly represented in contemporary Latin charters as 'Ermonie'; and the maiden name of the countess was Anne Welle, while her husband, the earl, was on his mother's side a d'Arcy. The resemblance of these names to Anelida and Arcite, when taken in conjunction with the equivalence of Ormonde and Ermony, constitutes a considerable presumption in favor of Tupper's theory; but there is no positive evidence in its support. The only reason for believing that the marriage in question was an unhappy one is the existence of two illegitimate sons of the Earl of Ormonde, who may perfectly well have antedated his marriage to Anne Welle. In the poem, moreover, Arcite's new love never granted him any grace (lines 188, 189). Professor Tupper suggests a number of further identifications, such as that of Theseus with Lionel, Duke of Clarence, which are much less plausible.

Miss M. Fabin, *Modern Language Notes*, 34. 266–272, argues that *Anelida* is indebted to *Le Lai de la Souscie* of Machaut.

Page 69, *line* 7. Cf. note on page 6, line 1, above.

Page 69, *line* 24. For a further account of the troubles of the mediæval author with his copyists, see the article by R. K. Root, 'Publication before Printing,' *Publications of the Modern Language Association*, 28. 417–431 (1913). See also E. P. Kuhl's 'A Note on Chaucer's Adam,' *Modern Language Notes*, 29. 263–264 (1914).

Page 72, *line* 13. See the article by J. L. Lowes, 'The Chaucerian "Merciles Beaute" and three poems of Deschamps's,' *Modern Language Review*, 5. 33–39 (1910).

Page 73. We now know, thanks to the brilliant discovery of Miss Edith Rickert, *Modern Philology*, 11. 209–225 (1913), that the *balade*, *Truth*, is addressed to Chaucer's friend, Sir Philip la Vache. The word 'vache' in the envoy should, therefore, be printed with a capital V. La Vache was son-in-law to Chaucer's friend, Sir Lewis Clifford. Miss Rickert has recorded the main facts of his career.

Page 76. In *Modern Language Notes*, 27. 45–48 (1912),

Professor J. L. Lowes discusses the reference in the *Envoy to Bukton* to captivity in Frisia, and suggests that the poem might have been written at any time between 1393 and 1396. Professor Kittredge, *Modern Language Notes*, 24. 14–15 (1909) cites from Deschamps some interesting parallels in dispraise of marriage.

Page 86. Professor Kittredge has suggested, *Modern Philology*, 14. 129–134 (1917), that 'litel Lowis' may have been the son of Chaucer's friend, Sir Lewis Clifford, and the 'son' of the poet only by affectionate adoption.

Page 151. The closest parallel to the framework of the *Canterbury Tales* is furnished by the prose *Novelle* of Giovanni Sercambi of Lucca written some time later than 1374. In this collection, the tales, though narrated by a single speaker, are addressed to a group of travelers on a journey through Italy. Brief interludes describe the doings of the company on the way. There is a 'president' who exercises a function somewhat analogous to that of Chaucer's Host. It is possible that Chaucer may have known Sercambi's work; but his debt to it, if any, is of a very general nature. He does not seem to have utilized any of the individual tales of the collection. The *Novelle* have survived only in a single manuscript, which has never been printed in its entirety. The best discussion of the matter is Professor Karl Young's essay, 'The Plan of the Canterbury Tales,' *Kittredge Anniversary Papers*, pp. 405–417 (1913). The first scholar to call attention to the parallel was H. B. Hinckley in his *Notes on Chaucer* (Northampton, Mass.. 1907).

Page 152. The student who wishes to venture into the tangled problem of the order of the groups of the *Canterbury Tales* will do well to begin with Miss E. P. Hammond's discussion, *Chaucer, a Bibliographical Manual*, pp. 158–172, 241–264. It must be remembered that the unity of Group B, as adopted by Furnivall for the Chaucer Society and observed in modern editions, rests on the authority of a single and otherwise unreliable manuscript. This manuscript (Selden B 14 of the Bodleian Library) is the only one which reads 'Shipman' in line B 1179. Instead, we find the word 'Squier' in all but one of the remaining manuscripts which contain this link; in that the word 'Sompnour' is substituted. The Selden manuscript is the only one in which the *Shipman's Tale* follows immediately the *Man of Law's Tale*. In the remaining manuscripts the Man of Law is followed by the Squire or by the Wife of Bath. The link which in Skeat's edition is called the 'Shipman's Prologue' should instead be called the 'Man of Law's Epilogue.' Scholars to-day consider the *Man of Law's Tale* with its introductory lines and this epilogue as one group, which they designate as B^1. The group which begins with the *Shipman's Tale* and ends with the Nun's Priest's epilogue is designated B^2.

The position assigned by Furnivall to C immediately after B^2 is entirely arbitrary. In all existing manuscripts except Selden B 14, where it is found between G and H, it immediately *precedes* B^2. Professor Samuel Moore, *Publications of the Modern Language Association*, 30. 116–123 (1915), has accordingly argued that the proper order is A, B^1, C, B^2, D, etc. This seems more probable than the order A, C, B^1, B^2, D, urged by G. Shipley in *Modern Language Notes*, 10. 260–279 (1895).

When Chaucer died, the *Canterbury Tales* were still unfinished. It seems clear that the pile of manuscript which he left gave no certain indication of the order in which he intended to incorporate the various fragments into a unified whole. Perhaps he himself had had no settled intention in the matter. Various scribes tried in various ways to arrange the sequence; and the result was the discord which now exists in the surviving manuscripts. The modern editor must similarly do the best he can to arrive at an arrangement which, if not Chaucer's own, shall in its avoidance of inconsistencies be one which Chaucer might have approved. He will consider primarily the geographical allusions in the various fragments and the references from one fragment to another, and will consider only secondarily the order presented in the existing manuscripts. From this point of view the order devised by Furnivall and adopted by Skeat in his edition remains a reasonably satisfactory solution; even though we grant, as seems probable, that Chaucer had no hand in the linking together of B^1 and B^2, and that he thought of C as preceding B^2.

Skeat's Chaucer Society volume, *The Evolution of the Canterbury Tales* (1907), confuses rather than clarifies the problem.

Page 173. See the discussion of the Miller and the Reeve by Dr. W. C. Curry, *Publications of the Modern Language Association*, 35. 189–209 (1920).

Page 175. For a parallel to Chaucer's apology for his indecent tales, see the article by R. K. Root, 'Chaucer and the Decameron,' *Englische Studien*, 44. 1–7 (1911).

Page 191. For a full and very interesting discussion of the *Prioress's Tale* and of the various versions of the story in mediæval literature, see Professor Carleton Brown's Chaucer Society volume, *A Study of the Miracle of Our Lady told by Chaucer's Prioress* (1910).

Page 223. See Dr. W. C. Curry's interesting article, 'The Secret of Chaucer's Pardoner,' *Journal of English and Germanic Philology*, 18. 593–606 (1919).

Page 253. On the Clerk of Oxford, see the article by Professor H. S. V. Jones in *Publications of the Modern Language Association*, 27. 106–115 (1912).

Page 255. Dr. W. E. Farnham has argued, *Modern Language Notes*, 33. 193–203 (1913), that Chaucer had access to the Italian version of Griselda as well as to Petrarch's Latin. Professor Cook has suggested, *Romanic Review*, 8. 210 (1917), that Chaucer consulted a French translation of Boccaccio's tale.

Page 270. A little further light has been thrown on the sources of the *Squire's Tale* by Professor H. S. V. Jones in *Publications of the Modern Language Association*, 20. 346–359 (1905), and by Professor J. L. Lowes in *Washington University Studies*, Vol. I, Part II, pp. 3–18 (St. Louis, 1913).

Page 273. The fidelity of the *Franklin's Tale* to its Breton setting is admirably discussed by Professor J. S. P. Tatlock in his Chaucer Society volume, *The Scene of the Franklin's Tale Visited* (1914). Mr. Tatlock believes that Chaucer has with deliberate art given to a story derived from other sources —

including the *Filocolo* of Boccaccio — the character of a Breton lay. See also the article by J. L. Lowes, 'The Franklin's Tale, the Teseide, and the Filocolo,' *Modern Philology*, 15. 689–728 (1918). Professor Lowes has shown conclusively that in numerous passages of the *Franklin's Tale* Chaucer has drawn on the *Teseide* of Boccaccio. He argues also for Chaucer's debt to the *Filocolo*. In spite of important differences, the *Franklin's Tale* is closer to the version in the *Filocolo* than to any other known version of the story; and there is no reason why Chaucer may not have known this work of Boccaccio. The facts can, however, be equally well explained on the assumption of a lost *fabliau* which was the ultimate common source of the Italian and the English tales.

See also Professor Tatlock's article, 'Astrology and Magic in Chaucer's Franklin's Tale,' *Kittredge Anniversary Papers*, pp. 339–350 (Boston, 1913), and Professor W. M. Hart's essay on the narrative art of the *Franklin's Tale* and its relation to the Breton lay in *Haverford Essays*, pp. 185–234 (Haverford, Pa., 1909).

Page 277. The student who wishes to understand the type of composition, of which the Second Nun's legend of St. Cecilia is an example, should consult Professor G. H. Gerould's scholarly book, *Saints' Legends* (Boston and New York, 1916). The *Second Nun's Tale* is discussed on pages 239–244. See also Professor Carleton Brown's 'The Prologue of Chaucer's "Lyf of Seint Cecile,"' *Modern Philology*, 9. 1–16 (1911), and the papers by Professor J. L. Lowes in *Publications of the Modern Language Association*, 26. 315–323 (1911) and 29. 129–133 (1914).

Page 288. See the article on 'Chaucer's Retractations,' by Professor J. S. P. Tatlock, in *Publications of the Modern Language Association*, 28. 521–529 (1913).

INDEX

INDEX